WILDLIFE

OF THE

CARIBBEAN

Herbert A. Raffaele

and James W. Wiley

Princeton University Press

Princeton and Oxford

PRINCETON  POCKET GUIDES

Wildlife of Australia, by Iain Campbell and Sam Woods

Wildlife of East Africa, by Martin B. Withers and David Hosking

Wildlife of the Galápagos, by Julian Fitter, Daniel Fitter, and David Hosking

Wildlife of Southern Africa, by Martin B. Withers and David Hosking

Wildlife of the Caribbean, by Herbert A. Raffaele and James W. Wiley

Coral Reef Fishes: Indo-Pacific and Caribbean, Revised Edition, by Ewald Lieske and Robert Myers

A Field Guide to the Birds of New Zealand, by Julian Fitter

The Kingdon Pocket Guide to African Mammals, by Jonathan Kingdon

Mammals of China, edited by Andrew T. Smith and Yan Xie

Reptiles and Amphibians of East Africa, by Stephen Spawls, Kim M. Howell, and Robert C. Drewes

———————

Published by Princeton University Press, 41 William Street, Princeton, New Jersey 08540

In the United Kingdom: Princeton University Press, 6 Oxford Street, Woodstock, Oxfordshire OX20 1TW

nathist.princeton.edu

ISBN 978-0-691-15382-7

Library of Congress Control Number: 2013945434

British Library Cataloging-in-Publication Data is available

This book has been composed in Myriad Pro

Printed on acid-free paper ∞

Edited and design by D & N Publishing, Wiltshire, UK

Printed in China

10 9 8 7 6 5 4 3 2 1

CONTENTS

ACKNOWLEDGMENTS

We are pleased to recognize the many individuals who assisted us in compiling material for this guide. We especially thank the artists Kristin Williams and Nils Navarro for the original works they produced. Robert Kirk, our managing editor at Princeton University Press, provided extensive and invaluable assistance in obtaining illustrations and photographs for the book. Catherine Levy and José Colón offered valuable editorial suggestions, and Ms. Levy also prepared a draft write-up of the Jamaican Ameiva. We thank Kimberly John for preparing draft write-ups and obtaining images of the freshwater fish and shrimp. A comprehensive list of credits can be found at the back of the book.

We especially wish to thank our wives, Jan Raffaele and Beth Wiley, for their support and encouragement during this time-consuming endeavor, as well as for their assistance in editing the manuscript.

INTRODUCTION

GOAL

The primary goal of this guide is to promote an interest in the natural world of the Caribbean islands. The book is intended to serve as a practical guide for local people and tourists alike. We presume its users have no particular experience or expertise with nature, so, to make identification easier, illustrations or photographs accompany every species description. In some cases, particularly plants, more than one picture is provided.

Aid in identification of commonly encountered species is a primary objective, an aim we supplement with text that attempts to highlight interesting facts about the species presented. By promoting interest in the Caribbean's extraordinary fauna and flora, we hope to enhance appreciation of and respect for nature. After all, it is only when we appreciate nature that we will ever take steps to conserve it.

GEOGRAPHIC COVERAGE

The Caribbean, also commonly referred to as the West Indies, is taken to include all islands of the Bahamas, Greater Antilles, Virgin Islands, Cayman Islands, and Lesser Antilles. Other adjacent islands, particularly San Andres and Providencia, while sharing many of the species in this book, are not specifically referred to in the text.

Omitted are Trinidad, Tobago, and other islands off the north coast of South America. These islands, though sharing many introduced plants and much marine life with the other Caribbean islands, differ substantially in their fauna and flora, thus their omission.

Finally, the coasts of the continental mainlands adjacent to the Caribbean are not included, due to their plant and animal species being decidedly different from those of the islands covered in this book.

SPECIES COVERAGE

The text presents accounts of 451 species of both terrestrial and marine animals and plants that occur in the Caribbean. Species were selected primarily based upon their likelihood of being seen. As a consequence, species included are typically either highly conspicuous, widely distributed, very common, or a combination of all three. A few exceptions, such as the Cuban Solenodon and Rhinoceros Iguana, are presented because of their uniqueness to the Caribbean as well as for their strikingly unusual characteristics. There is a heavier focus on birds, a more attention-getting portion of our natural world, than on plants or on deepwater reef fish that are common but more difficult to see.

Terrestrial species are treated first, marine species subsequently. The distinction between terrestrial and marine, however, is somewhat arbitrary. Crabs are an excellent example. A number of species are quite terrestrial, occurring some distance from streams, ponds, or the sea most of the year, yet they may be dependent upon such water bodies to spawn. A similar situation occurs in fish. Some "marine" species stray up rivers and streams, while some "freshwater" fish migrate to the sea to lay their eggs. Species in the latter category are treated in the section entitled Terrestrial Life.

Overall the book is a sampler. It aims to include conspicuous and widespread species from a broad range of organisms the novice is most likely to observe and inquire about. A reference section is provided in the back for individuals interested in more comprehensive guides to particular species groups.

SPECIES ACCOUNTS

Each account begins with a Key Features section that highlights the primary characteristics used to identify that particular animal or plant. We have tried to keep this section brief, since the accompanying photos and illustrations are the most valuable tool for identification. As few species as possible are presented on each page to allow for enlargement of the pictures, making identification a bit easier. To some extent, species of similar appearance are grouped close to one another to facilitate comparison.

The section entitled Status and Range includes much additional information, such as details regarding habitat; uses of the species for food, medicine, or the like; other species names; and interesting anecdotes.

Either a photo or illustration is included for each species. For species with variable coloration due to age, season, or gender, the most conspicuous form is depicted, sometimes accompanied by one or more other forms.

A few accounts refer to a higher taxonomic grouping rather than to one particular species. This is the case where there are many species of very similar appearance, such as with the prickly pear cacti and royal palms. When an account addresses a group of species, the common name of the group is not capitalized, except when used in a heading. Also, the scientific name for such a group is represented by a single name (the genus) followed by "spp." An example is the royal palms, *Roystonea* spp.

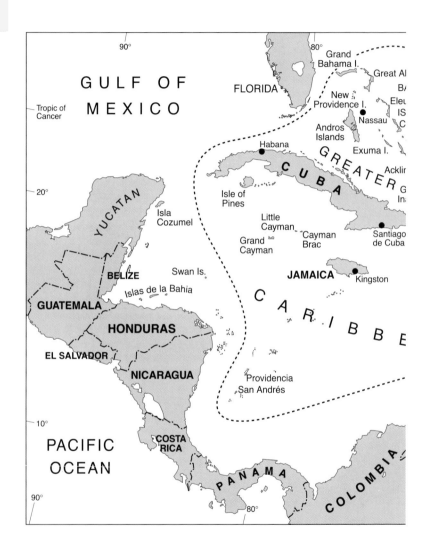

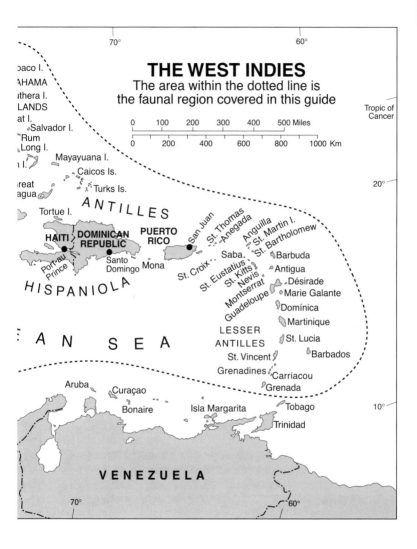

THE WEST INDIES
The area within the dotted line is
the faunal region covered in this guide

| 0 | 100 | 200 | 300 | 400 | 500 Miles |
| 0 | 200 | 400 | 600 | 800 | 1000 Km |

Tropic of
Cancer

70°

60°

20°

ɔaco I.
ΛHAMA
ithera I.
LANDS
at I.
Salvador I.
Rum
Long I.
ı I.
Mayayuana I.
Caicos Is.
Turks Is.

reat
agua

Tortue I.

A N T I L L E S

HAITI
DOMINICAN
REPUBLIC
PUERTO
RICO
San Juan
St. Thomas
Anegada
Anguilla
St. Martin I.
St. Bartholomew

Port-au
Prince
Santo
Domingo
Mona
St. Croix
Saba
St. Eustatius
St. Kitts
Nevis
Montserrat
Guadeloupe
St. Barbuda
Antigua
Désirade
Marie Galante
Domínica
Martinique

H I S P A N I O L A

LESSER
ANTILLES
St. Lucia
Barbados

A N   S E A

St. Vincent
Grenadines
Carriacou
Grenada

Aruba
Curaçao
Bonaire
Isla Margarita
Tobago
Trinidad

10°

V E N E Z U E L A

70°

60°

THE ISLANDS

GEOGRAPHY

The Caribbean islands fall into several groups. The four largest islands—Cuba, Jamaica, Hispaniola, and Puerto Rico—comprise the Greater Antilles; all are long and narrow and stretch from east to west. To the north of the Greater Antilles are the Bahamas, or Bahamas Bank, a cluster of more than seven hundred small, low-lying islands and cays, which includes the Turks and Caicos. To the east of Puerto Rico are the Virgin Islands, followed by the southward-arching Lesser Antilles, stretching from Anguilla in the north to Grenada in the south.

CLIMATE

The islands of the Caribbean are characteristically warm, sunny, and humid year round. The average annual temperature is approximately 26°C (79°F), though it varies moderately with season. The northeast trade winds blow steadily at 16–32 km (10–20 mi.) per hour, providing a pleasant cooling effect.

Temperatures drop with increased elevation; thus high mountain areas often require a sweatshirt and rain gear. Rainfall is decidedly more variable than temperature, this especially being the case on mountainous islands. The mountains serve as barriers to clouds moving in from the northeast. They stack up over the eastern parts of the islands and deposit most of their moisture as rain and mist. Parts of the island of Dominica receive 900 cm (350 in.) of rain per year due to this phenomenon. The leeward sides of the mountains, contrarily, are dry, the southwest portions of each island generally being the driest. Such areas are semiarid and may receive but a few centimeters of rain per year. Flat islands tend to be semiarid. The second half of each year is wetter than the first, the hurricane season ranging from July through October.

BIOGEOGRAPHY

GEOGRAPHIC ISOLATION AND THE COLONIZATION OF ISLANDS

The Caribbean, with Barbados and the Bahamas being major exceptions, are of volcanic origin and originally erupted from the ocean floor. This being the case, organisms that colonized these islands had to arrive by crossing open ocean, sometimes for great distances. The sea is an effective barrier to dispersal, so relatively few continental organisms have succeeded in reaching this region and becoming established. Hardy fliers such as birds and bats were most successful. Also, plants with tiny wind-borne seeds or with seeds fed upon by birds and carried in their digestive tracts colonized relatively easily. On the other hand, terrestrial mammals, delicate butterflies, and freshwater fish were rarely able to reach the islands.

Another inhibitor to colonization is the limited number of ecological niches available on islands. An animal's niche refers to the specific set of environmental conditions that the species needs to survive. This includes the availability of food, habitat types, nest sites, and shelter. Island size, elevation, and distance from major landmasses from which organisms have to travel, all play significant roles in the potential of a colonizing species to reach and survive on the island. The vast majority of attempts fail. It is for this reason the Caribbean's fauna and flora are not represented by as large a number of species as adjacent continental areas.

UNIQUENESS OF ISLAND SPECIES

The selective process of island colonization explains the relative lack of species diversity. A second outcome, however, is that islands possess large numbers of endemic species—species that occur no place else in the world. Island species tend to become endemic due to their isolation. When genes are not shared between populations for many generations, those populations tend to become increasingly different from one another. Over millennia this leads to such substantive differences that were an island species to come into contact with members of its ancestral stock, they would be unable to breed with one another. Thus, the island form would have evolved into an endemic species.

A consequence of this phenomenon is that what the Caribbean lacks in species diversity, it more than makes up for in uniqueness. This inverse relationship between diversity and uniqueness is typical of oceanic islands such as those in the Caribbean. To take the matter one step further, the greater the distance an island is from a continent (assuming islands are of similar size and elevation), the fewer plant and animal species it will support but the greater the distinctiveness of those species. As an example, compare Trinidad and Tobago with Puerto Rico. Trinidad and Tobago are two sister islands lying off South America, to which they were once connected by a land bridge. Their combined land mass is little more than half that of Puerto Rico, but their native avifauna totals approximately four hundred species, nearly twice that of Puerto Rico's. However, all the bird species on Trinidad and Tobago, with the sole exception of an endemic guan, are found either on the South American mainland or elsewhere. Contrarily, Puerto Rico's native avifauna totals only two hundred and forty species but includes sixteen endemic species, which, except for two occurring in the nearby Virgin Islands, are found nowhere else in the world.

Unfortunately, the isolation that permits evolution of many unique species also makes them highly vulnerable to environmental threats and ultimately to extinction. Oceanic island environments lack the diversity of predators and competitors present on continents. As a result, species that colonize successfully have an easy time, so to speak, since they do not have to be as wary. Over time, island species tend to lose many of the traits for discerning and avoiding predators that mainland species possess. Regrettably, recent colonization by humans has dramatically changed the dynamic of islands due to an array of human impacts, including the introduction of predatory species that were unable to reach such islands of their own accord. Island species, having lost their predator avoidance mechanisms, have suffered accordingly.

LOST FAUNAS

The Caribbean of today is quite different from the little-disturbed islands Christopher Columbus and his mariners encountered little more than five hundred years ago. Columbus described the island forests as being comprised of "trees that brushed the stars." Those original forests are gone. They were cut long ago for ship-building materials, to open lands for agriculture, for house construction, and for charcoal, among other uses. Wholesale deforestation was not the only early problem causing dramatic ecosystem change. Several exotic species were intentionally or accidentally introduced into the islands, where they outcompeted or preyed upon the local fauna. After hundreds of years of human impacts, the original delicate ecosystems of the Caribbean have been replaced by a complex of urban areas, degraded natural habitats, and a few preserved remnants of what once was. So much has been lost.

The casual visitor to these islands will be surprised at some of the forms that once existed here. Cuba can boast of animals of truly gigantic proportions, yet it is also home to one of the world's smallest vertebrates.

Not all of the fauna discussed here disappeared because of human activities. Some species were gone long before humans first stepped ashore on the islands. Those were victims of changing environmental conditions or simply disappeared as a result of an evolutionary experiment that did not pan out.

Three major periods of extinction transpired in the Caribbean. The first occurred during the Pleistocene, approximately ten thousand years ago, when climate change resulted in the global melting of glaciers and a resultant rise in sea level, which flooded low-lying areas, greatly reducing the sizes of some islands and overwashing others. At that time, several islands we now classify as having humid, lush tropical habitats were dominated by drier, palm savannas, with flora and fauna adapted to that climate. This climatic shift resulted in dramatic responses in the plant and animal makeup of the islands, some species becoming extinct and others, with good dispersal potential, relocating to more favorable environments.

The second period of extinction probably began with the arrival of Amerindians, perhaps about forty-five hundred years ago. Although little direct evidence shows the effects of early native peoples on their island environments, undoubtedly many of the large and slow-moving terrestrial mammals and flightless birds of the region were aggressively hunted and thereby suffered population declines. Humans then, as today, made direct use of wildlife—they ate them. In fact, we know of some extinct species because of their remains in human refuse heaps.

The third extinction period began with the arrival of European explorers and colonists and extends through today's intensive development. The extensive and rapid effects of habitat alteration, and introduction of exotic predators, competitors, and disease, have caused the decline and extinction of many more species.

Unfortunately, we know very little about early ecosystems on many of the Caribbean islands, where relatively few fossils of animals have been unearthed. In part this is because some islands lend themselves better to the preservation of fossil specimens. Some islands have caves where predatory animals carried their prey and left the remains in an environment favorable to their preservation.

A few islands such as Cuba had petroleum seeps where animals became mired and preserved in tar. Also, not all islands had the type of predators, such as large predatory birds, that captured prey and deposited their remains in sites suitable for preservation. This inadequate fossil record makes it difficult to fully appreciate the prehistoric ecosystems of the Caribbean. Nevertheless, what we do have gives a fascinating glimpse into the wondrous lost world of the islands, allowing us to envision the curious fauna that formerly existed here.

The long isolation of the Caribbean islands from the mainland is well exemplified by the mammalian fauna. Apart from bats, there is solid evidence of only four major groups of native land mammals in the Caribbean: insectivores, sloths, rodents, and primates. Among these, possibly the sloth representatives are the most surprising—surprising because these large, sedentary beasts would seem unlikely colonists to islands. But these sloths apparently had an exceptional ability to cross water barriers. All ground sloths are now extinct, but at one time these animals were apparently quite abundant. A single deposit within a Cuban cave yielded remains of more than two hundred individuals.

Another surprise is that several of the Caribbean islands were formerly inhabited by primates other than humans. There are no monkeys in the Caribbean today other than introduced species. Only a few thousand years ago, however, distinct endemic monkeys inhabited Cuba, Hispaniola, and Jamaica. Most of these probably had disappeared before European colonization, although a Jamaican species appears to have survived until after 1500, so that early explorers may have seen a monkey swinging through the primal forests.

The original mammal fauna of the Caribbean was especially rich in rodent species. This richness is in good part because, next to bats, rodents are by far the most successful mammalian colonizers of islands. Many of the Caribbean rodents were once extraordinarily abundant, some cave deposits containing thousands of specimens. Though some forms have survived, many more have disappeared forever, most likely the result of human activities. Hutias were prized by Amerindians as food, and the rodents' remains are common in their garbage piles.

Members of the extinct so-called giant hutias occurred in several of the Greater and northern Lesser Antillean islands. A Jamaican species of this group may have weighed as much as 40–50 kg (90–110 lb.), whereas another, the Blunt-toothed Mouse (*Amblyrhiza inundata*), not a mouse at all, which lived in St. Martin and Anguilla, attained almost bear size, weighing up to 150 kg (330 lb.). By comparison, today's hutias rarely weigh more than 2 kg (4.5 lb.).

Perhaps the most intriguing of the Caribbean mammals are the insectivores. The largest forms are the two living species of solenodon, known from Cuba and Hispaniola. A third fossil species has also been described from the latter island. At least eight species of smaller insectivores in the genus *Nesophontes* occurred through the Greater Antilles. Although *Nesophontes* are

Cuban Solenodon

11

known only from fossil remains, some are so recent that hope exists that a protected pocket of such animals may yet survive in some remote site.

The absence of native predatory mammals in the Caribbean left an open niche that was filled by large meat-eating birds. Most of these ancient raptors are now extinct, and many were of great size.

Raptorial birds were the principal predators of the Caribbean's mammals and were responsible for much of what we know of the fossil record, because they left evidence of their depredations in caves and other sites. These raptors were particularly diverse and included some truly fantastic forms. Cuba, with its varied large mammal fauna, had a particularly interesting assortment of raptors. Among these was a gigantic Cuban eagle, larger than any living eagle. A Cuban condor, approximately the size of the present-day Andean Condor, with its 3-m (10-ft.) wingspan, probably fed on the decaying remains of extinct ground sloths and a terrestrial tortoise.

Along with the condors, eagles, and other day-active raptors, nocturnal raptors were also an important component of the Caribbean's meat-eating birds. Among these was a giant barn owl from Haiti and other large, robust barn owls from Great Exuma, New Providence, and Cuba. Also, the Titanic Owl is known from several localities in Cuba. The breastbone and wings of the Titanic Owl were much smaller than flying birds, which suggests this owl was flightless. Perhaps it could glide to some extent, but capturing its ground sloth prey probably required little flying ability. Extinction of the large mammalian prey would have driven the Titanic Owl, Cuban Eagle, and other carnivorous birds to a similar demise.

The absence of mammalian predators allowed several avian forms to evolve toward flightlessness. This included some rails and an ibis. Among other unique birds that have disappeared from the region are a small goose, snipe, woodcock, swift, and quail-dove.

We closely associate parrots and their kin with the tropics, and these splendid birds formerly occurred through most of the Caribbean. Three genera of parrots inhabited the Caribbean: macaws, parakeets, and Amazon parrots. Gaps in parrot distribution suggest several extinctions, and there are as many as fifteen or sixteen species of Caribbean parrots that are believed to have existed, based on drawings or descriptions from early literature. Indeed, some of the best evidence of their former existence comes from the logs of early explorers and descriptions by colonists who harvested these macaws, parrots, and parakeets for the pot. Some, such as the supposed species of Amazon parrot from Guadeloupe and Martinique, are likely valid, because parrots of this genus occur on nearby St. Vincent, St. Lucia, and Dominica, as well as throughout the Greater Antilles. In the Caribbean the only macaw to survive long enough for specimens to be preserved was the Cuban Macaw, which probably became extinct in the mid-1860s. Old accounts suggest the possibility of another seven or eight macaws in both the Greater and Lesser Antilles.

Although the fossil record for reptiles and amphibians is poor, likely these animals suffered the same extinction patterns experienced by birds and mammals as the seas rose and fell, climates changed, and humans altered the island environments.

Picturing a past Cuba with huge flightless owls shuffling through the savanna while colorful macaws and giant eagles flew overhead boggles one's imagination.

So much has been lost. Yet many of the extinctions in the distant past were a natural result of evolving ecosystems. Unfortunately, current extinction and extirpation rates, virtually all human induced, may far exceed any that occurred in past epochs. Much more stands to be lost unless the accelerating rate of species endangerment is somehow checked.

HABITATS

TROPICAL RAIN FORESTS

Zebra Butterfly

Tropical rain forests are the most luxuriant of all tropical forest types because they receive some 200 cm (80 in.) of rain annually and are wet ten or so months of the year. Rain forests are found in lowland and mountainous areas, primarily on the windward side of high mountains. The vegetation is evergreen, grows in layers, and the tallest trees reach to 30 m (100 ft.) or more in height. With higher elevations, temperatures fall and rain increases. Surfaces become thickly encrusted with ferns, mosses, bromeliads, and orchids. The highest-elevation forests, usually enshrouded in clouds, are referred to as *cloud forests*. Moisture derives not only from rain but also from heavy mist of the clouds that obscure the mountain peaks. The uppermost forests of high, wet mountains are often stunted, the result of the high precipitation, poor soils, and strong winds, and are referred to as *dwarf forests* or *elfin forests*. Unfortunately, most rain forests, particularly those of the lowlands, have been severely degraded or destroyed in the Caribbean.

TROPICAL DRY (OR DECIDUOUS) FORESTS

These forests and woodlands occur in areas that receive approximately 75–130 cm (30–50 in.) of rain annually and are characterized by five to seven humid months. Dry forests are often found on the leeward sides of mountains. More open than wet forests, the trees rarely exceed 9 m (30 ft.) in height and lose their leaves during the dry season. Because the sun penetrates the more open canopy, ground cover is often dense, composed of thorny brush, and thereby quite difficult to penetrate.

SAVANNAS

Prior to European colonization savannas were not widely distributed in the Caribbean. Now these flat, dry grasslands containing scattered trees and palms are found on most islands where man has removed the original vegetation through burning and other forms of land conversion. Natural savannas occurred only in

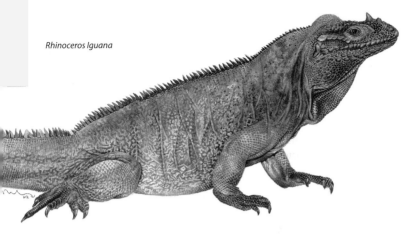

Rhinoceros Iguana

areas of seasonal drought and hard, coarse soils, such as in several expanses of Cuba, Hispaniola, and the northern Bahamas.

TROPICAL KARSTIC (MOGOTE) FORESTS

Mogotes, also referred to as *haystack hills* and, in Jamaica, *cockpit country*, are tightly spaced limestone hills with intervening valleys and sinks, giving an inverted egg-carton appearance to the area from an aerial view. The formation is characterized by dry, well-drained, and thin soils, although vegetation is typically lush and dense, particularly in the deeper soils of the sinks and valleys. Still, trees may reach upward of 25 m (80 ft.) in height. The karstic forests are quite difficult to hike through, unless one follows an established trail. This habitat is confined to the islands of the Greater Antilles.

THORNY WOODLANDS AND CACTUS SCRUB

These vegetative types are found on flat islands and dry leeward coasts, which generally receive less than 75 cm (30 in.) of rain and experience only three to four humid months per year. The habitat consists of low trees, seldom more than 2 m (6–7 ft.) tall, but so dense that they are almost impenetrable. Cactus scrub is more open and typified by abundant columnar cacti. Thorny woodlands and cactus scrub cover much of the Bahamas.

MANGROVE SWAMPS

Originally encircling the bays and other protected shorelines of most islands, mangroves have been widely destroyed to open such areas to other uses, from marinas to shrimp farms. Though important for storm protection, reef fish nurseries, and soil stabilization among other benefits, mangrove habitat continues to decline. The Caribbean's four species of mangrove display varying tolerances to salt and water depth. As a result they generally grow in sequence from Red Mangrove, the most seaward of the species, to Black Mangrove,

White Mangrove, and then Button Mangrove as one proceeds incrementally to higher ground.

CORAL REEFS

Coral reefs represent the most distinctive and fascinating habitat within the marine environment. Perhaps the most biologically diverse environment known, coral reefs occur in clear, shallow waters throughout the Caribbean and most of the tropical and subtropical waters of the Earth. Stony corals form the core of the reef community. Such corals are actually colonies of small organisms called *polyps* (see the text on corals for more details, pp.268–73) connected to one another by their external skeletons. Numerous other species are associated with these corals either as a food source, for protective cover, or as a base upon which to attach or build their own burrows, among other reasons. Such species include fish, sponges, crustaceans, mollusks, marine worms, coelenterates, and bryozoans, among many other types of marine organisms. Regrettably, reefs are very sensitive to environmental change, and thus there are many threats to their survival. Among these are pollution and runoff from adjacent land areas, dredging and the sedimentation derived from it, coral harvesting, blasting to harvest fish, and disease. Coupled with these threats are broader threats resulting from sea level rise, increased water temperature, and changes in acidity. Benefits provided by reef communities include, among others, support of major fish and shellfish industries, ecotourism, buffering of coastal areas from storm impacts, and marine species for the aquarium trade.

HURRICANES AND THEIR INFLUENCE ON HABITATS AND WILDLIFE

Hurricanes are a fact of life in the Caribbean. These savage storms have been shaping island environments for millennia, and, in fact, indigenous island plant and animal communities are adapted to survive them. Indeed, some species and habitats are dependent on these irregular storms to disperse and invigorate them. Still, we rightly fear hurricanes as agents of great destruction of property and even life. Certainly, they greatly alter habitats and affect wildlife dependent upon those habitats, including killing some individuals outright. As we learn more about hurricanes, however, we find that the effects are not felt as severely during the high winds and heavy rains as the storm passes over an island, but rather in the aftermath of the event when forests are opened up to greater exposure to sunlight, thereby altering humidity and wind patterns. Birds dependent on fruits may find these completely stripped from trees. Many trees may lose their leaves entirely, leaving numerous creatures without protective cover and exposing them to predation. On the other hand, some insect-feeding species and large predators may increase in numbers as they take advantage of exposed food resources.

These impressive storms serve an important function in estuarine and mangrove lagoon areas, scouring the basins of accumulated deposits of soils, redistributing nutrients, and providing reenergized habitats for organisms such as larval fish and invertebrates.

Hurricanes usually develop from August through October, typically as a result of a powerful upward air current arising out of the eastern Caribbean or eastern Atlantic Ocean off Africa. This upward air movement creates a circular area of exceptionally low pressure that spirals inward (counterclockwise in the Northern Hemisphere) around the storm's calm center, or *eye*. The heaviest damage occurs near the center of the storm, but dangerous weather may extend over an area 1,000 km (600 mi.) in diameter. Generally, hurricanes bring torrential rains; as much as 46 cm (18 in.) in one twenty-four-hour period has been recorded. Except at the eye, wind speeds are awesome, with velocities of 120+ kph (75+ mph) being common, and gusts near the center exceeding 320 kph (200 mph)! A hurricane's path is unpredictable, given the state of our technology, but in the Caribbean most tend to wobble slowly westward, at about 16 kph (10 mph), passing by or through the Lesser Antilles and then the Greater Antilles. Thereafter, the storm typically curves to the northeast or north, either slamming into the southeastern coast of the United States or petering out in the mid-Atlantic Ocean.

The routes of such storms are random, or *stochastic*, meaning we cannot predict when one will strike an individual island. For that reason, an island may be spared a direct hit by a hurricane for decades. Yet when a severe storm does hit, it can cause massive damage. On the other hand, storm-damaged trees provide cavities for shelter and nest sites for many animals, such as parrots. As one gazes at the vast and severe damage resulting from a recent hurricane, it is sometimes difficult to imagine good coming from the dramatically changed landscape, which to some resembles the aftermath of a powerful explosive. Nevertheless, some good there is, if one undertakes to find it.

FOLKLORE

Culturally, the Caribbean is an extraordinarily diverse region, and the folklore surrounding its plants and animals reflect that diversity. In Cuba, in previous centuries, the red breast of the Cuban Trogon was considered representative of the king of Spain's red sash; consequently, any negative aspersions cast about the bird were considered an insult to the king and were punished. In Jamaica, the calling of an owl near one's dwelling at night is said to portend death. In Puerto Rico, anole lizards are believed to be useful for extracting splinters. There are many, many other such tales. Regrettably, as fascinating as these may be, most have no basis in fact, and, more important, many result in the hostile treatment if not destruction of entirely innocent animals and plants. As a result, it is important that we all become aware of what is truth and what is fiction; that we recognize that the vast majority of the organisms of the Caribbean are harmless; that we understand that most native species serve important ecological functions; and perhaps of greatest importance, that an extraordinary number of the species around us are unique to the Caribbean, if not to one particular island, making them especially worthy of our pride, as they are unique to where we live. In the end, their disappearance would be a loss for all of humanity.

ENVIRONMENTAL THREATS AND CONSERVATION

ENVIRONMENTAL THREATS

High atop Mt. Misery among the rain and fog, the Mountain Blacksmith wailed away to no avail, calling and calling but evoking no response. As the rain grew heavier and the wind stronger, even this hearty soul gave up his familiar refrain, heard on the mountain from time immemorial, to shelter in a dense thicket as protection from the oncoming storm. But this was not just the kind of storm so common to these inhospitable climes, the kind that had given this formidable mountain its name. This was one of the great tempests of the century, sweeping up from the southeast, expanding as it came and thundering over St. Kitts, the tiny island the Mountain Blacksmith called home, like a tsunami striking an open beach.

Little in the storm's path remained unscathed—man made or otherwise. Boats, docks, houses, and churches; crops, woodlands, fields, and forests; all were wrought asunder by this great storm, setting the prosperity of the island back decades. And what of the Mountain Blacksmith? The storm virtually sealed his fate. Though he is reportedly seen from time to time, it is more likely than not that he has disappeared from the landscape forever—another uniquely Caribbean feature lost for all time to a changing world.

And what remains to remind us of the Mountain Blacksmith? Specimens in a museum—for the Mountain Blacksmith was a bird, a bird with a distinctive, clinking call that reminded one of a human blacksmith hammering away at his anvil time after time after time. In life, also like a blacksmith, it was robust, with a massive bill and stocky build. Its almost entirely black plumage served only to set off the reddish-orange markings on its throat and eyebrow and beneath its tail. The little we know of the Mountain Blacksmith, which left us now the better part of a century ago, can best be derived from the observation of its much smaller cousin, the Puerto Rican Bullfinch, which survives on that neighboring island to the north.

Doubtless the Mountain Blacksmith was a bird of dense forest and forest edges, particularly of thick undergrowth, which on St. Kitts at the time of European colonization likely extended virtually from seashore to mountaintop, providing ample habitat for the Mountain Blacksmith and allowing it to span the length and breadth of its island home. Increased colonization, however, brought the clearing of the lowlands and the gradual expansion of agricultural crops farther and farther up the slopes of all the foothills and ultimately Mt. Misery itself. This rapid and dramatic conversion from forest to other land uses was a substantial setback for the Mountain Blacksmith, which was incapable of adapting to fields of sugarcane and expanses of open pastureland—much as the advent of the automobile signaled the demise of human blacksmiths.

European colonization brought other threats to the Mountain Blacksmith beyond those of direct destruction of its living quarters. Various predators that threatened the birds, their eggs, and their young were introduced into St. Kitts— rats and cats and, perhaps worst of all, the African Green Monkey, which forayed well up onto Mt. Misery, the last bastion of the Mountain Blacksmith. Some believe it is the monkey that served the *coup de grace* to the Mountain Blacksmith, but this is not likely the case. While it is probable that the monkey indeed helped push the Mountain Blacksmith to the edge—making the bird's existence so precarious that the smallest additional perturbation could do it in—that is where a hurricane such as the one described may have come into play. With the Mountain Blacksmith now confined to tiny remnant forest plots, a direct hit by a severe hurricane could have been the last straw.

That the Mountain Blacksmith succumbed as described above is conjecture, but that it is gone, there is now little doubt.

The case of the Mountain Blacksmith is in no way unique. Regrettably, similar scenarios have been played out in very much the same way throughout the Caribbean and, in fact, throughout the world. Not surprisingly, islands, such as those of the Caribbean, are especially susceptible to extinctions of this sort because, by their very nature, they provide a species limited geographic areas on which to eke out its existence. Also, because many oceanic islands have existed in the absence of predatory mammals such as rats, cats, and mongooses, indigenous species lack some of the predator-avoidance adaptations inherent in their continental counterparts and suffer the consequences when such predators are introduced. As a result, a disproportionate share of the threatened and endangered species of the world are island forms.

According to the latest summary of both critically endangered and endangered species in the Caribbean, prepared by the International Union for the Conservation of Nature, the numbers break out as follows:

Animal Group	Critically Endangered	Endangered
Mammals	7	11
Birds	11	19
Reptiles	22	21
Amphibians	68	63

Let's look at the principal causes of endangerment and some of the Caribbean species they have affected:

HABITAT DESTRUCTION AND ALTERATION

The destruction and modification of natural habitats throughout the Caribbean is far and away the major cause of species decline whether one looks island by island or on a region-wide basis. Habitat destruction has derived from a wide variety of causes, including clearing land for home building, agriculture, industry, resorts, port facilities, ranching, timber harvesting, and charcoal production, among others. Not only is the loss of habitat disastrous for some animal and plant species, but in many cases it is irreversible. Linked to the destruction of habitats is their alteration. Even forests that remain uncut, wetlands that remain unfilled, and savannas that remain unurbanized have been substantially modified. In fact, not a single remaining natural habitat in the Caribbean remains unaltered. Almost every freshwater wetland in the Caribbean is marred by canals, constructed long ago to better control mosquitoes and the spread of malaria. Grasslands, one of the few habitats that has actually increased in extent, are so infested with alien plants as to be unrecognizable from pre-colonial days. Arid scrublands, another habitat that has arguably increased in acreage, are so heavily browsed by introduced goats and cattle, not to mention harvested for charcoal, that their current vegetative state—thorny, scrawny, and low-growing— differs dramatically from their natural condition.

Yellow-striped Dwarf Frog

Which organisms have suffered most from habitat destruction? There's quite a list. Most noticeably we can point to species heavily dependent on forests, particularly, all of the parrots and parakeets, forest hawks, and some of the quail-doves and songbirds.

INTRODUCED PREDATORS

Norway and Black Rats were introduced into the Caribbean so long ago that their impacts on the local fauna are poorly understood, though they are well known for taking the eggs and young of birds. The impact of the Javan Mongoose, introduced in the late 1880s and early 1900s to many islands, can be more clearly seen. Brought to the islands to control rat infestations in the region's priceless sugarcane plantations, the mongoose did not hesitate to add to its diet the multitude of native organisms formerly common to the islands. By as early as 1900 mongoose populations had burgeoned, while ground-dwelling species such as lizards, snakes, ground-doves, goatsuckers, and some owls had taken a dramatic nosedive. In Jamaica in 1948 the endemic rock iguana was believed extinct, but fortunately it was rediscovered in 1990 and a headstarting program was initiated. The greatest threat to the iguana was mongooses feeding on hatchlings. Another preeminent case demonstrating the impact of the mongoose on local faunas is that of the St. Croix Ground Lizard, which was wiped out on that island, where the mongoose became common, but continued to survive in numbers on offshore Protestant and Green Cays where mongooses had not invaded.

Fortuitously, over time mongoose populations declined, apparently a result of the species virtually eating itself out of house and home. This provided enough of a respite for ground-dwelling creatures that some of them have managed a comeback. The Puerto Rican Nightjar, Short-eared Owl, and a number of quail-doves likely owe their recoveries to the stabilization of mongoose populations at a lower level or to human-generated conservation actions, rather than to any adaptation they have made.

The mongoose is not the only predator necessitating concern. Feral pigs on Mona Island off Puerto Rico have been known to dig up rock iguana nests so efficiently as to destroy every egg during particularly bad years. On Abaco in the Bahamas, feral cats have been documented as major predators on that island's unique ground-nesting Rose-throated Parrot. Were we to know the impact of introduced predators on the Caribbean's fascinating native lizards and snakes, we would doubtless have a horror story of devastation.

OVERHUNTING AND OVERHARVESTING

Hunting wild game has been a basic component of human society since it first evolved. The extinctions of wild animals, including renowned species such as Wooly Mammoth, Mastodon, and Giant Sloth, among others, as far back as the Pleistocene ten thousand or more years ago, are believed to have resulted from overhunting by humans. In fact, increasing evidence from around the world suggests that the first global wave of human colonization—that undertaken by early indigenous societies many centuries before colonization by Europeans—resulted in extinctions on a massive scale. The demise of the thousand-pound Elephant Bird of Madagascar and the 3.7 m (12 ft.) tall Giant Moa of New Zealand are but a few dramatic examples. Suffice it to say that increased growth and expansion of human populations coupled with ever improving weapons has only served to exacerbate the potential threat to wildlife from uncontrolled hunting.

The Caribbean islands, like most regions of the world, have addressed this matter by the promulgation of hunting laws and regulations that aim to control the excessive taking of wildlife for food or sport. Regrettably, the shortage of solid scientific data on which to base hunting regulations, the lack of strong enforcement capabilities to control illegal hunting, combined with weak public support for such laws, result in overhunting remaining as a threat to various species throughout the region.

Larger animals of every type, whether fish or fowl, lizard or mammal, often suffer from overhunting, at least on a local scale. Among the lizards, the large rock iguanas of the genus *Cyclura* are an example. The Mountain Chicken, a large endemic frog of Dominica is a prized local food source. The West Indian Manatee, formerly abundant through much of the Caribbean, is now on the verge of extirpation due to overharvesting for its flesh. Numerous bird species, particularly among the waterfowl, doves, and to a lesser extent the parrots, are well known cases. Land crabs have declined dramatically from overharvesting, as have numbers of native marine organisms such as the Queen Conch, Spiny Lobster, and various groupers, to name a few.

In some cases, the eggs or young of local fauna are harvested rather than the adults. Eggs and sometimes young of many seabirds, for example, may be taken in great quantities while the adult birds are ignored. Eggs of marine turtles are also prized, though the adults of some species such as the Green Turtle are taken as well.

There is no doubt that hunting and harvesting of wildlife have historic roots in many Caribbean cultures. At the same time, such practices have had to be discontinued or dramatically curtailed in many localities due to resource depletion. It is only through the establishment of sustainable management practices that the fauna of the Caribbean can continue to serve as a harvestable and huntable resource.

WILDLIFE TRADE

International transport and trade of Caribbean fauna and flora has doubtless occurred since colonization by the Amerindians. It is believed that several Caribbean macaws and small mammals, some now extinct, were transported from island to island in Amerindian canoes. In recent centuries, ton upon ton of West Indian Manatees was shipped from the Caribbean to South America for sale in local meat markets. To this day trade in exotic species such as parrots, butterflies, and orchids has significantly impacted some Caribbean species.

The Convention on International Trade of Endangered Species (CITES), to which most Caribbean countries are party, attempts to regulate international trade of plants and animals. Effective implementation of this convention could potentially lead to sustainable commerce of the region's flora and fauna.

PESTICIDES AND CONTAMINANTS

The impact of DDT and other pesticides have been well documented with regard to their effects on birdlife. A number of species that migrate to the Caribbean, of which the Osprey and Peregrine Falcon are examples, are still recovering from these deleterious effects. However, to date, evidence has yet to be gathered demonstrating a serious influence of pesticides and other toxic chemicals on year-round resident organisms. This may be more a result of the lack of data being generated rather than evidence that such impacts do not occur.

INVASIVE SPECIES

Many species, in addition to the introduced predators discussed above, have been brought to the Caribbean. Consequently, numerous species of foreign plants and animals now call the Caribbean their home. Introduced crocodilians are resident in Puerto Rico wetlands. Green Iguanas now reside in Virgin Islands mangroves. South American parrots are faring well in central Martinique. African finches thrive in Dominican Republic scrublands and occur on Jamaica as well. And the list goes on and on. The reasons leading to the introduction of such an array of exotic species is lengthy: beautification, a new food source, control of some pest, sheer accident. The bottom line is that most are here to stay. Their potential impacts should be recognized and dealt with, and measures to control such introductions in the future should seriously be considered.

The potential impacts of alien species vary. Some are obvious. Introducing crocodiles to wetlands near rural communities is fraught with the potential for direct physical danger to humans. Introducing "rice birds" such as the Java Sparrow and Nutmeg Mannikin to rice-producing islands can have serious economic consequences. And then there are the less obvious downsides of such introductions. Alien diseases to which local species are unaccustomed might spread across an island or through the entire region. Introduced species might compete with local forms for food or nest sites. Or exotic species might simply become a downright pest.

One invasive species of particular concern is the Shiny Cowbird of South America. Virtually unknown from the Caribbean prior to the twentieth century, this bird has now spread through the entire region. Being a nest parasite, the Shiny Cowbird does not build a nest but rather goes to the nests of other birds, where it replaces their eggs with its own. Being a generalist with regard to this habit, it is a threat to many species of birds. In the Caribbean local orioles and blackbirds are particularly susceptible, and Puerto Rico's Yellow-shouldered Blackbird verges on extinction as a result of Shiny Cowbird parasitism. Many other lowland Caribbean blackbirds may follow suit. Special attention should be kept among the islands for potential impacts from this insidious bird.

The problem of invasive species has impacted the Caribbean to such an extent that we shall explore it in a bit more detail. For many reasons, the Caribbean has accumulated an astounding variety of exotic plants and animals. Native habitats of the Caribbean have been seriously disrupted by the introduction of these exotic plants and animals. Whereas these introductions may be viewed by some as offsetting the loss of species through extinctions and extirpations, exotic species do not always fit smoothly into their new environment. Some become aggressive predators of or competitors with native species. Native species that have developed on remote oceanic islands in the absence of such predators or competitors are usually at a great disadvantage and may easily fall victim to such exotic invaders.

The history of introductions to the islands of the Caribbean is a long one, predating the arrival of Europeans in the region. Even so, the rate of introductions, as in other parts of the world, has greatly accelerated with the shrinking Earth's increased travel and communication. Rapid and frequent transportation among the islands and mainlands has provided easy access to what were formerly remote regions. Furthermore, our society's increasing interest in stocking gardens with exotic plants and in keeping exotic pets has also facilitated the rate of exotics becoming established in the region. Many of these introduced organisms may pose problems to the islands for a range of reasons, including a propensity to feed on food crops or carry exotic diseases, or because they challenge the existence of native species.

On the positive side, on rare occasions some islands may be viewed as important sanctuaries for exotic species experiencing severe population declines or facing extinction in their native ranges elsewhere in the world. For example, the Cuban Rock Iguana is under threat in its native range, but introduced populations in Puerto Rico thrive. It is conceivable that Puerto Rican populations of such species may someday be valuable reservoirs for reintroducing those species into their native lands.

Most species are unsuccessful at colonization. Nevertheless, the variety of species that have become permanent residents of the region is impressive, one might say frightening, when considering the ecological harm done by some of these organisms.

PLANTS

Because of the extensive cutting and modification of natural forests, widespread agriculture, and introduction of a large number of exotic species, little remains of the original vegetation in much of the Caribbean, particularly in the lowlands. Many introduced tree and other plant species have become naturalized on the islands, now appearing native. What better examples than Sugarcane, the Mango, and the Flamboyant Tree?

The Caribbean's native vegetation developed in the absence of large herbivorous mammals and may have been quite susceptible to introduced goats and cattle. Dry forests, particularly, have been severely damaged by grazing animals.

ANIMALS

The introduction of animals has had enormous effects on island ecosystems throughout the world. The most disruptive species include vertebrate and invertebrate predators and herbivorous mammals. Most extinctions of birds and mammals in the Caribbean have been attributed to habitat loss and the introduction of rats, cats, dogs, and mongooses.

Introduced mammals: Probably the earliest introductions of mammals were made by Amerindians commuting among the islands and carrying with them both pets and food animals to provide meat during long journeys. Thus, some mammals such as the Paca and Agouti from South America may have received assistance in reaching the Lesser Antilles.

Later introductions were made by European explorers and colonists. Finding no source of large animals for meat, they established populations of goats, pigs, horses, and cattle on the islands. The long-term result of these introductions has been widespread modification of natural habitats, including their being cut to provide grazing lands. In addition, pigs have proven major predators of some native birds and reptiles.

Some mammals, like the Javan Mongoose, were introduced purposefully, whereas others were accidental. As mentioned previously, the mongoose was introduced to the Caribbean from 1872 to 1925 to help control rats and snakes. Instead of ridding those islands of rats, however, the mongoose eliminated several species of native animals. Cats and dogs are particularly destructive to native wildlife on small islands. Because they were introduced into the Caribbean hundreds of years before the mongoose, it is difficult to determine the damage they inflicted on native animal populations.

House Rats undoubtedly accompanied Columbus, uninvited, on his first voyage to the New World in 1492, and they probably beat the travel-weary sailors ashore. Certainly the mariners were glad to get rid of some of their guests, but the introduction was not done on purpose. Exotic rats and mice are now widespread in the Caribbean and have been implicated in the declines of several native mammals, birds, and reptiles.

Well-meaning people have introduced some fairly bizarre mammals to the Caribbean. Sloths, anteaters, and armadillos were once introduced into Jamaica. Some, like the White-tailed Deer introduced from North America, were brought to provide big game for hunters. The White-lipped Peccary and Collared Peccary were introduced into Cuba for that purpose, most recently on game ranches that also possess zebras, black buck, and other hoof stock. Early on, Cuba experimented with various beasts of burden, including the Dromedary and Llama.

Populations of African Green and Mona Monkeys are established on several of the Lesser Antilles. They probably descended from pets brought by African slave traders in the 1600s. Apparently the African Green Monkey initially increased rapidly on Barbados, then crashed in the eighteenth century because of bounty hunting and loss of forest habitat. It later increased again in the 1950s after some areas had become reforested.

Several primates, including the Rhesus Monkey, Patas Monkey, and Pigtail Macaque, were introduced into islands off Puerto Rico to study their social behavior and other aspects of primate biology. Unfortunately, some have escaped to the mainland and multiplied. There they may be a threat to native fauna as well as causing damage to crops. Rhesus Monkeys introduced into Puerto Rico's Desecheo Island are suspect in the near complete loss of the largest booby nesting colony in the Caribbean, as well as the decline of some reptiles.

Introduced birds: Most introductions of birds were probably accidental releases, but some were purposeful. Northern Bobwhite, introduced as game, survives through much of its Caribbean range but tenuously, probably because of intense predation by the mongoose. The well-established Troupial and Turkey Vulture were also introduced intentionally into Puerto Rico and other islands, and many species of cage birds have become established in the islands. Whereas certain exotics (e.g., some estrildid finches inhabiting grasslands) have had no apparent effect on native wildlife or plants, others are a current or potential threat to native wildlife or crops. The House Sparrow and European Starling have become well established in several island metropolitan areas within the last fifty years, and the exotic Hill Myna and White-vented Myna compete with native cavity nesting species such as the Puerto Rican Screech-Owl. At least eight species of exotic parrots breed in Puerto Rico and pose a threat to the endangered Puerto Rican Parrot as competitors for nest sites and food resources, and perhaps through interbreeding and disease transmission.

The Shiny Cowbird, mentioned earlier, was indirectly aided in its invasion of the Caribbean. The cowbird "island hopped" north from South America through the Caribbean as native forests were cut to make way for agriculture and pastures.

Introduced reptiles and amphibians: Several introduced reptiles and amphibians have become established in the Caribbean. Caimans, probably escaped or released pets, occur in Puerto Rico and Cuba. The Green Iguana was apparently introduced into several islands. The Red-footed Tortoise has been introduced into the Virgin Islands.

Native to tropical America, the Marine Toad was introduced into various Caribbean islands to control insect pests of sugarcane. The toad proliferated and helped to reduce cane pests, but it also competes with native species for food, habitat, and spawning sites.

Introduced freshwater fish: Numerous introduced species were released into native waters from aquarium stocks. Some, including several types of bass, were established as game species. Other efforts, such as those to establish Rainbow Trout, have met with failure because these temperate fish were unable to reproduce in the warm waters of the islands.

Introduced invertebrates: Native populations of freshwater snails, including *Physa cubensis*, have been affected by several introduced snails. An African species (*Tarebia granifera*) is now the most abundant snail in Puerto Rico. At least one introduced snail species has had a more direct effect on man. *Australorbis glabratus*, a possible introduction from South America, is an intermediate host to the debilitating human parasite that causes schistosomiasis, a serious ailment of the intestines and liver.

The European Honeybee, now established throughout the islands, was introduced by the earliest colonists. Honeybees have proven to be fierce competitors for natural cavities used as nests and roost sites by several native species. Recently, the Africanized Honeybee has been found in the Caribbean. This aggressive bee poses an even more serious threat to native cavity nesters and to humans unfamiliar with its aggressiveness.

CLIMATE CHANGE

The phenomenon of climate change, primarily influenced by the emission of greenhouse gases such as carbon dioxide into the atmosphere from businesses, homes, vehicles, and other human-made sources, has the potential to have catastrophic impacts on the fauna and flora of the Caribbean. Climate change is more than sea level rise—much more. It is irregular weather patterns, increased storm intensities, droughts, floods, nothing particularly good for any location no less an archipelago of small islands nestled in a hurricane belt. Already unclear causes, very possibly the result of our changing climate, have led to the extinction of extraordinary species such as the Golden Coqui, which has completely disappeared from intact forests in the Sierra de Cayey in Puerto Rico. A bromeliad dweller, this frog has gone unsighted since 1981. The list of such mysteriously disappearing species is growing, and there is every reason to expect its growth to accelerate. This is because the effects of climate change being observed today are actually the result of greenhouse gas emissions that occurred over twenty years ago. It is this lengthy lag time—the time between when emissions actually occur and when their impacts become evident—that is one of the great unknowns and ominous threats of climate change. There is little doubt that the impacts of climate change to the fauna and flora of the Caribbean will grow rapidly in years to come. How effectively we are able to adapt our conservation strategies to cope with this burgeoning threat will greatly influence the survival of more plant and animal species, both terrestrial and marine, than anyone might care to imagine.

CONSERVATION IN PRACTICE

The Caribbean is a large region; consequently, conservation efforts, programs, management infrastructures, and the like vary widely. Only a few examples will be presented here of some important or unique initiatives underway within the region.

The single greatest need in the Caribbean with regard to conservation is the need for the establishment of positive environmental values and attitudes among the islands. Until people develop pride in their local natural resources, or derive some value from them, these resources are susceptible to degradation. The development of a positive values system and pride among local islanders has the direct benefit of leading to much more dedicated and comprehensive conservation initiatives.

Fortuitously, it is in the Caribbean, on the island of St. Lucia, that one of the most exciting and effective conservation initiatives anywhere in the world was developed. That initiative, referred to as Conservation through Pride and implemented via a conservation education campaign, was created around the St. Lucia Parrot, which, at the time, had declined to number only about a hundred birds in the wild. On the verge of extinction, this parrot, locally known as "the Jacquot," was used as the symbol and "spokesperson" of an outreach campaign aimed to reach virtually every St. Lucian on the island. First, the "parrot" (a person in a parrot outfit) visited every school on St. Lucia and met with virtually every student. Schoolchildren were engaged in art contests, puppet shows, and many other activities oriented toward expanding their knowledge of and respect for the parrot and the habitats upon which it depends. A newsletter was produced on a regular basis and distributed far and wide. Community groups were visited, as were politicians and other decision-makers, to bolster their support of the initiative. Conservation through Pride went so far as to have local musicians write songs singing the praises of the Jacquot, and it had local clergy give sermons lauding the importance of conservation as a human endeavor.

The Jacquot was presented as something uniquely St. Lucian, which it is: a beautiful bird found only on this small island and nowhere else in the world; a global heritage entirely within the hands of St. Lucians to manage; something special that people would come from far and wide to see. As the campaign took off, positive developments began to occur on all fronts. Local businesses, recognizing the increased popularity of the bird, augmented their contributions to expand this conservation effort. The general citizenry, which had long prized the Jacquot as a cage bird, turned in their pets so that they could be bred or returned to the wild. In one extraordinary case, a local taxi driver, learning that his passenger wanted to be driven to the forest to collect a Jacquot for shipment abroad, drove the surprised fellow to the police station instead!

One might ask the outcome of this year-long intensive effort. Post-campaign surveys showed a significant boost in the attitudes of St. Lucians regarding the importance of conservation. Now, decades later, the St. Lucia Parrot is reported to number over one thousand birds, a dramatic increase, its population growing to the point that it is actually becoming a pest to local citrus farmers!

The extraordinary success of Conservation through Pride did not go unnoticed, leading other islands of the Caribbean to implement similar campaigns. St. Vincent and Dominica mirrored the St. Lucia effort, using their endemic parrots, the St. Vincent and Imperial Parrots respectively. Grenada, not possessing a parrot, used the endemic Grenada Dove to mount its campaign. Jamaica, despite having two endemic parrots, chose to feature an endemic butterfly, the largest in the world, as the campaign's spokesperson. Presently, in the Dominican Republic, one of its todies is serving as that local initiative's trademark.

St. Lucia Parrot

Little by little, Conservation through Pride campaigns have spread not only through the Caribbean but throughout the world. And everywhere the results have been the same—highly positive. The small island of St. Lucia, and its local creators of the Conservation through Pride campaign, deserve special credit for this extraordinary contribution to the toolkit available to conservationists worldwide.

Another major conservation initiative was begun by the Society for the Conservation and Study of Caribbean Birds. The effort focuses on the West Indian Whistling-Duck, a waterfowl species native only to the Caribbean. The society uses this duck as a flagship to draw attention to the plight of wetlands in the region. Education and outreach are the primary thrust of the initiative, with special attention directed toward training elementary school teachers to incorporate wetlands conservation into their classrooms. A major outcome was the creation of a teacher's manual for this purpose, but other results include a wide range of materials from slide presentations to puppet shows and coloring books, all aimed at stimulating local interest and support for conserving this resident duck and local wetlands. Some monitoring is also conducted on the West Indian Whistling-Duck, a difficult-to-find bird, a species active primarily at night and one that roosts in vegetated swamps during the day. One of the most significant developments from this initiative to date, besides the teacher and classroom materials produced, has been the establishment in the Cayman Islands of a well-signed interpretive trail in a wetland of importance to the duck. The initiative stands virtually alone as an example of inter-island cooperation in the conservation of wetlands and the species on which they depend.

A unique and highly successful conservation tool popular in the Caribbean is the environmentally oriented radio soap opera. Radio in the Caribbean remains widely listened to today; thus, the broadcasting of conservation-oriented soap operas has served to dramatically enhance social consciousness. Refined by the group PCI Media Impact, these soaps serve as a powerful tool to arouse public conscientiousness and influence local behavior. Various soap opera series have been run that have led to positive public responses with regard to the conservation of marine turtle eggs, the threats to endangered parrots, and other environmental concerns.

As discussed earlier, numerous exotic species have been introduced into the Caribbean, where many have taken hold, flourished, and have affected native species in negative ways, some to the point of extinction. The likely elimination of the Jamaican Petrel by the Javan Mongoose is an example. Consequently, the removal of introduced species, in selective cases, can help to restore native forms in dramatic fashion. In fact, the removal of exotic pest species from small islands is one of the least expensive and most cost-effective conservation tools when compared to the benefits gained. Such efforts have proven a resounding success with regard to the St. Croix Ground Lizard, Antiguan Racer, and various seabird colonies, among others. The organization Island Conservation has demonstrated great leadership in prioritizing islands that could benefit from invasive species removal and the implementation of effective removal techniques.

The Caribbean is home to many other wildlife conservation efforts. Endemic Bird Day, an initiative built around the pride local people should have in species found on their islands and nowhere else in the world, has become highly popular and successful throughout the region. Haiti is considering incorporation of native birds onto its currency so as to foment local interest in that nation's avifauna. Puerto Rico supports one of the world's most long-term parrot conservation programs in an effort to sustain its critically endangered parrot. Cuba has dedicated impressive resources to an extensive program to conserve representative ecosystems the length and breadth of the island. It is also actively engaged in trying to save the last remnant population of the Ivory-billed Woodpecker, a species already extinct in the United States. Various islands are preparing booklets on their common birds for use in local schools and to stimulate the lay public's interest and appreciation of birds. Haiti, Dominica, and Puerto Rico have done so to date.

So, much is underway, all of this in addition to the gradually increasing base of protected areas, both terrestrial and marine, being designated within the region. This array of initiatives is beginning to produce a cadre of individuals prepared to face the many conservation challenges that lie ahead. The future of the Caribbean's fauna and flora is in their hands.

TERRESTRIAL LIFE

FLAMBOYANT TREE OR ROYAL POINCIANA *Delonix regia*

KEY FEATURES This small to medium-size deciduous tree grows to 15 m (50 ft.) high and 60 cm (2 ft.) in trunk diameter. It is covered with brilliant masses of large, orange-red flowers mostly from May to July or August. Even when flowers are absent, it is easily identified by the feathery foliage and the giant flat, blackish or dark brown pods that resemble machetes.

seed pods

STATUS AND RANGE Widespread in the Caribbean where planted to beautify highways, streets, parks, and gardens of both moist and dry areas. Primarily coastal but also occurs at moderate elevations. Also a shade tree and used as a living fencepost. It sometimes escapes from cultivation and becomes naturalized. Native to Madagascar, it is one of the most extensively planted ornamental trees in tropical and subtropical regions of the world. This is the national flower of St. Kitts and Nevis and the national tree of St. Maarten.

flowers and seed pods

AFRICAN TULIPTREE
Spathodea campanulata

KEY FEATURES A large tree best recognized by the treetop clusters of tubular, tulip-like, flame-colored flowers 10 cm (4 in.) long that are present year-round. The seedpods are large, erect, green to dark brown, and up to 25 cm (10 in.) long. They characteristically point upward at the branch tips. The tree grows to 25 m (80 ft.) high and 45 cm (1.5 ft.) in trunk diameter, with a dense irregular crown. It has leaves year-round or nearly so. The trunks of larger trees possess tall narrow buttresses at their base.

STATUS AND RANGE Widespread in the Caribbean where cultivated for ornament and shade, growing in coastal limestone, on coastal plains, and in lower mountain regions. It is an introduced species native to West Africa that has become established throughout the warmer climates of the world. Other names include Flame of the Forest and Fountain Tree.

YELLOW CASSIA *Senna siamea*

KEY FEATURES A straight-trunked, medium-size broad-leaved evergreen tree to 18 m (60 ft.) in height and 30 cm (1 ft.) in trunk diameter. The crown is generally erect, not spreading like most similar species. Flowers are bright yellow and numerous, the five rounded petals forming erect large terminal clusters. The abundant dark brown pods are long, narrow, and flat. They split open to release the seeds.

STATUS AND RANGE Occurring through the Greater Antilles (uncommon in Jamaica) and on many Lesser Antilles islands, this tree is principally used for ornament, shade, and windbreaks. It is commonly planted along highways and streets and in parks and yards, in moist and dry coastal, moist limestone, and lower mountain regions. This exotic has escaped and is naturalized locally. Native of southeastern Asia but spread by cultivation.

seed pods

WHITE CEDAR *Tabebuia heterophylla*

KEY FEATURES A small to medium-size, mostly deciduous tree attaining 18 m (60 ft.) in height and 45 cm (1.5 ft.) in trunk diameter, with an erect trunk and narrow crown. The tree is covered in beautiful masses of showy pink, tubular five-lobed flowers 5–9 cm (2–3.5 in.) long primarily from March to July. It has dark brown cigarlike pods approximately 20 cm (8 in.) long.

STATUS AND RANGE This tree occurs in the Bahamas, Greater Antilles, Cayman Islands, Virgin Islands, and throughout the Lesser Antilles to Grenada and Barbados. It is widespread in forests, abandoned pastures, secondary forests, forest plantations, and along roads and city streets. The species prefers full sun and tolerates poor soils. It is native to the Caribbean where widely cultivated. Another name, Pink Trumpet Tree, derives from its gorgeous flowers. Related species have flowers of different colors, including red and yellow.

33

BUTTERFLY BAUHINIA *Bauhinia monandra*

KEY FEATURES Small, broad-leaved evergreen tree, to 9 m (30 ft.) high and 30 cm (1 ft.) in trunk diameter. The unusual leaves, from which its name is derived, are butterflylike, with eleven or thirteen main veins radiating from the heart-shaped base. Note the flowers—large, showy, and pink, with spoon-shaped petals. The pods are flat, about 20 cm (8 in.) long and 2.5 cm (1 in.) wide.
STATUS AND RANGE This tree occurs from Cuba to Barbados. It is planted for its large ornamental flowers, suggestive of orchids, and odd-shaped leaves. Escapes from cultivation become naturalized along roads and rivers and form thickets in coastal, limestone, and lower mountain regions. This is an introduced species native to southeastern Asia. Other names include Orchid Tree, Napoleon's Plume, and Bull Hoof, due to the shape of the leaves.

QUEEN OF FLOWERS *Lagerstroemia speciosa*

KEY FEATURES A small, cultivated tree to 9 m (30 ft.) high, with a trunk to 20 cm (8 in.) in diameter. The dense crown is rounded or widely spreading. The beautiful lavender or purple flowers, 5–6 cm (2–2.5 in.) across with six rounded, crinkled and wavy-edged, spreading petals, form large, loosely branched, terminal clusters 15–46 cm (6–18 in.) long. Seed capsules are grayish brown, rounded, and split into six parts, and they shed many brown-winged seeds.

STATUS AND RANGE Planted for ornament and shade, along streets and in gardens. It sometimes escapes from cultivation. Native from India to southern China, Malay Peninsula, Philippines, East Indies, and northern Australia. Also called Giant Crape Myrtle and Pride of India. The related Crape Myrtle (*L. indica*), which displays showy, light purple flower clusters, is also widely introduced, particularly in Jamaica and Puerto Rico.

INDIA-RUBBER FIG OR RUBBER PLANT *Ficus elastica*

KEY FEATURES A medium-size to large evergreen tree to 18 m (60 ft.) in height and 1 m (3 ft.) in trunk diameter, with an extensive superficial root system and numerous aerial roots about the trunk. The large, leathery, oblong or elliptical, shiny green leaves, 10–30 cm (4–12 in.) long and 5–8 cm (2–3 in.) broad, are distinctive. Its small, figlike fruits are oblong, greenish yellow, paired, and stalkless. They are located at the base of leaves.

STATUS AND RANGE Widely planted in Cuba, Hispaniola, Puerto Rico, Virgin Islands, and Guadeloupe for ornament and shade along streets and in parks and gardens. The flower is pollinated only by a particular species of fig wasp. Where the wasp is absent the tree is reproduced using cuttings. The tree's latex can be used to make rubber, but commercial rubber is primarily extracted from a different tree species. The India-rubber Fig has been introduced throughout the world's warm climates but is native to tropical Asia from India to Malaya. Many species of *Ficus* occur in the Caribbean, a number of them having berries attractive to birds.

CAUTION The milky latex or sap is an irritant.

aerial roots

fruit on tree

NORFOLK ISLAND PINE
Araucaria heterophylla

KEY FEATURES A symmetrical evergreen tree, to 24 m (80 ft.) high, with a straight trunk up to 1 m (3 ft.) in diameter, enlarged at the base or with small broad buttresses. Note the narrow, highly symmetrical conical form of the dark green foliage. The horizontal branches are in whorls and the many slender ropelike twigs are arranged in a horizontal plane. Its leaves are needlelike, though on large trees they are broad and scale-like, crowded, and extending on all sides of the twig. The cone is rounded, hard, and 10–13 cm (4–5 in.) long.

STATUS AND RANGE An introduced ornamental on a number of islands in the Caribbean, where often cultivated around city homes in moist regions. Introduced widely in warmer regions of the world, it is native only on Norfolk Island in the South Pacific.

cones

ROYAL PALM *Roystonea* spp.

KEY FEATURES Several species of royal palms occur in the Caribbean. Most are similar in appearance. They are grand trees, some growing to over 30 m (100 ft.) tall, possessing distinctive long, slender trunks, some gently tapered, and bulging above the base. The trunk is topped by a conspicuous, pale-green leaf sheath that, in turn, is crowned by a dense cluster of drooping fronds.

crown

fruiting body

STATUS AND RANGE One of the most regal of roadside trees, the majestic Royal Palm lives up to its name. Most Caribbean islands host a native species, but Jamaica has two and Cuba five. Royal Palms are planted widely along roads and in large gardens and many other decorated landscapes. In the wild they are generally common in forests, pastures, and along river banks. *Roystonea stellata*, endemic to Cuba, is endangered and may now be extinct. Another species, extinct for millennia in the Dominican Republic, is known only from its flowers preserved in amber. Royal Palms generally occur in rich, well-watered soils. Their "hearts" are sometimes eaten for food and their seeds serve as a substitute for coffee. They are native to the Caribbean, Central America, Mexico, and the southern tip of Florida. This is the national tree of Cuba.

INDIAN ALMOND *Terminalia catappa*

KEY FEATURES A medium-size, broad-leaved, often evergreen tree, to 15 m (50 ft.) in height and 30 cm (1 ft.) in trunk diameter, sometimes larger and with small buttresses. Note the distinctive, large leathery leaves, broadest at the tip, turning reddish before falling. With age the tree becomes broader at the top, resulting in one of its local names—Umbrella Tree. Branches are horizontal, emerging in tiers. The flowers

are small and greenish white, in narrow lateral clusters. The distinctive fruit contains a large, edible nut.

STATUS AND RANGE A hardy and salt-tolerant introduced tree commonly planted for shade and ornament, especially along roadsides and sandy seashores. It has become naturalized and has escaped from cultivation. When red the fruit contains an edible nut that tastes like the true almond, though the trees are not closely related. Fruits are buoyant and spread by floating away from the parent plant. The leaves and bark serve in traditional medicine. Native of Malaysia, Indonesia, northern Australia, and Polynesia. Other names include Broadleaf and Seaside Almond.

fruit

SILK-COTTON TREE
Ceiba pentandra

KEY FEATURES This giant, buttressed, deciduous tree, one of the largest in tropical America, grows to 60 m (200 ft.) or more in height and 3 m (10 ft.) in diameter. The massive buttresses extend horizontally out from the trunk base as much as 3 m (10 ft.) and are almost as high. The crown is distinctively broad and flat. The pale-pink flowers are numerous. Seed capsules contain many seeds and woolly fibers.

STATUS AND RANGE Scattered and widely distributed along riverbanks and open hillsides on coastal plains and in lower mountain regions, it is most common in drier areas. Trees are occasionally planted for shade and ornament, and in many tropical towns a giant spreading Silk-Cotton Tree occupies the center of the plaza. Fibers surrounding the seeds are cottonlike and referred to as kapok, another name for the tree. Kapok was formerly popular for stuffing mattresses and upholstery, for insulation, and to fill life preservers because of its buoyancy. The bark has various medicinal uses, and the trunk was valued for making dugout canoes. The flower is bat pollinated. This tree was sacred to the Amerindians; thus even today, in Jamaica, it is believed one should not cut it down without first appeasing the spirit within—usually by sprinkling white rum around. Most likely the tree is native to tropical America, but it has been cultivated for so long that its origin is unknown.

buttress roots

hanging seed pods

thorny trunk

seed pod and kapok

WEST INDIAN LOCUST *Hymenaea courbaril*

KEY FEATURES Most readily identified by its distinctive, dark-brown seedpods each reminiscent of a large toe, giving rise to some of the tree's local names. A broad-leaved evergreen tree to 20 m (65 ft.) in height. It sometimes has buttresses. The leaves are compound, consisting of two almost stalkless, unequal-sided, oblong, shiny-green leaflets. The flowers are large, whitish, and numerous in erect terminal clusters.

STATUS AND RANGE Scattered in forests, pastures, and along roadsides in moist and dry coastal and limestone regions. It is native to the Caribbean though absent from the Bahamas. Other names include Stinking Toe or Old Man's Toe tree, derived from the seedpod, which is toe shaped. The powdery pulp of the fruit has a foul smell but a sweet taste enjoyed by many local people. Tree sap is used in repairing dental cavities and making varnish. Extracts from the tree serve in many traditional medicines. Jewelry is made from the seeds, and the wood is a popular lumber. The night-blooming flowers are pollinated by nectar-feeding bats. In the Dominican Republic, sap from this tree that has hardened into amber is invaluable for the study of fossil organisms trapped in the sap millions of years ago.

green seed pods

seed pods

LIGNUM VITAE *Guaiacum officinale*

KEY FEATURES A handsome small evergreen tree, generally to 9 m (30 ft.) high, with a short trunk to 46 cm (18 in.) in diameter and a dense, rounded crown with dark-green foliage. The bark is light brown, smooth, and mottled, peeling off in

thin scales. The flowers are pale to deep blue, with five petals spreading starlike in showy terminal and lateral clusters. Seed capsules are flattened, heart shaped, orange brown, and broad.

STATUS AND RANGE Occurs in forests, thickets, and pastures in dry coastal and dry limestone regions. It is occasionally planted as an ornamental. This is the densest of commercial woods, readily sinking in water. It has numerous commercial uses, a common one being for mortars and pestles. The name *Lignum Vitae*, Latin for "wood of life," likely derives from its many traditional medicinal uses. Native to the Bahamas, Greater Antilles, and south to Martinique in the Lesser Antilles as well as Central America, northern South America, and southern Florida in the United States. This is the national flower of Jamaica. Early English Christmas carols speak of "wassail bowls" that were often made from Lignum Vitae. Wassail is a spiced ale or mulled wine drunk during Christmastime.

seed pods

MANGO *Mangifera indica*

KEY FEATURES Most easily distinguished when fruiting, the large, elliptical yellow mangos hanging in clusters all over the tree. A medium-size to large broad-leaved evergreen attaining 20 m (65 ft.) in height with a stout trunk to 1 m (3 ft.) in diameter. The crown is round, with very dense leaves that are large, leathery, dark green, and lance shaped. Numerous small, yellow-green to pink five-parted flowers form large, showy terminal clusters.

STATUS AND RANGE This popular introduced fruit and shade tree is commonly planted around houses and found along roads throughout the Caribbean where the seeds drop and germinate. It bears

one of the finest tropical fruits, popular the world over. The fruit has a thin, easily peeled outer skin, edible flesh, and a single, large seed. Mango trees commonly escape from cultivation and are naturalized widely. Native of tropical Asia, probably from India east to Vietnam, it has been cultivated in India for more than four thousand years.

fruit on tree

43

PAPAYA OR PAWPAW *Carica papaya*

KEY FEATURES A very slender tree or shrub, 2–6 m (6–20 ft.) in height, with a straight, leaf-scarred trunk, usually with no branches and crowned with a cluster of large, deeply lobed leaves. It is evergreen and has a distinctive pungent odor. The large oblong or rounded fruits, which turn orange when ripe, are clustered at the base of the leaves or down the length of the trunk and contain numerous round, black seeds.

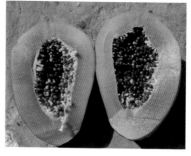

STATUS AND RANGE Widely cultivated throughout the Caribbean for its delicious edible fruits, it also grows wild. Probably originally from Central America, but its origin now is obscure since it was cultivated long before the European settlement of the New World. The plant is used as a hair conditioner and has many reputed medicinal uses. In some areas meat is wrapped in the leaves to tenderize it before cooking. The name derives from the indigenous Carib language.

fruit

AVOCADO *Persea americana*

KEY FEATURES A small to medium-size deciduous tree attaining 9 m (30 ft.) in height and 45 cm (1.5 ft.) in trunk diameter, with a symmetrical narrow or rounded crown. The distinctive fruit is shiny pale green, pear shaped or nearly round, about 10–13 cm (4–5 in.) long with oily green-and-yellow flesh and one very large seed. The leaves are elliptical, slightly thickened, and crowded near twig tips.

STATUS AND RANGE Planted throughout many habitats, most commonly on coasts and in moist limestone and lower mountain regions. It is escaped or naturalized in many places. The fruit is highly edible and is grown in plantations. It is the core ingredient in the dish guacamole. Perhaps native to the Caribbean, though uncertain. Native of tropical America, but cultivated for so long that its origin is obscured.

hanging fruit

ACKEE *Blighia sapida*

KEY FEATURES A broad-leaved evergreen, 10 m (40 ft.) tall with a short trunk and dense crown of spreading branches. The distinctive fruit turns from green to bright red and yellowish pink. When ripe it breaks open, displaying three

large black seeds and white or yellowish pulpy flesh.

STATUS AND RANGE This introduced species is most common in Jamaica, where it occurs from sea level to 900 m (3,000 ft.). It is Jamaica's national fruit and, combined with salt fish, the national dish. It is also a significant export crop from that island. Frequently planted around homes, this tree is far less common on other islands. It was originally transported to Jamaica with the slave trade and subsequently brought by Captain William Bligh to England in 1793. It was from these specimens that the species was first described scientifically and named in his honor. The tree also occurs in Cuba, Haiti, Puerto Rico, Antigua, Barbuda, Barbados, and Grenada. It is native to West Africa.

CAUTION The fruit is highly poisonous if not harvested and cooked properly.

hanging fruit

fruit open

BREADFRUIT *Artocarpus altilis*

KEY FEATURES Note the distinctive large fruit, nearly round, with a rough, spiny-looking surface. The tree's huge, deeply lobed, shiny, dark-green leaves aid in identification. This tree, usually evergreen but losing its leaves in some localities, is medium size to 18 m (60 ft.) high and 60 cm (2 ft.) or more in trunk diameter. Most parts of the tree exude a milky latex sap when cut.

STATUS AND RANGE
A handsome tree widely planted throughout the Caribbean for its edible fruits, which are a staple in many regions. It is one of the most prolific of fruit trees and was originally brought to the region as a food for slaves. The tree is also valued for shade and for its attractive foliage. Various parts of the tree have uses, including for boat building and for medicinal purposes. The tree was introduced into the Caribbean in 1793 from Tahiti. An earlier attempt to introduce the tree became history due to a mutiny on the *Bounty*—the ship transporting the seedlings. The tree is native to Malaya and the western Pacific islands, from which Polynesians first established it far outside its native range.

JACKFRUIT *Artocarpus heterophyllus*

KEY FEATURES A small to medium-size broad-leaved evergreen tree to 12 m (40 ft.) in height and 30 cm (1 ft.) in trunk diameter. The leaves are dark green, leathery, and slightly shiny. Fruits are huge, typically 30–60 cm (1–2 ft.) long and 15–30 cm (0.5–1 ft.) in diameter, elliptical, irregularly shaped, yellow green, and covered with sharp conical spines. A milky latex sap is exuded when the tree is cut.

STATUS AND RANGE A cultivated relative of the breadfruit, though much less common. It is occasionally planted in gardens for ornament, shade, or the large edible fruits. Both the pulp and seeds are edible when cooked, plus the plant has a number of medicinal uses. The fruits grow to be the largest in the world, reaching over 36 kg (80 lb.) in weight and 90 cm (3 ft.) in length. The tree is native to tropical Asia from India to Malaya and the East Indies, where it has been cultivated for thousands of years.

SOURSOP *Annona muricata*

KEY FEATURES A small broad-leaved evergreen tree attaining 6 m (20 ft.) in height and 15 cm (6 in.) in trunk diameter. The distinctive fruit, covered with many curved, fleshy spines, is green and fleshy, 30 cm (1 ft.) long, heart shaped, and often asymmetric.

STATUS AND RANGE Planted for its fruits, it also grows wild or becomes naturalized in thickets, pastures, and along roads, most often on coasts, but also on lower mountain slopes. The fruit is widely used as a juice and in desserts. The fruit, seeds, and leaves are also used for medicinal purposes, and recent reports suggest it may possess anticancer benefits. At the same time, the tea has been reported to lead to Parkinson's disease in Guadeloupe. Likely native to the Caribbean since it was reported as common by the earliest Spanish explorers, but it may have been introduced from northern South America by Amerindians. Also native to Mesoamerica. Another name is Corossol.

CHINESE HIBISCUS *Hibiscus rosa-sinensis*

KEY FEATURES Note the showy, trumpet-shaped flowers with five spreading petals and a long, protruding pistil covered with stamens. Typically a bright red, it also occurs in other colors. It grows as an evergreen shrub or small tree attaining a height of 4.5 m (15 ft.), commonly with several stems radiating from the base.

STATUS AND RANGE A popular ornamental garden plant throughout the Caribbean, often used as a hedge and grown for its stunning blossoms. It sometimes occurs in old fields and disturbed sites near abandoned habitations. In Jamaica and other islands the plant is made into a sweet drink. It also serves in traditional medicines. Introduced throughout warmer regions of the world, but native to tropical Asia, apparently China to India. There are a number of related species. This is Puerto Rico's official flower. Other English names, Shoeflower and Shoeblack, derive from use of the petals to blacken shoes.

PURPLE BOUGAINVILLEA *Bougainvillea spectabilis*

KEY FEATURES A spectacular, vividly colored vine, the beautiful colors deriving from the large bracts, which are modified leaves. These surround the inconspicuous flowers. Its vibrant colors include purple, magenta, pink, red, and white, among others. Generally evergreen, this spiny vine forms a dense cover.
STATUS AND RANGE Common and widespread in the Caribbean on terraces, patios, walls, and fences. Without support it forms a broad, sprawling shrub or ground cover. The species tolerates dry weather, at which time the bracts come into full bloom. Native to South America, it has been introduced throughout warmer climates of the world. There are a number of related species. This is Grenada's national flower.
CAUTION The sap can be an irritant.

ALLAMANDA OR YELLOW BELL *Allamanda cathartica*

KEY FEATURES Note the distinctive showy, yellow flowers of this vine or shrub. The lance-shaped leaves are shiny green. It is an evergreen and may bloom year-round.
STATUS AND RANGE A widely introduced garden plant in the Caribbean, often trimmed as a hedge. It has various medicinal properties, but all parts of the plant are toxic. Stripes deep in the corolla serve to help guide insects to the nectar within. The plant is native to Brazil but is now distributed widely in the tropics. Also known as Golden Trumpet.

FRANGIPANI *Plumeria rubra*

KEY FEATURES A small ornamental tree becoming 5–8 m (15–25 ft.) tall, with an open crown of a few thick spreading branches and beautiful clusters of large fragrant, waxy red, yellow, or white flowers often with yellow at the center. The few stout fleshy branches contain whitish latex and bear crowded leaves at the ends. Its leaves are long, broad, shiny-green above and somewhat hairy beneath, with prominent parallel veins coming off a central rib. The seedpods are cigar shaped and grow to 25 cm (10 in.) in length.
STATUS AND RANGE Commonly planted throughout the Caribbean as an ornamental in gardens and parks, from which it occasionally escapes from cultivation. It also grows in dry, rocky, and windy areas. The Frangipani caterpillar (*Pseudosphinx tetrio*), which matures to be the sphinx moth, is easily recognizable for its red head and black body with yellow bands. The caterpillars can defoliate a tree within a few days, but they usually do not kill it. Frangipani is an introduced species, native from southern Mexico to northern South America.

GARDEN CROTON *Codiaeum variegatum*

KEY FEATURES Distinguished by its striking leaves, which are variably colored green, yellow, red, purple, bronze, pink, or almost any combination of these. The leaves are large, leathery, glossy, and vary in shape. Typically an evergreen shrub reaching 1.8 m (6 ft.) or more in height, but often trimmed as a hedge. Many different varieties have been bred.

STATUS AND RANGE One of the most commonly cultivated ornamental plants in the Caribbean in gardens, around houses, and along roadsides. The sap is toxic but is also used in herbal medicines. The plant is often used on graves in rural areas, because of its ability to regenerate after drought, a symbol of rebirth. Native to southern India, Malaysia, and Indonesia to Australia and Polynesia.

PERIWINKLE *Catharanthus roseus*

KEY FEATURES A low-growing evergreen plant with glossy green leaves and showy white or pinkish flowers with red at the center. Flowering occurs through most of the year.

STATUS AND RANGE A common ornamental plant of gardens and roadsides, particularly in poor soils. It is not suitable for indoor planting due to the unpleasant odor it generates when cut. The plant is native to Madagascar and is widely used for medicinal purposes, including as an anticancer drug. Other names include Ramgoat Roses, Churchyard Blossom, and Old Maid.

POINSETTIA *Euphorbia pulcherrima*

KEY FEATURES An evergreen shrub or small tree 3–4.5 m (10–15 ft.) high, with branching trunks and a thin, flat-topped, spreading crown. When nights are long, the plant's distinctive large bracts, which are modified leaves, turn a brilliant red, orange red, or yellow. With many homes now having outside guard lights, fewer large Poinsettias are found in gardens than formerly.

STATUS AND RANGE Introduced to Hispaniola, Cuba, Puerto Rico, Virgin Islands, Barbados, and Jamaica, where it is a common ornamental that escapes from cultivation along roadsides and in thickets. It has been used to produce dye and in traditional medicines. Much folklore has developed around this plant, particularly in association with Christmas. Native to western Mexico, but widely cultivated throughout the tropics. The national flower of Trinidad and Tobago.

pale bracts

red bracts

YELLOW TRUMPETBUSH *Tecoma stans*

KEY FEATURES An evergreen shrub or small tree, 3–8 m (10–25 ft.) high, characterized by many large, bell-shaped, bright-yellow clustered flowers 4–5 cm (1.5–2 in.) and long and narrow, dark-brown cigarlike pods 10–20 cm (4–8 in.) in length.

STATUS AND RANGE Widespread, it is primarily used as an ornamental for its showy flowers, particularly along roadsides and fences, but also on open hillsides; escapes cultivation in waste places, scrublands, and coppice borders. Most prevalent in dry, sunny areas. Native to continental subtropical and tropical America and the Caribbean. The official flower of the Bahamas and U.S. Virgin Islands. Other names include Yellow Elder and Torch Wood.

seed pods

OLEANDER *Nerium oleander*

KEY FEATURES A rounded, spreading evergreen shrub commonly 2–4.5 m
(6–15 ft.) high, but sometimes a small tree to 6 m (20 ft.) high and 8 cm (3 in.)
in trunk diameter. It has conspicuous tubular flowers that are five lobed, about
2.5 cm (1 in.) long and 5 cm (2 in.) broad, varying in color from red to pink to
white. The long, slender leaves are leathery, shiny green, pointed at both ends,
and mostly in threes. The plant usually has a very pleasant fragrance.

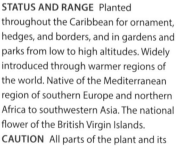

STATUS AND RANGE Planted
throughout the Caribbean for ornament,
hedges, and borders, and in gardens and
parks from low to high altitudes. Widely
introduced through warmer regions of
the world. Native of the Mediterranean
region of southern Europe and northern
Africa to southwestern Asia. The national
flower of the British Virgin Islands.

CAUTION All parts of the plant and its
whitish sap are poisonous to humans
and animals. In the most severe cases,
death has resulted from eating a few
leaves or flowers. Some insects are
immune to the toxins.

IXORA OR **JUNGLE FLAME** *Ixora coccinea*

KEY FEATURES Note the clusters of red flowers, each with four petals. This dense evergreen shrub grows to 2m (6 ft.) tall and possesses dark leaves. It flowers nearly year-round.

STATUS AND RANGE A widely introduced ornamental, common as a hedge or in flower beds. Native to Southeast Asia and India. Also known as Flame of the Woods. There are approximately five hundred species in the genus, but few are cultivated.

PURPLE QUEEN OR PURPLE HEART *Tradescantia pallida*

KEY FEATURES A low-growing, creeping plant readily distinguished by its entirely purple stems, leaves, and flowers.
STATUS AND RANGE Often cultivated as a house and garden plant, where it forms dense ground cover in both sunny and shady areas. Native to southeastern United States, Mexico, and parts of the Caribbean.
CAUTION The sap can cause skin irritation.

flower

WANDERING JEW *Tradescantia zebrina*

KEY FEATURES A low-growing, trailing plant no more than 0.3 m (1 ft.) tall, creating dense ground cover. Note the distinctive lance-shaped leaves banded purple, green, and white. The stems and lower leaf faces are purple. Flowers are tiny and pink.
STATUS AND RANGE Common in gardens and cultivated areas, from which it often spreads to shady, moist trails, road edges, and coppices. Native of Mexico and Guatemala, but naturalized widely in the Caribbean.
CAUTION The sap can cause skin irritation.

OYSTER PLANT *Tradescantia spathacea*

KEY FEATURES A low-growing plant approximately 0.5 m (1.5 ft.) in height. It has long, slender leaves distinctively green above and purple below. The tiny white flowers are nestled among the plant's large leaves, which gives rise to one of the plant's local names—Moses in the Bulrushes.

STATUS AND RANGE Typically open, rocky areas, around abandoned homesteads, and cultivated in gardens. Naturalized widely in the Caribbean, but native to southern Mexico and northern Central America.

CAUTION The sap can cause skin irritation.

SUGARCANE *Saccharum officinarum*

KEY FEATURES A huge perennial grass to 3 or 4 m (10–13 ft.) tall. The stalk is segmented, marked by distinct nodes. Long, bladelike leaves extend from the upper portion of the plant and, when mature, a large, plumelike, silvery flower head emerges.

STATUS AND RANGE Formerly planted throughout coastal and lower mountain valleys, where it was cultivated extensively in plantations, it is now less abundant. It is also in family gardens and former agricultural lands. A major source of the world's sugar supply, it was for centuries the primary agricultural crop of many Caribbean islands. Its importance is diminishing but remains significant on some islands. Sugarcane is one of the most efficient users of solar energy among all plants and thus grows very rapidly. That, among other reasons, has resulted in its importance in creating biofuels such as ethanol. Probably native of tropical East Asia.

stalk

flower spike

BANANA *Musa* spp.

KEY FEATURES A perennial tree-like herb of many varieties, sizes, and fruit types. All have soft, thick stems and are spread by underground roots called suckers to form clumps. Their spectacular long, broad leaves are easily tattered by strong winds. *Musa paradisiaca* forms a large clump to 6 m (20 ft.) tall, with leaves to 3 m (9 ft.) and a drooping flower stalk containing powdery purple bracts; fruits (usually seedy and inedible) sometimes follow.

STATUS AND RANGE Common in moist areas, particularly plantations, abandoned cultivated sites, and as an ornamental in gardens and around homes. The Edible Banana (*Musa acuminata*) is a perennial tree or shrub. The popular plantain, or cooking banana, is a sterile hybrid of similar appearance. These species and their relatives are widely cultivated in the Caribbean but are often ravaged by hurricanes and strong winds. The genus contains about forty species, most of which are native to tropical Africa and Asia.

flower

COFFEE *Coffea arabica*

KEY FEATURES Generally an evergreen shrub with compact, spreading foliage that if not pruned becomes a small tree 3.5–4.5 m (12–15 ft.) high and 5–8 cm (2–3 in.) in trunk diameter. Its leaves are shiny, dark green, and have an undulating upper surface. The fragrant white flowers, several together, form at the leaf bases. The bright-red berries are elliptical and contain usually two large brown seeds, the coffee beans.

STATUS AND RANGE The source of one of the world's most popular beverages. Coffee plantations are on mountains, chiefly at elevations from 250–900 m (800–3,000 ft.). Planted and escaping from cultivation or naturalized. Native of Abyssinia but introduced to Arabia (fourteenth century) and extensively planted and escaping through the tropics.

flowers

fruit

SWEET ORANGE
Citrus sinensis

KEY FEATURES This best known and most popular of the citrus fruits is a small, broad-leaved evergreen tree becoming 6–9 m (20–30 ft.) tall and 15–25 cm (6–10 in.) or more in trunk diameter, with a rounded crown. The fragrant white flowers have five petals. The conspicuous fruit known by all is approximately 7 cm (2.5 in.) and orange in color when ripe.

STATUS AND RANGE Planted extensively as a fruit tree and ornamental, often grown in coffee plantations. It occasionally escapes from cultivation and becomes naturalized. This is the most commonly grown tree fruit in the world. Probably native to southern China, Vietnam, or other southeastern Asiatic regions but no longer found in the wild.

63

GRAPEFRUIT *Citrus paradisi*

KEY FEATURES A small, aromatic evergreen tree with glossy, dark-green leaves, generally 4.5–6 m (15–20 ft.) high and 15 cm (6 in.) in trunk diameter, the crown rounded and spreading. The large, fragrant white flowers have four petals. The familiar large, round fruit, 9–13 cm (3.5–5 in.) in diameter, is pale yellow at maturity.

STATUS AND RANGE Commonly grown in plantations, especially in moist coastal regions. Many survive in abandoned plantations. Thought to have originated in the Caribbean on Barbados as a hybrid of two introduced species, the Pummelo (*Citrus maxima*) and the Sweet Orange. It is now widespread throughout the tropics. The name derives from the large fruits appearing to hang like clusters of grapes. An attempt in 1962 in the United States to change the name to one more attractive to consumers failed.

PINEAPPLE *Ananas comosus*

KEY FEATURES A rosette of narrow, waxy leaves 0.75–1.5 m (2.5–5 ft.) long, with spines on the edges, all emanating outward from a stalkless base. Its fruit, the pineapple known to all, grows up from the plant's center.

STATUS AND RANGE Widespread in lowland areas of the Caribbean either in plantations or individual gardens. The plant was introduced by the Amerindians and was reported by Christopher Columbus. Native to portions of Brazil and Paraguay, it now grows in all warm climates. Of the many bromeliad species, this is the only one cultivated for food.

COCONUT PALM *Cocos nucifera*

KEY FEATURES A medium-size palm, usually to 18 m (60 ft.) high, sometimes taller. The slender trunk bulges at the base and displays irregular rings closer to the crown. This palm often leans as a result of coastal breezes, an indication of primary wind direction. The familiar coconut fruit, hanging in clusters at the base of the fronds, consists of a green to light brown fibrous husk to 30 cm (12 in.) long, which encloses a hard shell and a very large hollow seed, with whitish, oily, edible flesh.

STATUS AND RANGE This graceful palm lining tropical shores and widely planted for fruit, shade, and ornament has become a symbol of the tropics. It commonly grows wild along sandy shores. The Coconut Palm has many uses and formerly was frequently planted in plantations. It is best known for its drinkable "water," the white flesh of its seed, which is edible and also processed to produce coconut "milk," and its use to produce oil. Coconut milk is reported to have medicinal properties. The species is naturalized throughout the Caribbean and the tropical shores of the world. The native land of this palm is unknown but thought to be Malaya or the Indo-Pacific region.

AUSTRALIAN PINE *Casuarina equisetifolia*

KEY FEATURES A slender, medium-size evergreen tree to 30 m (100 ft.) tall and 30–46 cm (1–1.5 ft.) in trunk diameter, with a thin crown and wiry, droopy, dark-green, needle-like twigs. Male and female flowers are numerous, small, and crowded in inconspicuous light- brown clusters, which are very attractive to bees. The fruit is a light-brown warty, cone-like ball.

STATUS AND RANGE Widespread in the Caribbean, where often used for street, park, ornamental, and windbreak plantings. It is sometimes trimmed into hedges. This exotic is frequently used for reforestation because of its rapid growth and adaptability to degraded sites. It is often seen on protected sandy seacoasts and less commonly on lower mountains. Native to tropical Asia and Australia.

RED MANGROVE *Rhizophora mangle*

KEY FEATURES Easily distinguished by its array of tall, arching prop roots, which look like crooked stilts supporting the tree in shallow salt or brackish water. These roots form dense, impenetrable thickets at tide level. A small broad-

leaved evergreen tree usually 4.5–8 m (15–25 ft.) in height, but sometimes much taller. The leaves are shiny green, slightly leathery, fleshy, and with two distinctive glands on each side of the short stem or petiole. The distinctive dark-brown fruits contain a growing seedling much larger than the fruit itself. **STATUS AND RANGE** Common along protected muddy seashores throughout the Caribbean except Dominica. Red Mangroves serve as an important buffer during storms, help stabilize shorelines, and are nurseries for many species of fish and other marine organisms. When the seeds drop from the tree, they float in the sea until they settle on sand or mud and the plant takes root. Native to tropical America and tropical West Africa.

fruit and seed

roots

BLACK MANGROVE
Avicennia germinans

KEY FEATURES Most readily distinguished by its saltwater habitat and profusion of pencil-like aerial roots or "pneumatophores," which stick out of the mud in which this tree prospers. Commonly a small, broad-leaved evergreen tree or shrub to 12 m (40 ft.) tall, with a rounded crown. The leaves are opposite, lance shaped, and leathery, the lower surface grayish green with a coat of fine hairs, giving a grayish color to the crown. Leaf surfaces often are salty to the taste. Its flowers are stalkless, white, and four lobed, many crowded in clusters. Seed capsules are yellowish green, elliptically flattened, and blunt pointed.

seeds

STATUS AND RANGE This is one of four species of mangrove trees that form swamp forests just above sea level in saltwater and brackish water along silty seashores, generally just above the high tide line. It sometimes penetrates inland along rivers. The aerial roots serve to provide oxygen to the tree, even when the underground roots are submerged. It occurs throughout the Caribbean, except Dominica. Native to tropical America.

aerial roots

SEA GRAPE *Coccoloba uvifera*

KEY FEATURES Varying in size from a low prostrate shrub on windswept beaches to a small, scraggly or widespreading tree to 9 m (30 ft.) in height and 30 cm (1 ft.) in trunk diameter. The leaves are rounded or kidney shaped, thick and leathery, 7.5–15 cm (3–6 in.) long and 10–20 cm (4–8 in.) wide, and heart shaped at the base. Note the distinct midrib on the leaf, its large veins, and the reddish coloration of young and very old leaves. Numerous small whitish or greenish-white flowers occur in narrow terminal and lateral clusters 10–23 cm (4–9 in.) long. The fruits are crowded in drooping, grapelike clusters and are edible.

STATUS AND RANGE Widespread in the Caribbean, where usually limited to sandy and rocky seashores and coastal thickets. This is one of the first woody species to become established on sandy shores. Because sea grape is hardier to exposure and more tolerant of salt than most trees, it is often planted as an ornamental or windbreak along the coast. Native to the Caribbean basin.

fruit

BEACH MORNING GLORY *Ipomoea pes-caprae*

KEY FEATURES A creeping vine of sandy beaches, displaying large, bell-shaped violet flowers. It has two-lobed leathery, pale-green leaves that give rise to one of its common names—Goat's Foot.

STATUS AND RANGE One of the most common and widely distributed plants throughout the Caribbean and tropical beaches around the world. This vine is highly tolerant of salt spray and is of major importance in stabilizing dunes. It is reputed to have some medicinal qualities.

PRICKLY PEAR CACTUS *Opuntia* spp.

KEY FEATURES Several species of prickly pear cactus occur in the Caribbean, some native and others introduced. These cacti are distinguished by their large flat, fleshy pads covered with sharp spines. The pads are actually modified branches, whereas the spines are modified leaves. Some prickly pears grow low over the ground, while others grow to several meters in height.

STATUS AND RANGE Generally common in dry forests and open scrublands of plains and hills at low elevations. It is often an undesirable plant where common. Some members of the genus are planted as ornamentals. Approximately two hundred species compose the genus, which ranges through much of the Americas. Many have been introduced into other parts of the world.

MONKEY PUZZLE EUPHORBIA OR MOTTLED SPURGE
Euphorbia lactea

KEY FEATURES A usually leafless but large evergreen shrub or small tree to 8 m (25 ft.) high and 15 cm (6 in.) in trunk diameter, with fleshy or succulent stems and many three-angled branches 2.5–8 cm (1–3 in.) across.

STATUS AND RANGE This introduced plant with succulent stems and water storage tissues is adapted to dry regions. It is grown for ornament, in rows as fences, and trimmed as hedges. Conspicuous, but only moderately common, it sometimes escapes from cultivation, spreading and forming thickets in some places. It is native to the East Indies. Another name is Jerusalem Candlestick.

CAUTION All parts of the plant are poisonous, particularly the white sap.

CENTURY PLANT *Agave* spp.

KEY FEATURES Century plants are succulents distinguished by a rosette of narrow, fleshy, sword-shaped leaves armed with sharp thorns, particularly at the leaf tip. When mature, they grow a central flowering stalk, in some species to a height of 4 m (13 ft.) or more. Flower clusters grow from this central stalk. After flowering, the plant dies.

STATUS AND RANGE Generally common in open arid areas often with little soil. Agaves are also popularly planted as ornamentals in gardens. Several species of century plant occur in the Caribbean, some endemic to one or a few islands, such as *Agave barbadensis* of Barbados. Others, such as *A. americana*, the national flower of Antigua and Barbuda, where it is known as Dagger's Log, are native to the southwestern United States and northern Mexico and have been introduced

into the Caribbean. Over two hundred species of century plants are known, most from Mexico. They have many popular uses, including as food and for the production of hemp, tequila, mescal, and medicines. The name *century plant* derives from the lengthy time it takes for this plant to flower, but normally this period is only a few years. Bats pollinate the flowers.

CAUTION The sap of this plant can be a severe irritant.

flower head

PINGUIN OR WILD PINEAPPLE *Bromelia pinguin*

KEY FEATURES A spiny plant with a rosette of narrow, fleshy leaves 1–2 m (3.3–6.5 ft.) long, all emanating outward from a stalkless base. A single, clustered flower head grows up from the plant's center.

STATUS AND RANGE Commonly used as a living hedgerow, the dense leaves and sharp thorns serve to impede the passage of cattle. Also grows along roadsides and open wastelands. Native to much of the Caribbean, Mexico, and Central and South America. Introduced into the Bahamas and Cayman Islands. There are over three thousand species of bromeliads. Many are "airplants," also called epiphytes. The name *airplant* derives from them rooting on a tree rather than the ground. They are particularly common in wet forests, where their exposed roots can easily acquire moisture.

LEADTREE *Leucaena leucocephala*

KEY FEATURES A small deciduous spreading tree or shrub 5–8 m (15–25 ft.) high and 5–10 cm (2–4 in.) in diameter. The numerous flowers form small, whitish round balls. It has numerous dark-brown seedpods, which are long, wide, flat, and thin, with raised borders. They usually form many clusters.

STATUS AND RANGE Common along roadsides and in old fields and thickets in dry limestone and dry coastal regions. It is native to the Caribbean and from southern Mexico to northern South America. The tree is naturalized in the southern United States and the Old World tropics. Its uses include as food, medicines, to stop erosion, as a living fence, as a windbreak, and to shade coffee. But it is highly invasive and a pest in many areas.

pods on tree

73

TURPENTINE TREE OR GUMBO-LIMBO *Bursera simaruba*

KEY FEATURES The bark is a distinctive reddish-brown or copper color, peeling off in papery flakes (giving it the local name Tourist's Nose Tree, for its resemblance to a sunburned visitor's nose). A medium-size aromatic, broad-

leaved deciduous tree 6–12 m (20–40 ft.) high, with a relatively thick trunk, 25–50 cm (1–2 ft.) in diameter, large spreading crooked branches, and thin foliage. The resin is grayish, with a turpentine-like taste. Crushed leaves, fruits, and twigs have a slightly pungent or turpentine odor.

STATUS AND RANGE Native to dry soils derived from limestone and also tolerant of low levels of salt. It is frequently used as a fencerow and roadside tree in coastal and lower mountain regions. Various parts of the tree are used for medicinal purposes, and the resin is used for glues and varnish. The tree's fruits are an important food for birds. Widespread, it is native to the Caribbean, southern Florida, and parts of Mexico and Central America. Its many local names include Mastic Tree, Incense Tree, Mulatto Tree, Naked Indian, and Gum Bark.

COMMON GUAVA *Psidium guajava*

KEY FEATURES Generally a shrub or low, widely spreading evergreen tree to 4.5 m (15 ft.) high with a seldom-straight trunk to 20 cm (8 in.) in diameter. The large white flowers are about 4 cm (1.5 in.) across with four or five large petals, mostly borne singly at the leaf bases. Its distinctive, edible fruits are rounded (sometimes pear-shaped), yellow when ripe, and 3–5 cm (1.3–2 in.) in diameter. Stems are four-sided.

STATUS AND RANGE The guava is commonly cultivated as a fruit tree. Paste, jelly, and juice are made from its fruits. It often forms thickets and spreads throughout pastures, chiefly on coastal plains but also in lower mountain regions. Native to the Caribbean and tropical America from Mexico into South America, the range greatly extended through cultivation.

CALABASH TREE *Crescentia cujete*

KEY FEATURES A small tree 9 m (30 ft.) or more in height and 30 cm (1 ft.) or more in trunk diameter, with few long, spreading branches. The sparseness of the branches, containing few secondary twigs, gives this tree a distinctive appearance. Also characteristic are the large, globe-shaped fruits, up to 30 cm (12 in.) in diameter. They are hard, glossy, green to brown in color, and resemble gourds. The spoon-shaped leaves are long, broad, and arranged in clusters along the stout branches. Pale-green, bell-shaped flowers are borne singly on the trunk and branches.

STATUS AND RANGE This tree is planted or seeded naturally in pastures, hillsides, roadsides, and around country homes in coastal, limestone, and lower mountain regions. It is more common in drier areas. The tree is widely planted through the tropics for its fruits, from which bowls, cups, jugs, water containers, and other utensils, as well as ornaments and musical instruments, are fashioned. Native to the Caribbean, wetter parts of Mexico, and Central America.

seed pods

MESQUITE *Prosopis juliflora*

KEY FEATURES A small deciduous, often flat-topped spiny tree or shrub, to 9 m (30 ft.) high, with a short, crooked trunk and a broad crown of very thin spreading foliage. Many small, pale-yellow flowers form narrow, drooping clusters. The seedpod is light yellowish-brown, flattened but thick, and the leaves consist of series of pairs of fine leaflets.

STATUS AND RANGE Introduced and naturalized in thickets and forests in arid limestone and dry coastal regions. It commonly invades pastures and is occasionally planted for ornament. This genus possesses enormous taproots, the record being 58 m (190 ft.), which serve to seek water deep below the surface. The wood is used for fenceposts, firewood, and charcoal, and the pods are nutritious for livestock. There are several similar species. Native from the southwestern United States to Columbia and Venezuela. It is widely introduced throughout the tropics, where it is a pest in many locations. Other names are Cashaw, Macca, and Cashee.

SWEET ACACIA OR NEEDLE BUSH *Vachellia farnesiana*

KEY FEATURES A spiny deciduous shrub or small tree, usually less than 3 m
(10 ft.) high, with conspicuous, fragrant yellow flowers clustered in bright-yellow
balls. The leaves are a series of delicate paired leaflets. Paired whitish spines occur
on the slightly zigzag twigs. The seedpods are dark brown to blackish.

STATUS AND RANGE Common in thickets
and forests in dry coastal and dry limestone
regions. It is occasionally cultivated around
houses and in gardens as an ornamental for its
flowers, shade, and green foliage. The flowers
are used in the perfume industry, and the seeds
are ground to make cooking oil. The name
Needle Bush derives from its thorny twigs.
Perhaps introduced and naturalized on most
islands, its native distribution is uncertain but
believed to be tropical America, including Cuba. Sweet Acacia occurs throughout
the tropics. Its former scientific name was *Acacia farnesiana*. Other names include
Cassie Flower and Cashaw.

seed pods

TAMARIND *Tamarindus indica*

KEY FEATURES A medium-size, short-trunked tree to 12 m (40 ft.) high and 1 m (3 ft.) in diameter or larger, with a rounded crown of dense, fine, feathery foliage. The showy flowers are pale yellow tinged with red, some forming terminal and lateral clusters 4–15 cm (1.5–6 in.) long. The distinctive seedpods are gray, rough, and thick.

STATUS AND RANGE Cultivated and naturalized throughout the Caribbean, where it is fairly common around houses, along roads, and on hillsides, mainly in dry coastal regions. It is planted for its fruits, as well as ornament and shade, and occasionally naturalized. The sour pulp around the seeds is popular in drinks, desserts such as tamarind balls, and in other recipes. Probably native to tropical Africa, but cultivated for so long its origins are obscure. The name derives from the Persian *tamar-i-hind*, meaning "date of India."

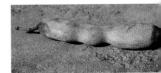

JERUSALEM THORN
Parkinsonia aculeata

KEY FEATURES A shrub or small spiny tree to 6 m (20 ft.) tall, with distinctive green bark. It often branches near the ground and has an open crown of spreading branches and thin drooping foliage. It is green throughout the year, though appearing leafless after the leaflets fall. The showy golden-yellow flowers have five petals and form loose clusters. Seedpods are brown, small, and slender.

STATUS AND RANGE Often planted as an ornamental along roads and found chiefly in dry coastal regions. "Jerusalem" does not refer to the city in the Middle East but rather is an anglicization of the Spanish word *girasol*, which means "turn to the sun." Native to southern Mexico and Central America, but cultivated, spreading, and naturalized south to Argentina and in the Caribbean.

WEST INDIAN LANTANA *Lantana camara*

KEY FEATURES Usually a low, much-branched evergreen shrub to about 2 m
(6 ft.), with stems and branches unarmed or with only a few weak prickles.
Most distinctive are its dense flowers with showy yellow to orange or red
clusters of blossoms.

STATUS AND RANGE
This species is cultivated
for its lovely flowers. It
often grows commonly
along roads and in waste
places, especially where
slightly moist. Native
to the Caribbean and
much of tropical and
subtropical America, it
has been introduced
widely around the
globe. Flower coloration
changes with maturity.
Other names include
Spanish Flag, Ham and
Eggs—derived from the
red and yellow flowers—
and Sage—based on
the fragrant scent of the
leaves when crushed.
Many strains have been
cultivated and over a
hundred species occur in
this genus.

COMMON BAMBOO *Bambusa vulgaris*

KEY FEATURES A giant evergreen grass to 15 m (50 ft.), with clustered, jointed hollow stems and feathery foliage.

STATUS AND RANGE Introduced and widespread in the Caribbean, it is commonly planted in moist soils, such as along streams and roadsides and for ornament because of its attractive foliage. Native to tropical Asia but widely planted throughout the tropics. This is the most widely grown bamboo throughout the tropics. Bamboos include some of the fastest growing plants in the world. They have been known to grow 100 cm (39 in.) per day. There are approximately seventy genera and fifteen hundred species of bamboos.

clump

CARIBBEAN TREE FERN *Cyathea arborea*

KEY FEATURES A small evergreen tree to 9 m (30 ft.) or more in height, with a stately crown of 10–18 large, lacelike leaves, mostly 2–3 m (6–10 ft.) long, unrolling from a coil at the apex. It has no obvious flowers, fruits, or seeds.

STATUS AND RANGE Occurs in lower to upper mountain forests as a small understory tree. It is especially common in open areas such as ravines, banks, and roadsides. The species colonizes disturbed land and is the most common tree fern in the Caribbean. Native to the Caribbean and eastern Mexico to northern South America. Tree fern trunks are widely used for raising orchids, resulting in the decline of some species. The Carib Amerindians reputedly used the hollow stems to preserve fire.

leaf

fruiting body with fruits

fruiting body with flowers

SIERRA PALM *Prestoea montana*

KEY FEATURES A small to medium-size palm to 15 m (50 ft.) tall, with a slender, erect trunk, often with tubercle-covered prop roots at the base. It has a thin, narrow evergreen crown of several very large spreading leaves with blades about 2 m (6 ft.) long. The large, distinctive fruiting body contains round, shiny black fruits 1 cm (0.4 in.) in diameter and slightly fleshy.

STATUS AND RANGE A common to abundant native palm forming pure forests in upper mountain regions of Cuba, Hispaniola, Puerto Rico, and most of the Lesser Antilles, descending down ravines into lower mountain forests to about 460 m (1,500 ft.). Another name is Mountain Cabbage.

TRUMPET TREE
Cecropia schreberiana

KEY FEATURES A medium-size, usually evergreen tree to 21 m (70 ft.) high, with a thin spreading crown of a few stout branches arising high on the trunk and curving upward. Note its few, very large, thick umbrellalike leaves to 75 cm (2.5 ft.) across, with whitish or silvery undersurfaces, which are readily seen when upturned by a breeze.

STATUS AND RANGE One of the most abundant trees in the Caribbean, occurring in moist and wet open areas and in forests both virgin and cutover. It is absent from drier regions. Because Trumpet Tree grows rapidly in nearly full sunlight, it is among the first to reforest cut or hurricane-damaged forested lands. Its open shade provides a good environment for the development of a new forest. In other regions an ant lives commensally with the tree, benefiting from its hollow stems and food-producing glands on the leaves, while in turn protecting the tree from herbivores. Native to the Caribbean, Mexico, and Central and South America. Another common name is Snake Wood. A related species, *C. peltata,* is common and has a similar geographic range.

CAMASEY OR **GRANADILLO BOBO** *Miconia* spp.

KEY FEATURES Camasey (*Miconia* and related genera) is represented by many species of small trees and shrubs in the Caribbean. *Miconia prasina* is an evergreen shrub or small tree to 8 m (25 ft.) high and 10 cm (4 in.) in trunk diameter, with opposite, narrowly elliptical leaves finely wavy-toothed, green, and slightly shiny on both sides; small, whitish flowers in large terminal clusters; and rounded, purplish-blue berries. Most species can be recognized by the oval-shaped leaves, which have three pronounced veins running from the base to the apex. The flowers of other species may be yellow or pink.

STATUS AND RANGE Common in moist coastal, moist limestone, and lower mountain forests in Cuba, Jamaica, Hispaniola, Puerto Rico, and some of the Lesser Antilles. Native to the Caribbean and southern Mexico to Peru, Bolivia, Paraguay, and Brazil.

AUTOGRAPH TREE *Clusia major*

KEY FEATURES A medium-size evergreen tree with a broad, spreading, dense crown, to 18 m (60 ft.) high, usually with prop roots. Its ovate, glossy leaves are thick, stiff, and leathery, while the white flowers are showy, spreading, and large. The seed capsules are nearly round, fleshy, and 5–6 cm (2–2.5 in.) in diameter. The sap is a yellow, resinous latex.

STATUS AND RANGE Common in forests on riverbanks and hillsides except in upper mountain regions. It often begins as an air plant or epiphyte, the seed germinating in the fork of a tree and sending long aerial roots to the ground. In time these rapidly growing roots come together and encircle the host tree, eventually forming a trunk around it and strangling the host to death. The thick, black sap of related *Clusia* species is sometimes used to mend pots. Native to the Caribbean and southeastern Mexico to northern South America. Other names include Wild-Mammee, Wild Man Support, and Copey Clusia.

prop roots

SWAMP BLOODWOOD *Pterocarpus officinalis*

KEY FEATURES A large evergreen tree to 27 m (90 ft.) tall, with a trunk to 90 cm (3 ft.) in diameter. Distinctive are its enormous narrow, planklike buttress roots, sometimes extending high up the trunk. The buttress roots generally curve snakelike along the forest floor.

STATUS AND RANGE It generally grows on the landward side of mangrove forests, but also in swamps and along stream banks up to about 460 m (1,500 ft.) elevation. Native to the Caribbean and southeastern Mexico to South America. The common name, among others such as Dragon's Blood Tree, derives from its red resin.

fruit

buttress roots

SWAMP CYRILLA OR PALO COLORADO *Cyrilla racemiflora*

KEY FEATURES A large evergreen tree to 18 m (60 ft.) high, with a crooked and twisted trunk, to 2 m (6 ft.) in diameter, and smooth, thin, reddish-brown bark that splits off in thin plates or scales. The leaves are leathery and lance shaped, usually turning red before falling, and are confined mainly to the top of a many-branched crown, which resembles a broom in appearance.

STATUS AND RANGE Over most of its wide range it is a small tree or shrub of swamps and river banks, but in the mountains of the Greater Antilles it becomes a large tree. An important nest tree for the endangered Puerto Rican Parrot. It may live to one thousand years of age. Native to the Caribbean and the southeastern United States south to northern Brazil. Other names include Beetwood and Pigeon Berry.

BULLWOOD OR MOTILLO *Sloanea berteriana*

KEY FEATURES A large, straight-trunked evergreen tree to 30 m (100 ft.) tall and trunk 90 cm (3 ft.) in diameter, with pronounced buttresses at the base. The leaves are elliptical and large, 15–45 cm (6–18 in.) long and 8–20 cm (3–8 in.) broad. Flowers are 2 cm (.75 in.) across, pale yellow, and form lateral clusters. Seed capsules are brown, elliptical, and 3 cm (1.2 in.) long.

STATUS AND RANGE A dominant native tree of lower mountain rain forests in Hispaniola and Puerto Rico, and from St. Kitts to Martinique. It usually grows in moist ravines and emerges above the forest. In Jamaica *S. jamaicensis*, an endemic known as Break-axe Tree or Ironwood, is also buttressed. It is found in forest and woodland on limestone.

TABONUCO OR CANDLEWOOD *Dacryodes excelsa*

KEY FEATURES An evergreen tree, usually tall—to 30 m (100 ft.) in height, the trunk to 1.5 m (5 ft.) in diameter—and distinguished at a distance by its size, white trunk, and dark-green foliage. The smooth, white bark peels off in thick flakes and exudes streaks of fragrant, whitish resin from cuts.

STATUS AND RANGE A native tree typical of lower wet forests in Puerto Rico and the Lesser Antilles from St. Kitts to Grenada, where it rises above the forest canopy. Amerindians used it to make canoes. Another local name is Mountain Gommier.

MANCHINEEL *Hippomane mancinella*

KEY FEATURES A broad-leaved evergreen tree to 12 m (40 ft.) in height with a trunk to 60 cm (2 ft.) in diameter, with widely forking branches and broad spreading crown. The fruit resembles a small apple or guava, often littering beaches. It is round, yellow green or yellowish, tinged with red. The leaves are long-stalked, shiny, leathery, yellow green, and elliptical, edged with tiny, wavy teeth.

STATUS AND RANGE Widespread and fairly common along and near sandy seashore, on rocky cliffs, and in coastal woods and thickets, sometimes singly, in both wet and dry areas. Native to the Caribbean.

CAUTION The deadly Manzanillo or Manchineel is the most poisonous tree in the islands and ranks among the most poisonous plants in tropical America; the attractive, palatable fruits cause serious illness or even death when eaten, and the milky sap is injurious both externally and internally. Other names are Poison Apple and Beach Apple.

FLORIDA POISONTREE OR POISONWOOD *Metopium toxiferum*

KEY FEATURES A small evergreen tree reaching 6 m (15–20 ft.) in height and a trunk diameter of 28 cm (11 in.) in diameter, related to poison ivy and poison oak. Its distinctive smooth, light-gray bark with yellow to brown spots peels off in thin scales or flakes, exposing the yellow to brown, thin inner layer.

STATUS AND RANGE A widespread native in the Caribbean, especially in dry limestone areas. It is also native to southern Florida. In Jamaica *M. brownei* is known as Hog Doctor, because it is said wild pigs rub their wounds on the bark, causing the sap to flow and leaving a black mark on the bark.

CAUTION Its caustic sap is poisonous to the touch and can cause a painful rash or swelling on contact with leaves or twigs. A related species, *M. brownei*, found in Cuba, Hispaniola, and Jamaica, also causes a painful rash when touched to the skin. A reputed antidote is red tea made from boiled *Bursera simaruba* leaves and applied as a salve or wash.

TOOTHED MAIDENPLUM
Comocladia dentata

KEY FEATURES A bush or small tree reaching 12 m (40 ft.) in height. Each leaf has leaflets arranged in seven or eight pairs, each lance shaped and with spiny-toothed margins, which gives rise to its English common name.

STATUS AND RANGE An abundant and persistent species in secondary vegetation, particularly in dry uplands. It is usually found in the forest understory. It is sometimes used as a homeopathic remedy for eye and skin ailments. The species is native to Cuba, Hispaniola, Puerto Rico, and the Virgin Islands, as well as southeastern North America.

CAUTION The milky sap is strongly caustic, producing burns on contact with the skin. The skin may become inflamed by merely brushing the plant or when standing underneath it. Other species of *Comocladia* occur in the Caribbean and produce similar skin eruptions.

SOUTHERN OPOSSUM *Didelphis marsupialis*

KEY FEATURES Large—head and body to 40 cm (15 in.)—with a conical snout. The body is gray and the naked ears are black. The species also has a distinctive long, naked tail. Opossums walk slowly and sometimes "play dead" when molested.

STATUS AND RANGE Common on Dominica, Martinique, St. Lucia, St. Vincent, and Grenada around villages, secondary forests, and river-edge vegetation. It is active at night, occurring on the ground or in trees. Being a marsupial, its young are weaned in a stomach pouch. Subsequently they are carried on the mother's back. The tail is prehensile enabling the opossum to hang by it from a branch. Whether the opossum is native or was introduced by man to the islands from mainland tropical America is unclear.

JAVAN MONGOOSE *Herpestes auropunctatus*

KEY FEATURES A slender, medium-size mammal—head and body 25–30 cm (10–12 in.). It is reddish brown, short legged, and weasellike, with a long, furry tail and slender snout.

STATUS AND RANGE Introduced into Jamaica in 1871, it was then intentionally spread through most of the Caribbean, with the aim of controlling rats in sugarcane fields. The species is common, occurring at most elevations. It inhabits plantations, scrub, dry and moist forest, and even the vicinity of human dwellings. Active by day, it is frequently seen prowling for prey or darting across a road. The diet is diverse and includes various invertebrates, lizards, snakes, frogs, small mammals, birds, and eggs. The mongoose, along with introduced rats, likely played a major role in the decline of ground-nesting birds in the Caribbean. The species is native to South and Southeast Asia, including Java.

BRAZILIAN AGOUTI *Dasyprocta leporina*

KEY FEATURES A medium-size rodent—head and body 45–60 cm (15–24 in.)—with much longer rear legs, no tail, and brown upper parts that become increasingly orange toward the hind quarters.

STATUS AND RANGE Occurs nearly throughout the Lesser Antilles, where it was probably introduced from South America by Amerindians. It was also introduced into St. Thomas (Virgin Islands) by Europeans. Related species have been introduced into the Bahamas, Cuba, and Cayman Islands. The agouti inhabits forests, brush, savannas, and cultivated areas, often near water and dense vegetation. It is primarily active by day except where extensively molested by people. Agoutis can travel with remarkable speed and agility when threatened and can jump vertically at least 2 m (6.5 ft.). Fruits and nuts are its primary food, which it holds in its front paws when feeding. Some nuts are buried during periods of excess; thus the agouti serves as an important seed disperser. It lives in burrows and is hunted for food in some areas.

SOUTHERN OPOSSUM

JAVAN MONGOOSE

BRAZILIAN AGOUTI

Hutias are endemic to the Caribbean. Of the twenty-six species, the majority are either extinct or endangered. While all hutia species have a similar body form, they vary substantially in size and from having a prehensile tail to one that is vestigial. Nineteen species were a food source for Amerindians in pre-Columbian times, which likely was an important factor in their decline. More recently, deforestation and predation by introduced carnivores have reduced their numbers. Hutias evolved from a South American ancestor that invaded the Caribbean perhaps twenty million years ago. Desmarest's Hutia of Cuba is the largest living hutia, reaching a weight of 8.5 kg (19 lb.). Most are brown, nocturnal, and herbivorous.

DESMAREST'S HUTIA *Capromys pilorides*

KEY FEATURES A medium-size, chunky, short-legged rodent—length 70–80 cm (28–32 in.). The fur-covered tail is about one-third the total body length. Body color varies substantially, being black, gray, brown, rusty, or pale buff, the underparts in some cases being paler. This is the largest of the living hutias. STATUS AND RANGE Endemic to Cuba and nearby islands, it is common and widespread but has declined in numbers. The species occupies a variety of habitats from swamps and mangroves to mountain forests and deserts. Usually in pairs, it lives in caves, among tree roots, or in rock crevices. Active primarily by day, it passes considerable time feeding in trees, and on occasion it sleeps in them. The diet consists primarily of fruits, leaves, and bark. This hutia's stomach is divided into three chambers, the most complex of any rodent.

JAMAICAN CONEY OR BROWN'S HUTIA *Geocapromys brownii*

KEY FEATURES A medium-size chunky, short-legged rodent—head and body length 33–46 cm (13–18 in.)—with a very short tail. The upper parts are yellowish gray, dark brown, or blackish, and the underparts are buffy gray or dusky brown. STATUS AND RANGE Endemic to Jamaica, where it occurs in increasingly small patches of remote forest in the central, eastern, and southern portions of the island. It is primarily nocturnal, herbivorous, and terrestrial, living in rocky areas and where it can dig burrows for protection and to reproduce. The species has declined drastically and is considered vulnerable to extinction. This is the only native land mammal on Jamaica besides bats.

BAHAMIAN HUTIA *Geocapromys ingrahami*

KEY FEATURES A medium-size chunky, short-legged rodent—head and body length 37–39 cm (15–16 in.)—with a very short tail. The fur is yellowish brown mixed with red or sprinkled with gray and black. STATUS AND RANGE Endemic to the Bahamas where formerly widespread, this hutia was reduced to a single locality—East Plana Key. Subsequently it was reintroduced into Little Wax Cay and Warderick Wells Cay in the Exumas island chain. It occurs in wooded and semiarid areas, foraging on the ground and in trees during the night. By day it remains underground in crevices or burrows.

DESMAREST'S HUTIA

JAMAICAN CONEY

BAHAMIAN HUTIA

CUBAN SOLENODON *Solenodon cubanus*

KEY FEATURES Medium-size—head and body length 28–32 cm (11–13 in.)—it has a long, pointed snout and a long, naked tail. The eyes are small and the body is reddish brown, turning black on the back and throat.

STATUS AND RANGE Endemic to Cuba, where it is rare and very local, restricted to the Sierra Maestra and Sierra de Toa in eastern Cuba. It occurs in forests and brushy areas, often around plantations. The species is active at night and takes shelter by day in caves, rocky crevices, hollow trees, logs, or burrows they dig themselves. It is unusual among mammals for having toxic saliva. The solenodon is endangered as a result of habitat loss and depredation by and competition with exotic mammals. A related species occurs in neighboring Hispaniola. It, too, is endangered. The solenodon is so unusual as to be placed in its own taxonomic family.

BATS

Bats are by far the best represented group of mammals in the Caribbean. This is doubtless due to their capacity to disperse relatively easily over the sea to reach remote islands. The richest bat faunas are on the largest islands, with Cuba supporting thirty-two species, Jamaica twenty-three, Hispaniola seventeen, and Puerto Rico sixteen. Though bats disperse with less difficulty than more terrestrial mammals, the remoteness of the Caribbean islands provided enough isolation so that over half of the species in the Greater Antilles evolved to become endemics. The bats of the Greater Antilles originally derived primarily from Central America, whereas those of the Lesser Antilles colonized from South America. Few species are included in this guide, due to the nocturnal nature of the group and the difficulty in observing them clearly. A consequence of the nocturnal habits of bats, along with their less than cuddly appearance, is that much folklore has developed about them, resulting in heavy persecution by humans. This is highly regrettable for a number of reasons, a major one being that bats provide great services to us by consuming vast numbers of noxious insects, pollinating various plants, and distributing their seeds. A number of plants are specifically adapted to attract bats as pollinators.

GREATER BULLDOG BAT *Noctilio leporinus*

KEY FEATURES A large bat—body length 10–13 cm (4–5 in.), with a wingspan of 50 cm (2 ft.). The upper parts are brown or gray in females and bright orange-rufous in males. The underparts range in color from cream to orange. It has a squared snout with no nose leaf. Most characteristic are its huge, clawed feet.

STATUS AND RANGE This bat is widespread but local in the Caribbean. It occurs in coastal areas, estuaries, lagoons, lowland lakes, and rivers, where it usually is seen flying low over calm water at night hunting for small fish. Prey is scooped from the water with the webbed tail and then clung to by the bat's hooklike claws. The species roosts in rock clefts and fissures, dark caves, and hollow trees. Flight is slow, with deliberate wing beats.

CUBAN SOLENODON

GREATER BULLDOG BAT

JAMAICAN FRUIT-EATING BAT *Artibeus jamaicensis*

KEY FEATURES A large bat—head and body length 9 cm (3.5 in.), with a wingspan of 40 cm (16 in.). Its coloration is dull brown to grayish above, with paler underparts. The muzzle is short and the snout broad, with a spear-shaped nose leaf. The chin bears a row of V- shaped small bumps, and the ears are medium-size and pointed. The bat lacks a tail.

STATUS AND RANGE Common throughout the Caribbean, though less so in the Bahamas. It frequents low- and middle-elevation wet and dry forests, where it feeds on a huge variety of fruits, especially figs and mangos. In actuality, the bat primarily squeezes the juice from the fruits and spits out the pulp. The flight is powerful but slow, and at the level of the vegetation. This bat roosts in trees and caves, but individuals generally travel alone. It serves as an important seed disperser and has been known to fly up to 15 km (9 mi.) to find fruiting trees. The species occurs as well in Central and South America.

ANTILLEAN FRUIT-EATING BAT *Brachyphylla cavernarum*

KEY FEATURES A large bat—head and body length 7–12 cm (3–5 in.)—the upper parts are pale yellow, the hairs tipped with brown. Patches on the neck, shoulders, and sides are paler. The underparts are brown. The muzzle is narrow tipped, with a stumpy nose leaf. The tail is vestigial.

STATUS AND RANGE Found only in the Caribbean, this bat occurs in Puerto Rico, the Virgin Islands, and Lesser Antilles south to St. Vincent and Barbados. It mainly roosts as colonies in caves, but also in buildings and sometimes under large leaves. An opportunistic feeder, its diet includes diverse fruits as well as flowers, pollen, nectar, and insects. A closely related species, the Cuban Fruit-eating Bat occurs in Cuba, Hispaniola, Jamaica, the Bahamas, and Cayman Islands.

BIG BROWN BAT *Eptesicus fuscus*

KEY FEATURES A large bat—head and body length 10 cm (4 in.), wingspan 30–36 cm (12–14 in.)—with rich, dark reddish-brown coloration. The snout is wide, short, and lacks a nose leaf. The ears are small, narrow, and pointed.

STATUS AND RANGE This bat occurs in the Bahamas, Greater Antilles, Dominica, and Barbados. It frequents moist forests or woodlands but is found in a diversity of other habitats. Males often roost alone, but females form maternity colonies. These may be in caves, tree cavities, rock crevices, or buildings. Flight is relatively ponderous and fluttering. Like many other bats, it navigates using very high pitched sounds emitted through the mouth or nose. The bat feeds on a wide array of nocturnal insects, including many detrimental beetles, all of which are caught in flight. Females can consume their body weight in a single night, making them of extraordinary value for noxious insect control. The species occurs through North and Central America.

JAMAICAN FRUIT-EATING BAT

ANTILLEAN FRUIT-EATING BAT

BIG BROWN BAT

WHITE-TAILED TROPICBIRD *Phaethon lepturus*

KEY FEATURES 81 cm (31 in.) with plumes, 37– 40 cm (15–16 in.) without plumes. White overall, with long trailing tail feathers and heavy black stripes on the upper wing and outer primaries. The bill is yellow or orange. Voice is a raspy *crick-et*.
STATUS AND RANGE Widespread in the Caribbean, where it occurs primarily at sea. While breeding it is locally common around nesting cliffs, primarily March through June (through October in the Bahamas). The typical tropicbird of the Bahamas, Greater Antilles, and Cayman Islands, it is scarcer in the Lesser Antilles, where it is replaced by the similar Red-billed Tropicbird, which has fine black barring on the back and a red bill. Tropicbirds have the capacity to safely drink seawater.

BROWN BOOBY *Sula leucogaster*

KEY FEATURES 71–76 cm (28–30 in.). Primarily dark brown, with a sharply demarcated white belly and abdomen. Voice is a hoarse *kak*.
STATUS AND RANGE Widespread in bays, coastal areas, and at sea. This species is a fairly common resident offshore throughout the Caribbean, while locally abundant near its breeding grounds. It is very rare or absent only from the northern Bahamas. Boobies dive into the sea for fish and squid. This species lays its eggs on the ground, thus requiring remote, predator-free islands for nesting.

BROWN PELICAN *Pelecanus occidentalis*

KEY FEATURES 107–137 cm (42–54 in.). Note its large size, massive bill, and dark coloration. In breeding plumage, the back of the head and neck are reddish brown.
STATUS AND RANGE Widespread in bays, lagoons, and other calm coastal waters. It is a common resident of the southern Bahamas, Greater Antilles, and locally in the northern Lesser Antilles east to Montserrat. The species is uncommon to rare through the rest of the Caribbean. Pelicans usually dive for fish, which they scoop up in their large bill pouches. They can become quite tame at fishing wharfs. Pelican populations have recovered successfully from a serious decline decades ago due to thinning of their shells by the pesticide DDT.

MAGNIFICENT FRIGATEBIRD *Fregata magnificens*

KEY FEATURES 94–104 cm (37–41 in.). Distinguished by its long, forked tail; long, slender, pointed wings sharply bent at the wrist; and habit of floating motionless in the air. Adult male is black, and during courtship the inflatable throat pouch is bright red. Adult female is blackish with a white breast. Immature is blackish with a white head and breast.
STATUS AND RANGE A common and widespread, but somewhat local resident of bays, inshore waters, and offshore cays throughout the Caribbean. Though strictly a seabird, the frigatebird does not dive into or land on the water. It obtains fish by either scooping them from the surface or robbing them from other smaller, slower flying seabirds. The bones of this extraordinary aerialist are riddled with air sacks, making them so light that in sum they weigh less than the bird's feathers.

WHITE-TAILED TROPICBIRD

imm.

adult

BROWN BOOBY

adult

non-br. adult

br.

imm.

BROWN PELICAN

adult ♂

imm.

adult ♀

adult ♂

MAGNIFICENT FRIGATEBIRD

LAUGHING GULL *Leucophaeus atricilla*

KEY FEATURES 38–43 cm (15–17 in.). Breeding adult has a distinctive black head. In the nonbreeding adult the head is white, the mantle gray, and the bill black. First year bird has a noticeably white rump, gray sides and back, and broad black tail band. Voice is squawky, variable *caw* and *caw-aw*; also a laughlike *kaka-ka-ka-ka-ka-ka-kaa-kaa-kaaa-kaaa*.

STATUS AND RANGE A widespread resident of the Caribbean, where it breeds locally. It is generally common April through September in calm coastal waters, though irregular and rare through most of the Caribbean the remainder of year.

RING-BILLED GULL *Larus delawarensis*

KEY FEATURES 46–51 cm (18–20 in.). Fairly large, with a medium-size bill. Breeding adult has white head and underparts, gray wings and back, black wing tips, and ring around its bill.

STATUS AND RANGE Widespread in coastal harbors, lagoons, and open ground from parking lots to grassy fields. It often occurs in urban areas. The species is fairly common but local as a nonbreeding resident of the northern Bahamas and Puerto Rico; uncommon in the southern Bahamas, Cuba, Hispaniola, Cayman Islands, and Barbados; and rare elsewhere. This gull occurs in all months, but primarily December through March. Numbers of this and other gulls are increasing in the Caribbean. This gull is omnivorous, eating everything from fish to garbage. It can be a predator on the eggs and chicks of other birds.

ROYAL TERN *Thalasseus maximus*

KEY FEATURES 46–53 cm (18–21 in.). A large tern with an orange-yellow bill and black crest. Breeding adult's crown is entirely black; nonbreeding's forehead is white. Voice is a harsh, high-pitched *kri-i-ik*.

STATUS AND RANGE Probably the most frequently seen tern of calm coastal waters in the Caribbean, where it is locally common in the Bahamas, Greater Antilles, Virgin and Cayman Islands, and fairly so in the Lesser Antilles. It breeds in colonies very locally on offshore islands, laying its eggs on the sand. In-shore terns in the Caribbean characteristically hover and then dive after their prey.

SANDWICH TERN *Thalasseus sandvicensis*

KEY FEATURES 41–46 cm (16–18 in.). A relatively large tern. The breeding adult appears white, with a shaggy black crest and slender black bill tipped with yellow. In a nonbreeding adult, the crown is white, flecked with black.

STATUS AND RANGE A widespread and common resident of coastal bays and lagoons in the Bahamas, Cuba, and seasonally so in Puerto Rico, it is uncommon in the Virgin Islands and possibly on Sombrero Island (Anguilla). Nonbreeding birds range to other islands, where the species is common in Jamaica, St. Bartholomew, and Antigua primarily October through March. It is uncommon in Hispaniola, St. Martin, Guadeloupe, Martinique, and Barbados and is rare elsewhere.

LAUGHING GULL

imm.

non-br. adult

br.

RING-BILLED GULL

br.

non-br. adult

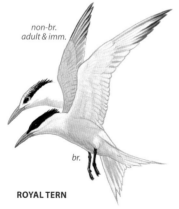

non-br. adult & imm.

br.

ROYAL TERN

SANDWICH TERN

br.

SOOTY TERN *Onychoprion fuscatus*

KEY FEATURES 38–43 cm (15–17 in.). Adult is blackish above and white below, with a deeply forked tail. The outer tail feathers and forehead are white. Immature is dark brown, with whitish spots on mantle and wings; tail less deeply forked. Voice is a distinctive, plaintive *wide-a-wake* or *wacky-wack*.

STATUS AND RANGE Generally a common breeding resident throughout the Caribbean from May through August, but rare in other months. It primarily occurs far offshore, where it feeds on fish and squid. Nesting is on offshore islands in large colonies. Some Sooty Terns from the Caribbean migrate to Africa's shores.

BROWN NODDY *Anous stolidus*

KEY FEATURES 38–40 cm (15–16 in.). Adult is entirely dark brown except for its silvery-white forecrown. Voice is a harsh *karrk*.

STATUS AND RANGE A locally common and widespread resident throughout the Bahamas, Greater Antilles, Virgin Islands, and Lesser Antilles. Away from its breeding islets it is usually seen only at sea far offshore. Young can outweigh their parents by the age of six weeks.

NEOTROPIC CORMORANT *Phalacrocorax brasilianus*

KEY FEATURES 63–69 cm (25–27 in.). A large black waterbird with a long neck and hooked bill. It often sits with its wings spread. Immature is brown above and paler below.

STATUS AND RANGE A common resident of inland freshwater bodies and coastal waters in Cuba, and locally in the Bahamas. The species is expanding its range eastward in the Caribbean. Cormorants eat fish, which they pursue under water. Lacking the oil glands of other waterbirds, cormorants perch with spread wings to dry their feathers.

MARSH AND WETLAND BIRDS

ANHINGA *Anhinga anhinga*

KEY FEATURES 85 cm (34 in.). A large, long-necked waterbird possessing a long tail, pointed bill, and large whitish patches on its back and upper wing. Adult male is glossy black. Adult female is light brown from head to breast. Immature is brown above, tan below.

STATUS AND RANGE A common resident of shallow, calm waters, either fresh or brackish, in Cuba. Sometimes referred to as the Snake-bird, it can gradually submerge beneath the water so that only its snakelike neck and head protrude above the surface. The long, sharp bill serves to spear its primary prey—fish. Like cormorants, the Anhinga often sits with its wings spread to dry its feathers.

adult

SOOTY TERN

adult

BROWN NODDY

non-br.
adult

br.

imm.

NEOTROPIC CORMORANT

adult
♀

adult
♂ br.

adult
♀

ANHINGA

WHITE IBIS *Eudocimus albus*

KEY FEATURES 56–71 cm (22–28 in.). A fairly large wading bird with a distinctively long, down-curved, reddish bill. Adult is white; immature, brown with a white belly and rump. In flight, note the outstretched neck, black wingtips, and curved bill.

STATUS AND RANGE A common resident of freshwater swamps, rice fields, and saltwater lagoons in Cuba and Hispaniola, locally so in Puerto Rico, uncommon and local in Jamaica, and a rare nonbreeding resident of the Bahamas. Ibises typically occur in loose flocks and nest colonially. They feed on a wide variety of animal matter.

ROSEATE SPOONBILL *Platalea ajaja*

KEY FEATURES 66–81 cm (26–32 in.). Adult is a large, pink wading bird with a long, spatulalike bill. Immature is white with some pink.

STATUS AND RANGE A locally common resident of shallow, saltwater lagoons and edges of mudflats in Cuba and Hispaniola. In the Bahamas it is a common resident of Great Inagua, uncommon on Andros, and rare on Caicos. The spoonbill feeds on small aquatic organisms by sweeping its head back and forth with its bill in the water. It typically occurs in flocks.

AMERICAN FLAMINGO *Phoenicopterus ruber*

KEY FEATURES 107–122 cm (42–48 in.). A very large, distinctive pink bird with long legs and neck and a strangely curved bill. Immature is much paler. Voice consists of gooselike honks.

STATUS AND RANGE An abundant resident of shallow lagoons and coastal estuaries on Great Inagua in the Bahamas and common but a very local resident of Cuba and Hispaniola. It is rare and very local in Jamaica and Puerto Rico, but numbers are increasing. Flamingos feed with their head upside down and use their peculiar bills to strain minute organisms and algae from the water. They often occur in large flocks.

adult

adult

WHITE IBIS

imm.

adult

imm.

ROSEATE SPOONBILL

adult

adult

AMERICAN FLAMINGO

adult

imm.

LITTLE BLUE HERON *Egretta caerulea*

KEY FEATURES 56–71 cm (22–28 in.). A medium-size heron with a grayish bill tipped with black. Adult is entirely dark gray. Immature is white, sometimes mottled with dark feathers.

STATUS AND RANGE A common resident throughout the Caribbean, where it occurs in calm, shallow freshwater and saltwater areas as well as swift-flowing rivers and streams. It slowly stalks its prey, primarily fish, but also eats many other organisms, including frogs, lizards, and mice. Nesting is colonial, in trees.

TRICOLORED HERON *Egretta tricolor*

KEY FEATURES 61–71 cm (24–28 in.). A medium-size gray heron with a white belly and undertail coverts. Immature is browner.

STATUS AND RANGE A common resident of mangrove swamps and saltwater lagoons in the Bahamas, Greater Antilles, and Virgin and Cayman Islands. Generally it is rare in the Lesser Antilles. This heron sometimes occurs in freshwater wetlands. It feeds primarily on fish, which it stalks stealthily in shallow waters. Nesting is colonial, in trees.

SNOWY EGRET *Egretta thula*

KEY FEATURES 51–71 cm (20–28 in.). A medium-size white heron with black legs, yellow feet, and yellow in front of the eye. The long, slender bill is entirely black.

STATUS AND RANGE A common resident of the Bahamas, Greater Antilles, Virgin and Cayman Islands, Antigua, Guadeloupe, and Barbados. It is generally an uncommon nonbreeding resident or transient elsewhere in the Lesser Antilles, though it breeds on St. Martin. Freshwater swamps are its primary habitat, but it also occurs along river banks and saltwater lagoons. Fish are its primary food, which it frequently hunts by standing immobile in shallow water waiting for unwary prey to come within range of its spearlike bill.

REDDISH EGRET *Egretta rufescens*

KEY FEATURES 69–81 cm (27–32 in.). A medium-size heron of varying coloration. In the adult, note the black-tipped bill, pinkish at the base, the ruffled neck feathers, and its behavior of dancing in the water. Dark phase is grayish, the head and neck reddish brown. In the white phase, plumage is entirely white. The immature bill is entirely dark and the neck feathers unruffled.

STATUS AND RANGE A locally common resident of shallow, protected coastal waters and, less frequently, swamp edges in the Bahamas and Cuba. It is uncommon in the Cayman Islands and Hispaniola, and is uncommon and very local in Jamaica. This is the most active of herons when searching for prey, primarily fish. It runs, hops, and spreads its wings, giving the impression of a dance.

adult

imm. molting

imm.

LITTLE BLUE HERON

adult

TRICOLORED HERON

adult

SNOWY EGRET

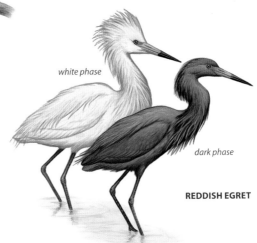

white phase

dark phase

REDDISH EGRET

CATTLE EGRET *Bubulcus ibis*

KEY FEATURES 48–64 cm (19–25 in.). A small white heron with a short, stout, yellowish bill. It is the only heron typically found away from water. Breeding birds have a tan wash on the crown, breast, and upper back.

STATUS AND RANGE A common resident throughout the Caribbean. Large numbers of these herons are regularly seen in pastures and fields, often around cattle, which serve to scare up insects, small lizards, and mice upon which the birds prey. The Cattle Egret, originally confined to the Eastern Hemisphere, expanded its range naturally to the Western Hemisphere over a century ago and is now widespread from South America to Canada. Large roosts occur in mangroves, dense woods, and, curiously, on electrical transformers.

GREAT EGRET *Ardea alba*

KEY FEATURES 89–107 cm (35–42 in.). A large white heron with a yellow bill and black legs.

STATUS AND RANGE A common resident of large freshwater and saltwater swamps, grassy marshes, river banks, and shallows behind reefs in the Bahamas, Greater Antilles, Antigua, and Guadeloupe, though uncommon in the Virgin Islands. It is a common nonbreeding resident of the Cayman Islands, St. Bartholomew, and Barbados, but uncommon elsewhere in the Lesser Antilles from September through April. The plumes of this elegant bird and of the Snowy Egret were formerly popular in women's hats, which led to a dramatic decline in their numbers, but both species have recovered.

GREAT BLUE HERON *Ardea herodias*

KEY FEATURES 107–132 cm (42–52 in.). By far the largest heron in the region. Dark phase: primarily gray, with a black eyebrow stripe. White phase: white plumage, with a yellow bill and legs.

STATUS AND RANGE A common nonbreeding resident of ponds and lagoons in the Bahamas, Greater Antilles, and Virgin and Cayman Islands primarily October through April, it is uncommon in the Lesser Antilles. During other months, it is decidedly uncommon anywhere in the region. White-phase birds are extremely rare in the Caribbean. Like all other herons and egrets, the Great Blue tucks its neck in an S when in flight.

CATTLE EGRET

br.

non-br. adult

GREAT EGRET

br.

GREAT BLUE HERON

dark phase

YELLOW-CROWNED NIGHT-HERON *Nyctanassa violacea*

KEY FEATURES 56–71 cm (22–28 in.). A medium-size heron of chunky appearance. Adult has distinctive gray underparts and black-and-white head markings. Immature is grayish brown with white flecks. Voice is a distinctive *quark*.

STATUS AND RANGE The species frequents mangrove swamps, but also freshwater areas, mudflats, and dry thickets. It is a common resident of the Bahamas, Greater Antilles, Virgin and Cayman Islands, and northern Lesser Antilles and is generally uncommon south of Barbuda. Primarily nocturnal, its heavy bill is adapted for feeding on hard-shelled crustaceans such as crabs.

BLACK-CROWNED NIGHT-HERON *Nycticorax nycticorax*

KEY FEATURES 58–71 cm (23–28 in.). A medium-size heron of chunky appearance. Adult has a black crown and back with a white face, underparts, and head plumes. Immature is brown with white flecks. Voice is a distinctive *quark*.

STATUS AND RANGE An uncommon and local resident of freshwater swamps, brackish lagoons, and salt ponds in the Bahamas, Greater Antilles, and Virgin and Cayman Islands. It is an uncommon to rare nonbreeding resident of the Lesser Antilles from October through April. Primarily nocturnal, this heron often is found standing motionless in reeds or on mangrove roots over shallow water.

GREEN HERON *Butorides virescens*

KEY FEATURES 40–48 cm (16–19 in.). A small, short-necked heron with dark coloration and greenish-yellow to orangish legs. Breeding adult's legs are bright orange. Immature is heavily streaked below. Voice is a distinctive, piercing *skyow* when flushed; a softer series of *kek*, *kak*, or *que* notes when undisturbed.

STATUS AND RANGE A common resident throughout the Caribbean, occurring at all water bodies, both fresh and saline. Usually solitary, it is frequently discovered by its piercing call. This heron typically perches motionless on a limb low over the water, waiting for unsuspecting prey to come within range of its sharp bill.

PURPLE GALLINULE *Porphyrio martinica*

KEY FEATURES 33 cm (13 in.). Adult is a chickenlike waterbird, bluish purple in color with yellow legs and a bluish-white frontal shield. Immature is golden brown, with bluish wings. Voice is a high-pitched, melodious *klee-klee*.

STATUS AND RANGE A common resident of freshwater bodies with dense vegetation in Cuba, Hispaniola, and Puerto Rico, while uncommon in Jamaica and the Cayman Islands. In the Bahamas it is an uncommon migrant on the larger northern islands August through October and March through May. It is rare and local elsewhere. The Purple Gallinule has very long toes, enabling it to walk on water lilies and other aquatic vegetation without sinking into the water.

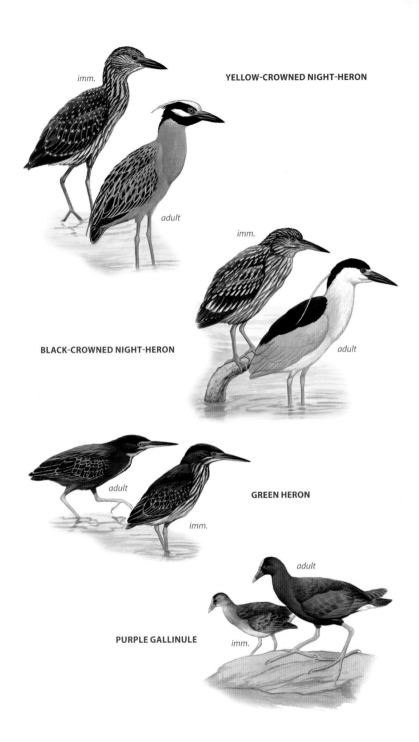

imm.

YELLOW-CROWNED NIGHT-HERON

adult

imm.

BLACK-CROWNED NIGHT-HERON

adult

adult

GREEN HERON

imm.

adult

PURPLE GALLINULE

imm.

COMMON GALLINULE *Gallinula galeata*

KEY FEATURES 34 cm (13.5 in.). A black, ducklike waterbird with red bill tipped with yellow, a red frontal shield, and a white line down its flank. It head bobs as it swims. Voice is a piercing, laughlike cackle, slowing at the end: *ki-ki-ki-ki-ka, kaa, kaaa*.

STATUS AND RANGE Generally a common resident of most wetlands with water plants throughout the Caribbean. The bird is not shy and is usually quite noisy and conspicuous among aquatic vegetation or on open water nearby. It feeds on both plant and animal matter.

AMERICAN COOT *Fulica americana*

KEY FEATURES 38–40 cm (15–16 in.). A ducklike waterbird with a pointed bill. It bobs its head while swimming. Adult is grayish black overall with a white bill and undertail coverts. Nearly identical to the Caribbean Coot, this bird's frontal shield above its forehead is dark.

STATUS AND RANGE An uncommon breeding resident on open freshwater bodies in the Bahamas, Cuba, Jamaica, Hispaniola, and the Cayman Islands, primarily from May through August. Migrants augment numbers from September through April, making it common throughout the Bahamas, Greater Antilles, and Cayman Islands during these months. It is uncommon and occasionally breeds in the Virgin Islands and is rare in the Lesser Antilles. Coots are excellent divers and usually occur in flocks. The toes of coots are lobed, but the lobes are not connected, as in ducks.

CARIBBEAN COOT *Fulica caribaea*

KEY FEATURES 38–40 cm (15–16 in.). A ducklike waterbird with a pointed bill. It swims with its head bobbing. It is nearly identical to the American Coot, but the frontal shield above its forehead is white, extending onto the crown.

STATUS AND RANGE A common resident of open water bodies in Puerto Rico, uncommon and local in Hispaniola, but a rare resident of Jamaica and the Virgin Islands and a wanderer in the Lesser Antilles. Species numbers have declined substantially to the point where this coot is considered threatened with extinction. Causes of the decline include habitat loss and degradation, overhunting, and introduced predators.

CLAPPER RAIL *Rallus longirostris*

KEY FEATURES 36 cm (14 in.). A gray, chickenlike waterbird with a long, slender bill. Voice is a loud, grating cackle *kek-kek-kek-kek …*, slowing at the end.

STATUS AND RANGE A common resident of salt marshes and mangroves in the Bahamas, Cuba, and Puerto Rico; locally so in Jamaica, Hispaniola, the Virgin Islands, and Barbuda; and rare and local on St. Kitts, Guadeloupe, and Martinique. The Clapper Rail, like others of the group, stalks around in the dense vegetation bordering saline wetlands. It rarely flies, preferring to run for cover. Most active at dawn and dusk, it is far more often heard than seen.

COMMON GALLINULE

adult

AMERICAN COOT

adult

imm.

adult

CARIBBEAN COOT

CLAPPER RAIL

NORTHERN JACANA *Jacana spinosa*

KEY FEATURES 19–23 cm (7.5–9 in.). A medium-size, chickenlike waterbird with large yellow wing patches and extremely long, slender, greenish toes. Adult is deep reddish-brown with a blackish head and neck and yellow bill and forehead shield. Immature has whitish underparts and eyebrow stripe. Flight is low over the water, with shallow wingbeats and dangling legs. Voice is a sharp, repeated cackle.

STATUS AND RANGE A common resident of ponds and lake edges with large-leaved floating vegetation in Cuba, Jamaica, and Hispaniola. Its huge toes enable it to walk on floating vegetation without sinking. Unusual among birds, the male is smaller than the female, incubates the eggs, and cares for the young. Among some jacanas the female has several mates.

WHITE-CHEEKED PINTAIL *Anas bahamensis*

KEY FEATURES 38–48 cm (15–19 in.). Note the red bill mark and white cheek. The wing patch is green, edged with buff.

STATUS AND RANGE A locally common resident of calm shallow water, both fresh and saline, in the Bahamas, Cuba, Puerto Rico, Virgin Islands, and Antigua. It is locally uncommon in Hispaniola and uncommon to rare in most of the northern Lesser Antilles and Barbados. This duck is considered threatened due to habitat loss, overhunting, and predation by the mongoose and other predators on eggs and nestlings.

BLUE-WINGED TEAL *Anas discors*

KEY FEATURES 38–40 cm (15–16 in.). A small duck with a blue forewing. Female and nonbreeding male are mottled brown with a green speculum. In the breeding male, note the white face crescent.

STATUS AND RANGE The most common nonbreeding duck in the Caribbean, it occurs primarily from October through April. It feeds on seeds, plant matter, and aquatic invertebrates in the shallows of both fresh and saltwater bodies.

NORTHERN SHOVELER *Anas clypeata*

KEY FEATURES 43–53 cm (17–21 in.). The unusually large bill is distinctive. Male: Note the green head, white breast, and reddish-brown sides. Female is mottled brown.

STATUS AND RANGE A nonbreeding resident of shallow fresh and brackish water bodies throughout the Caribbean, primarily from October through May. It is common in Cuba; uncommon in the Bahamas, Hispaniola, Puerto Rico, and the Cayman Islands; and is rare in Jamaica and the Lesser Antilles. The unusual bill and specialized tongue serve to strain seeds, algae, and aquatic invertebrates from the water.

NORTHERN JACANA

imm.

adult

WHITE-CHEEKED PINTAIL

br. ♂

♀ &
non-br. ♂

BLUE-WINGED TEAL

♀ &
non-br. ♂

br. ♂

NORTHERN SHOVELER

♂

♀

♀

♂

AMERICAN WIGEON *Anas americana*

KEY FEATURES 46–56 cm (18–22 in.). Male is distinguished by the white crown, light-blue bill, and green eye-patch. Female is brownish, with a gray head and light blue bill.

STATUS AND RANGE A nonbreeding resident of shallow freshwater ponds and lakes throughout the Caribbean, principally October through April. It is common in Cuba; fairly common in Hispaniola; and uncommon to rare elsewhere. Aquatic vegetation is its primary food.

RUDDY DUCK *Oxyura jamaicensis*

KEY FEATURES 35–43 cm (14–17 in.). A small duck with a chunky body and erect tail. Male is reddish brown overall, with a white cheek patch and blue bill. Female and immature are mostly brown, with a whitish stripe below the eye.

STATUS AND RANGE A locally common resident of deep, open water bodies, both fresh and brackish, on New Providence in the Bahamas and the Greater Antilles. It is uncommon and local elsewhere in the Bahamas and rare in the Virgin Islands and Barbados. The Ruddy Duck lays huge eggs, the largest of any duck relative to its body size. This duck dives for food, primarily plant material, and most run over the water to take flight.

BIRDS OF MUDFLATS

RUDDY TURNSTONE *Arenaria interpres*

KEY FEATURES 21–23 cm (8–9 in.). Nonbreeding birds have noticeable dark breast markings and orange legs. Breeding birds have unusual black-and-white facial markings. These, along with the reddish-orange back are diagnostic. In flight, the bird has a distinctive white pattern on the upper wings, back, and tail. Voice is a loud, nasal *cuck-cuck-cuck*, increasing in volume.

STATUS AND RANGE A common nonbreeding resident of mudflats, pond edges, and sandy and rocky coasts throughout the Caribbean during most months. Turnstones occur in flocks and derive their name from the habit of flipping over stones and pebbles to search beneath them for invertebrate prey.

BLACK-BELLIED PLOVER *Pluvialis squatarola*

KEY FEATURES 26–34 cm (10–13.5 in.). A large, stocky shorebird with a short bill. Nonbreeding birds are a light mottled gray with indistinct contrast between the gray crown and whitish eyebrow stripe. This is the most frequently observed plumage in the Caribbean. In breeding birds the black underparts are distinctive. Voice is a plaintive *klee* or *klee-a-lee*.

STATUS AND RANGE A common nonbreeding resident of tidal mudflats and sometimes other coastal water edges in the Caribbean from August through May. It generally occurs in loose flocks. It probes in moist mud for invertebrate prey. Like most shorebirds in the region, it is a long-distance migrant.

AMERICAN WIGEON

♀

♂

♂

♀

♀ & imm.

non-br. ♂

br. ♂

br. ♂

♀ & imm.

RUDDY DUCK

non-br.

br.

non-br.

RUDDY TURNSTONE

non-br.

non-br.

br.

BLACK-BELLIED PLOVER

WILSON'S PLOVER *Charadrius wilsonia*

KEY FEATURES 18–20 cm (7–8 in.). Note this shorebird's broad breast band and thick, black bill. Adult male's breast band is black. Adult female and immature have a brown breast band. Voice is an emphatic, raspy whistle or a quick *ki-ki-ki*.
STATUS AND RANGE A common resident of salt pond borders in the Bahamas, Greater Antilles, Virgin Islands, and some northern Lesser Antilles. It is uncommon in the Cayman Islands and the Grenadines. The nest is a depression in the sand. Its food consists of various invertebrates, including fiddler crabs.

SEMIPALMATED PLOVER *Charadrius semipalmatus*

KEY FEATURES 18.5 cm (7.25 in.). A small shorebird with brown upper parts, a dark breast band, stubby bill, and orange legs. Sometimes the breast band shows only as bars on either side of the breast. Voice is a plaintive *weet*.
STATUS AND RANGE A common nonbreeding resident of tidal mudflats through most of the Caribbean from August through May, though most frequent in September and October. This tiny plover occurs most typically in small, loose groups that probe in moist mud for invertebrates.

KILLDEER *Charadrius vociferus*

KEY FEATURES 25 cm (9.75 in.). Readily identified by its two black breast bands. In flight, note the reddish-brown rump. Voice is a plaintive, high-pitched *kee* and *dee-de*.
STATUS AND RANGE A common resident of wet fields, short grass, muddy areas, and freshwater pond edges in the Bahamas and Greater Antilles, less so in the Virgin Islands. Migrants augment local numbers primarily from September through March. It is an uncommon nonbreeding resident of the Cayman Islands, northern Lesser Antilles, and Barbados and is rare to very rare elsewhere in the Lesser Antilles. The Killdeer does not typically flock and is more of an upland bird than other plovers in the region. Its name derives from the bird's call.

LESSER YELLOWLEGS *Tringa flavipes*

KEY FEATURES 25–28 cm (9.75–11 in.). A medium-size shorebird with orangish-yellow legs and a thin, straight bill. Voice is a one- or two-note *cu-cu*, softer and more nasal than the Greater Yellowlegs.
STATUS AND RANGE A nonbreeding resident throughout the Caribbean, it is most common during migration August through October and March through May. The species typically occurs in flocks and frequents mudflats and shallows of both freshwater and saltwater bodies, where it probes for invertebrates.

WILSON'S PLOVER

♀

♂

SEMIPALMATED PLOVER

br.

non-br.

adult

KILLDEER

LESSER YELLOWLEGS

WILLET *Tringa semipalmata*

KEY FEATURES 38–40 cm (15–16 in.). A large shorebird of light-gray coloration with gray legs and a relatively thick bill. In flight, note the distinctive black-and-white wing pattern. Voice is a sharp *chip-chip-chip*; also a sharp whistle.

STATUS AND RANGE A resident of tidal flats and borders of saltwater and freshwater bodies in the Bahamas, Greater Antilles, and Cayman Islands, where it is most common from August through November. It is uncommon to rare elsewhere. Unlike most other shorebirds in the region, the Willet does not typically flock.

SPOTTED SANDPIPER *Actitis macularius*

KEY FEATURES 18–20 cm (7–8 in.). Most readily identified by its distinctive teetering walk. Nonbreeding birds have white underparts with a dark mark on side of neck; the bill base is orangish. Breeding birds have noticeable dark spots on the underparts and the orange bill has a black tip. Voice is a whistled *we-weet*.

STATUS AND RANGE Generally a common nonbreeding resident along edges of mangroves, coastlines, and streams throughout the Caribbean from August through May, it is less common during other months. This sandpiper does not typically flock. It deliberately walks along water borders searching carefully for prey, frequently teetering as it goes.

SEMIPALMATED SANDPIPER *Calidris pusilla*

KEY FEATURES 14–16.5 cm (5.5–6.5 in.). A small shorebird with black legs and a medium-length black bill that is slightly longer and more drooped at the tip in the female than in the male. This is the principal small sandpiper to know well. Nonbreeding is grayish brown above, whitish below. Breeding has a finely barred upper breast and reddish-brown tints on upper parts. Voice is a soft chatter; also a fairly deep, hoarse *cherk*.

STATUS AND RANGE Generally a common nonbreeding resident of mudflats and still water edges from puddles to salt ponds in most of Caribbean from August through October. This species often occurs in large flocks, sometimes numbering in the hundreds or even thousands.

BLACK-NECKED STILT *Himantopus mexicanus*

KEY FEATURES 34–39 cm (13.5–15.5 in.). A large, noisy shorebird with long pink legs, black upper parts, and white underparts. Voice is a loud, raucous *wit, wit, wit, wit, wit.*

STATUS AND RANGE Widespread throughout the Caribbean on mudflats, salt ponds, and open mangrove swamps. A common breeding resident March through October in the southern and central Bahamas, Greater Antilles, and Virgin and Cayman Islands. It is an uncommon to rare breeding resident of the northernmost Bahamas and is uncommon in the northern Lesser Antilles south to Guadeloupe. Stilts typically occur in flocks.

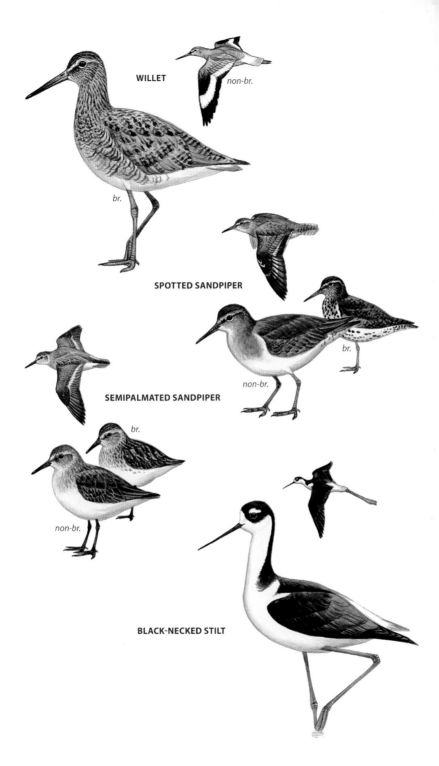

WILLET

non-br.

SPOTTED SANDPIPER

non-br. *br.*

SEMIPALMATED SANDPIPER

br.

non-br.

BLACK-NECKED STILT

br.

NORTHERN BOBWHITE *Colinus virginianus*

KEY FEATURES 25 cm (10 in.). A terrestrial bird resembling a small chicken. It is most frequently located by its distinctive call. Male has a white throat and eyebrow stripe. On females the throat and eyebrow stripe are tan. Voice is a clear, whistled *bob, bob-white*, rising at the end and often repeated.

STATUS AND RANGE A common resident of Cuba, where it inhabits scrubland and pasture with dense cover. This quail was introduced into and is now common in the northern Bahamas; it is uncommon in Hispaniola. Introductions on other islands have been unsuccessful. The Bobwhite typically occurs in flocks and does not flush until underfoot.

RED JUNGLEFOWL *Gallus gallus*

KEY FEATURES Male: 71 cm (28 in.); female: 43 cm (17 in.). Male (rooster) is a resplendently plumaged bird known to everyone; it has a red head comb and wattle and a long, bushy tail. Female (hen) is much smaller than the male, and with a smaller comb and wattle and brownish plumage. Voice is a universally recognized *cockadoodledoo*.

STATUS AND RANGE This is the wild version of the domesticated rooster and chicken. It has been introduced into many islands and is now feral very locally in the Dominican Republic, Puerto Rico, and the Grenadines. Domesticated birds are common on farms throughout the Caribbean. In the wild it occurs in dry and moist forests.

HELMETED GUINEAFOWL *Numida meleagris*

KEY FEATURES 53 cm (21 in.). A large terrestrial fowl of unusual body shape and distinctive dark-gray feathering with white spots. The head and neck are nearly naked. Voice is a wild cackle.

STATUS AND RANGE Introduced to the Caribbean, where it is widespread domestically in farmyards but locally feral. In the feral state it is fairly common locally in the Dominican Republic and rare in Cuba, Puerto Rico, the Virgin Islands (St. Croix), St. Martin (Isle Pinel), and Barbuda. Guineafowl occur primarily in dry scrubland and typically flock.

NORTHERN BOBWHITE

RED JUNGLEFOWL

HELMETED GUINEAFOWL

TURKEY VULTURE *Cathartes aura*

KEY FEATURES 68–80 cm (27–32 in.). A very large, blackish bird with a small, bare red head. In flight, it soars on dark two-toned wings held well above horizontal in a broad V.

STATUS AND RANGE A common and widespread resident of Cuba and Jamaica, while locally common in the northern Bahamas (Grand Bahama, Abaco, and Andros), northeastern Hispaniola, and southwestern Puerto Rico. The species occurs in open areas at all elevations. It feeds on carrion, which it detects using acute senses of sight and smell. Vultures often sunbathe on exposed perches with wings outstretched.

OSPREY *Pandion haliaetus*

KEY FEATURES 53–61 cm (21–24 in.). The widespread migratory race has a white head and dark bar behind the eye, while the resident race has a white head with only a trace of an eyestripe. The primarily white underparts contrast with the dark upper parts. In flight, the primarily white wings are characteristically bent at their dark wrist patch. Voice is a piercing whistle.

STATUS AND RANGE A nonbreeding resident throughout the Caribbean primarily from September through April, it is common in the Bahamas, Greater Antilles, and the Virgin and Cayman Islands and is uncommon in the Lesser Antilles. This hawk breeds only in the Bahamas and Cuba. The Osprey occurs around all calm fresh or saltwater bodies. It eats only fish it is specially adapted to capture. When hunting the Osprey hovers and then plunges, talons first, into the water after its prey.

SNAIL KITE *Rostrhamus sociabilis*

KEY FEATURES 43–48 cm (17–19 in.). Note the white rump and the conspicuous hooked bill. The legs, eyes, and mark between the eyes and bill are red. Adult male is blackish. Adult female is brown above and white below, heavily streaked with brown; white eyebrow stripe. Voice is a raspy, ratchetlike *ge-gege-ge*.

STATUS AND RANGE A common resident of Cuba, where its habitat is freshwater marshes, open swamps, reservoirs, rice fields, and canals. It forages by slowly flying over marshes with an active, flapping flight. Freshwater apple snails make up its entire diet.

TURKEY VULTURE

migratory race
OSPREY

adult

SNAIL KITE

adult
♂

adult
♀

adult
♂

adult
♀

BROAD-WINGED HAWK *Buteo platypterus*

KEY FEATURES 35–41 cm (14–16 in.). A medium-size, chunky hawk that alternately soars and flaps on broad, rounded wings. In the adult the tail is boldly banded black and white and the underparts are barred reddish-brown. In the immature the underparts are white and streaked with dark brown, and the tail bands are more numerous but less distinct. Voice is a thin, shrill squeal: *pweeeeeeeeee*.

STATUS AND RANGE A common resident of Cuba, Antigua, and Dominica south to Grenada, but rare and very local in Puerto Rico and uncommon on St. Kitts. Its habitat includes dense broad-leaved, mixed, and plantation forests at all elevations and less frequently open woodlands. On Antigua this hawk occurs in open woodlands and towns.

RED-TAILED HAWK *Buteo jamaicensis*

KEY FEATURES 48–64 cm (19–25 in.). A large hawk, dark brown above and white below, with dark belly stripes and a distinctive reddish tail. When immature the tail is grayish brown with faint bars and the underparts are more heavily streaked. Voice is a raspy *keeer-r-r-r*, slurring downward.

STATUS AND RANGE A common resident on larger islands of the northern Bahamas, Greater Antilles, Virgin Islands, St. Bartholomew, Saba, St. Kitts, and Nevis, but rare on St. Eustatius. This is a bird of open country, woodlands, forests, and towns at all elevations. It soars on broad, rounded wings and fanned tail. It feeds primarily on introduced rodents, lizards, snakes, birds, and large invertebrates.

AMERICAN KESTREL *Falco sparverius*

KEY FEATURES 23–30 cm (9–12 in.). A small falcon with a reddish-brown back (except the dark phase of the Cuban race *F. s. sparverioides*, which is dark gray). The tail is reddish, with a broad, black terminal band, and the face has two black bars. The underparts vary from white to reddish brown. Adult male has blue-gray wings; adult female, reddish-brown wings. Immature has dark breast streaks. Voice is a high-pitched *killi-killi-killi*.

STATUS AND RANGE A common resident of the Bahamas, Greater Antilles, Virgin Islands, and Lesser Antilles south to St. Lucia. It is rare farther south. In the Cayman Islands it is a fairly common migrant but does not breed. Typical habitats include dry, open lowlands with high perches from which it searches for prey. It also frequents palm savannas, towns, and forest edges in the mountains. The nest is in a tree cavity.

BROAD-WINGED HAWK

Puerto Rico race adult

St. Vincent, Barbados, Grenada race

adult

imm.

Dominica, Martinique, St. Lucia race

imm.

adult

RED-TAILED HAWK

imm.

adult

imm.

adult ♀ Hispaniola race

Cuba, Bahamas, Jamaica race

adult ♀

Hispaniola race

adult ♂

AMERICAN KESTREL

SCALY-NAPED PIGEON *Patagioenas squamosa*

KEY FEATURES 36–40 cm (14–16 in.). A large, slate-gray arboreal pigeon. Voice sounds like an emphatic *"Who are you!"*

STATUS AND RANGE Resident through much of the Caribbean, where it is common in Puerto Rico, the Virgin Islands, and much of the Lesser Antilles, while fairly common only locally in Hispaniola. In Cuba it is uncommon in the east and rare in the west. These islands comprise nearly its entire range. Typically a bird of mountain forests, it sometimes occurs in well-wooded lowlands. On St. Kitts and Barbados this pigeon frequents towns and villages. Overall, it has declined widely in the Caribbean primarily due to intensive hunting.

WHITE-CROWNED PIGEON *Patagioenas leucocephala*

KEY FEATURES 33–36 cm (13–14 in.). A dark-gray pigeon with a white crown. Voice sounds like *"Who took two?"* although faster and less deliberate than the Scaly-naped Pigeon. The second syllable rises.

STATUS AND RANGE A common breeding resident generally year-round in the Bahamas, Cuba, Jamaica, and Antigua; locally common in Hispaniola, Puerto Rico, and the Virgin Islands; and uncommon in the Cayman Islands, Anguilla, and St. Bartholomew. It is rare elsewhere in the Caribbean, the region that comprises nearly its entire range. This arboreal, gregarious pigeon inhabits coastal woodlands and mangroves when breeding, and when not breeding it sometimes ranges to the mountains.

ROCK PIGEON *Columba livia*

KEY FEATURES 33–36 cm (13–14 in.). A variably colored pigeon, it is often gray with a black tail band and white rump. Voice is a gentle cooing.

STATUS AND RANGE This is the common, resident pigeon of cities and towns through much of the Caribbean. It typically occurs in tight flocks. In a few locations it is semiferal and may be entirely feral. Native to temperate regions of the Eastern Hemisphere, it has been widely introduced elsewhere.

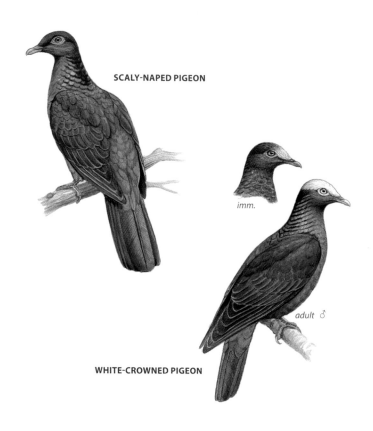

SCALY-NAPED PIGEON

imm.

adult ♂

WHITE-CROWNED PIGEON

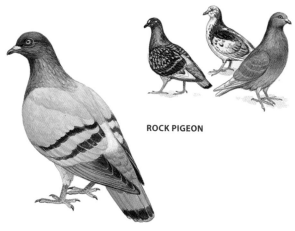

ROCK PIGEON

EURASIAN COLLARED-DOVE *Streptopelia decaocto*

KEY FEATURES 28–30 cm (11–12 in.). A medium-size, pale-gray dove with dark primaries and a black band on the hindneck. Voice is an often-repeated three-syllable *kuk-koooooooó-kook,* with brief pauses between phrases; also a harsh, nasal *mew* in flight or upon landing.

STATUS AND RANGE A common resident of the northern Bahamas while locally common and spreading in Cuba, Puerto Rico, Guadeloupe, and Martinique. The entire Caribbean may soon be colonized by this introduced species, which is native to Europe and Asia. It primarily inhabits urban areas, where it forages for seeds on the ground.

COMMON GROUND-DOVE *Columbina passerina*

KEY FEATURES 15–18 cm (5.75–7 in.). The only tiny dove in the Caribbean. Its plumage varies among islands, but all display a reddish-brown wing patch, which is conspicuous in flight. Voice consists of a monotonous, often-repeated call, either of single or double notes, *coo, coo, coo, coo …* or *co-coo, co-coo, co-coo …* or *hoop, hoop, hoop …* in staccato fashion.

STATUS AND RANGE A very common resident throughout the Caribbean in most lowland habitats except heavily wooded areas. Primarily ground dwelling, it sometimes seeks refuge in trees. Seeds are its principle food.

WHITE-WINGED DOVE *Zenaida asiatica*

KEY FEATURES 28–30 cm (11–12 in.). A medium-size dove distinguished by its large, white central wing patch. Voice consists of two calls. One call is *"Two bits for two"* on a single pitch. A second call is a yodellike cooing slurred between two notes.

STATUS AND RANGE Generally a common resident of the southern Bahamas, Cuba, Jamaica, Hispaniola, Puerto Rico, and Grand Cayman in scrubland, mangroves, open woodlands, and urban gardens primarily in coastal areas. It is uncommon in the northern Bahamas. The species is expanding eastward through the Caribbean. It frequently occurs in loose flocks.

EURASIAN COLLARED-DOVE

adult

COMMON GROUND-DOVE

adult

WHITE-WINGED DOVE

adult

ZENAIDA DOVE *Zenaida aurita*

KEY FEATURES 25–28 cm (10–11 in.). This medium-size dove is distinguished by a white band on the trailing edge of its secondaries and its rounded tail tipped with white. The Mourning Dove lacks white in its wings and has a longer, pointed tail. Voice is a gentle cooing, almost identical to the Mourning Dove—*coo-oo, coo, coo, coo,* the second syllable rising sharply. The call is rendered as *"Mar-y boil brown rice."*
STATUS AND RANGE A common resident throughout the Caribbean, though slightly less abundant in the southern Lesser Antilles, where the Eared Dove is more common. This dove occurs primarily in open areas, gardens, and hotel grounds, but also in open woodlands, scrub thickets, pine woods with dense understory, and lower mountain forests. It primarily frequents coastal areas.

EARED DOVE *Zenaida auriculata*

KEY FEATURES 22–25 cm (8.5–10 in.). A moderately small dove, grayish brown above with a few small black spots on its lower back. The underparts are entirely brown and the outer tail feathers have reddish-brown tips. It lacks white in the wings or tail. Voice is like the Zenaida Dove but shorter.
STATUS AND RANGE A common resident on St. Lucia, St. Vincent, the Grenadines, and Grenada, while very local on Barbados. The species is expanding its range northward in the Caribbean. It occurs in semiarid brushlands, primarily in the lowlands. This dove forages on the ground and sometimes occurs in large flocks.

MOURNING DOVE *Zenaida macroura*

KEY FEATURES 28–33 cm (11–13 in.). The long, wedge-shaped tail of this dove distinguishes it. The tail is fringed with white, while the wings lack it. Zenaida and White-winged Doves have white wing markings. Voice is a mournful cooing almost identical to the Zenaida Dove—*coo-oo, coo, coo, coo,* the second syllable rising sharply.
STATUS AND RANGE A locally common resident primarily in open lowlands, dry coastal forests, and agricultural lands, often near freshwater in the Bahamas and Greater Antilles. It also occurs in agricultural areas in the mountains. The species is expanding its range eastward in the Caribbean.

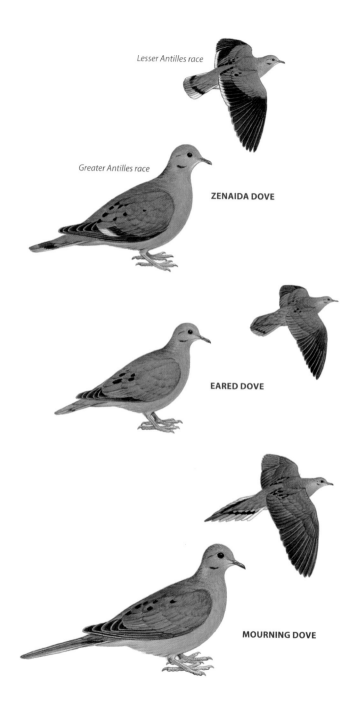

Lesser Antilles race

Greater Antilles race

ZENAIDA DOVE

EARED DOVE

MOURNING DOVE

MONK PARAKEET *Myiopsitta monachus*

KEY FEATURES 28 cm (11 in.). A fairly large parakeet, green above with a gray crown, throat, and breast. It has a long, pointed tail, and the flight feathers are blue. Voice is a raucous squawk.

STATUS AND RANGE Introduced into Puerto Rico, where it is locally abundant in coastal palm groves and urban gardens. It is also introduced but rare on Guadeloupe and in the Cayman Islands, where it occurs in George Town on Grand Cayman. Unusual among Western Hemisphere parrots, this species nests communally, a number of pairs collaborating to construct a large apartment complex of nests. The nests, sometimes constructed on electrical transmission poles, can be a nuisance by causing short circuits.

HISPANIOLAN PARAKEET *Aratinga chloroptera*

KEY FEATURES 30–33 cm (12–13 in.). A large parakeet with a long, pointed tail, white eye-ring, and red edge along the bend of the wing. In flight, red underwing coverts are visible. Voice is a screech.

STATUS AND RANGE Endemic to Hispaniola, where it is locally common in forests and woodlands at all elevations but is rapidly declining. In the Dominican Republic it occurs primarily in the Sierra de Baoruco and Sierra de Neiba. In Haiti the species is common in the Massif de la Selle and the La Citadelle area in the Massif du Nord. It is uncommon elsewhere in Haiti. This parakeet has been introduced into Guadeloupe, where it is very local. The bird is considered threatened due to habitat loss and overhunting. It nests in tree cavities and arboreal termite nests.

OLIVE-THROATED PARAKEET *Aratinga nana*

KEY FEATURES 30.5 cm (12 in.). A fairly large parakeet with a long, pointed tail. The underparts are dark brownish-olive and the bill and eye-ring are yellowish white. The Hispaniolan Parakeet, which overlaps in range, has red on the bend of the wing. Voice is a screech.

STATUS AND RANGE A common and widespread resident of Jamaica, where the species occupies scrub, woodlands, forests, croplands, and gardens from the coast to the lower mountains. It has been introduced into the Dominican Republic, where numbers are increasing.

GREEN-RUMPED PARROTLET *Forpus passerinus*

KEY FEATURES 13 cm (5 in.). A tiny parrot with a short tail and yellowish-white bill. In the male, the rump and wings are greenish blue. The female lacks blue in the wing and has a yellower breast. Voice is a shrill, squeaky chattering.

STATUS AND RANGE Introduced into Jamaica, where it is common and widespread primarily in open country, particularly drier lowlands and hills. The species was also introduced into Barbados. This parrotlet occurs in fast-flying, chattering flocks, which are sometimes a pest to grain crops such as corn. It is native to northern South America.

MONK PARAKEET

adult

HISPANIOLAN PARAKEET

adult

OLIVE-THROATED PARAKEET

adult

GREEN-RUMPED PARROTLET

adult

YELLOW-BILLED PARROT   *Amazona collaria*

KEY FEATURES 28–31 cm (11–12 in.). Note the pale yellow bill, white forehead and eye-ring, bluish forecrown and ear coverts, and maroon throat and base of tail. In flight, note the blue flight feathers and shallow wingbeats. Voice when perched is a high-pitched *tah-tah-eeeeep*; in flight the call is a bugling *tuk-tuk-tuk-taaah*, lower pitched and with the last syllable more drawn out than in the Black-billed Parrot.

STATUS AND RANGE Endemic to Jamaica. It is locally common and more widespread than the Black-billed Parrot, occurring primarily in mid-elevation wet forests of hills and mountains. This parrot is threatened, having declined as a result of habitat destruction and collection for the pet trade. It is a wary bird usually found in pairs or small flocks.

BLACK-BILLED PARROT   *Amazona agilis*

KEY FEATURES 26 cm (10 in.). Note the blackish bill and eye-ring. The tail base is red. The flight feathers are primarily blue, and some birds have a red wing patch visible in flight. Voice when perched is *rrak* and *muh-weep*, in flight *tuh-tuk*; also a sharp screech. Its calls are higher pitched than the Yellow-billed Parrot's.

STATUS AND RANGE Endemic to Jamaica. This parrot is fairly common in mid-level moist forests of hills and mountains, particularly on Mount Diablo and in Cockpit Country. It is scarcer in eastern Jamaica. The bird is threatened primarily as a result of habitat destruction and collecting for the pet trade.

ROSE-THROATED PARROT OR CUBAN PARROT
Amazona leucocephala

KEY FEATURES 28–33 cm (11–13 in.). Note this parrot's pale red chin, throat, and lower face, white forehead and eye-ring, and blue primaries. Its coloration is variable among islands. Voice is a noisy squawk, in flight a harsh *squawk-squawk*. Calls vary among populations.

STATUS AND RANGE The parrot occurs only in the Bahamas, Cuba, and Cayman Islands. In the Bahamas it occurs only on Abaco and Great Inagua, where it is fairly common. The species is locally common in Cuba and is fairly common on Grand Cayman and Cayman Brac. Its habitat includes forests at all elevations and palm savannas. This parrot is threatened for the same reasons described for other parrots in the region. The Abaco population in the Bahamas has the unique behavior of nesting in limestone crevices in the ground.

YELLOW-BILLED PARROT

BLACK-BILLED PARROT

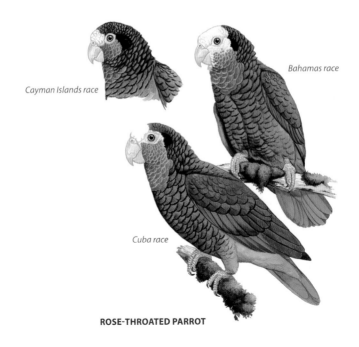

Cayman Islands race

Bahamas race

Cuba race

ROSE-THROATED PARROT

HISPANIOLAN PARROT *Amazona ventralis*

KEY FEATURES 28–31 cm (11–12 in.). This parrot has a distinctive white forehead, dark ear-spot, and maroon belly. In flight, the primaries and secondaries are bright blue. Voice in flight is a loud bugling; calls while perched include loud squawks and screeches.

STATUS AND RANGE Endemic to Hispaniola, where it occurs at all elevations in forests, woodlands, and scrub, but is locally common only in major forest reserves. This parrot has been introduced into Puerto Rico, where it is now very rare in forests and woodlands of foothills. It is threatened due to habitat loss, hunting, and collecting for the pet trade—both domestic and international.

PUERTO RICAN PARROT *Amazona vittata*

KEY FEATURES 30 cm (12 in.). Note the white eye-ring, red forehead, and two-toned blue primaries of this parrot. Voice consists of raucous squawks, including a distinct bugling flight call.

STATUS AND RANGE Endemic to Puerto Rico, where it is very rare and local, primarily in mid-elevation wet forests of eastern Puerto Rico and in Puerto Rico's Rio Abajo Commonwealth Forest and Maricao. The species is critically endangered principally due to habitat loss but also as a result of other causes. At one point the entire wild population consisted of only thirteen birds. Like almost all other parrots in the region, it nests in tree cavities and feeds on an array of wild fruits and seeds. The Rio Abajo and Maricao populations are the result of an ongoing reintroduction effort. Reintroductions are planned for other sites.

RED-NECKED PARROT *Amazona arausiaca*

KEY FEATURES 33–36 cm (13–14 in.). This parrot has a blue crown, face, and chin, a bright red spot on the throat, and a red wing patch. It is the smaller of the two parrots on Dominica. Voice is a two-syllable *rrr-eee,* like a drawn-out hiccup.

STATUS AND RANGE Endemic to Dominica, where it is critically endangered but increasing in numbers. The bird occurs in moist primary rain forests, generally at mid-elevations, and is locally common in the Northern Forest Reserve. It is endangered due to habitat destruction, being hunted for food, being captured for local and international pet trade, and hurricanes.

HISPANIOLAN PARROT

PUERTO RICAN PARROT

RED-NECKED PARROT

ST. LUCIA PARROT *Amazona versicolor*

KEY FEATURES 42–46 cm (16.5–18 in.). Note the violet-blue forehead, cheeks, and forecrown and the red band across the throat extending down the breast. The wings are green, with violet-blue primaries and a red patch. Voice is a raucous squawk.

STATUS AND RANGE Endemic to St. Lucia. This parrot is uncommon and local, primarily in moist mountain forests but also in secondary forests and cultivated areas. Once critically endangered, its entire population down to approximately a hundred birds in the 1970s, the species has recovered significantly to reportedly number over a thousand individuals at present. Threats included habitat destruction, illegal hunting, and capturing of parrots for local and international pet trade.

ST. VINCENT PARROT *Amazona guildingii*

KEY FEATURES 41–46 cm (16–18 in.). A large parrot, dramatically patterned and of variable coloration. Two major color phases—one predominantly green, the other golden brown. The creamy-white forehead shades to orange yellow on the hindcrown, the cheeks are violet blue, and the wings black with yellow-orange patches conspicuous in flight. The tail is orange at the base, with a wide central band of violet and a broad yellow tip. Voice is a loud, unparrotlike *gua, gua, gua* … in flight.

STATUS AND RANGE Endemic to St. Vincent. It is uncommon in mature moist mountain forests in the upper reaches of the Buccament, Cumberland, and Wallilabou valleys. This parrot is critically endangered, primarily as a result of forest clearing, but also due to the cutting of nest trees for charcoal, illegal hunting, and the pet trade.

IMPERIAL PARROT *Amazona imperialis*

KEY FEATURES 46–51 cm (18–20 in.). A large parrot with a dark maroon-purple head. The dark-violet band on its hindneck appears black in low light. The wings are green with a red speculum, and the primaries are a dull violet-blue. The underparts are purple violet from the breast to the abdomen. Voice in flight is a distinctive trumpeting, metallic *eeeee-er* that descends at the end; when perched, shrieks, squawks, whistles, and bubbly trills. It is more shrill and metallic than the Red-necked Parrot's.

STATUS AND RANGE Endemic to Dominica, where it is uncommon and local, primarily in mid- to high-elevation wet forests on Morne Diablotin in the Northern Forest Reserve. Numbers are slowly increasing. The species is critically endangered due to habitat destruction, being hunted for food, and being captured for the local and international pet trade.

ST. LUCIA PARROT

ST. VINCENT PARROT

IMPERIAL PARROT

GREAT LIZARD-CUCKOO *Coccyzus merlini*

KEY FEATURES 44–55 cm (17–22 in.). A large cuckoo with a long, tapered tail, the feathers tipped with white. The long bill is only slightly down-curved. Voice is a long, increasingly loud *ka-ka-ka-ka-ka* …

STATUS AND RANGE Known only from Cuba and the Bahamas. In Cuba it is common and widespread while in the Bahamas it is uncommon and limited to Andros, Eleuthera, and New Providence. While tame in Cuba, it is secretive in the Bahamas. The species occurs in wooded areas at all altitudes, showing a preference for bushy country with vines and dense vegetation. It feeds on lizards, small snakes, frogs, and sometimes mice and fruits.

PUERTO RICAN LIZARD-CUCKOO *Coccyzus vielloti*

KEY FEATURES 40–48 cm (16–1 9 in.). A large bird with a very long tail. The underparts are two toned, and the tail has large white spots. Voice is an emphatic *ka-ka-ka-ka* …, accelerating and becoming louder.

STATUS AND RANGE Endemic to Puerto Rico, where it is fairly common at all elevations in dense forests. This inconspicuous bird is usually detected by its call. It often sits quietly among dense vegetation and frequently tolerates being approached. The species feeds primarily on lizards and large insects.

CHESTNUT-BELLIED CUCKOO *Coccyzus pluvialis*

KEY FEATURES 48–56 cm (19–22 in.). A large bird with a long tail and down-curved bill. Note its primarily reddish underparts, except for the pale gray throat and upper breast. Voice is a throaty, accelerating *quawk-quawk-ak-ak-ak-ak-ak*.

STATUS AND RANGE Endemic to Jamaica, where it is common in open, wet forests at mid-elevations. It also occurs in open woodlands, dense second-growth forests, and gardens. This cuckoo moves slowly through the forest, where it feeds on a wide variety of prey, including insects, lizards, nestlings, eggs, and small mammals. It is more often heard than seen.

HISPANIOLAN LIZARD-CUCKOO *Coccyzus longirostris*

KEY FEATURES 41–46 cm (16–18 in.). A large bird with a pale-gray breast, long tail, and straight, slender bill. It has a reddish-brown wing patch. Voice is a throaty *ka-ka-ka-ka-ka-ka-ka-ka-kau-kau-ko-ko*, descending as it progresses.

STATUS AND RANGE Endemic to Hispaniola, where it is common at all elevations. This cuckoo inhabits forests and wooded areas, including shade coffee plantations. It is often seen moving deliberately through the vegetation, where it pursues lizards and large insects.

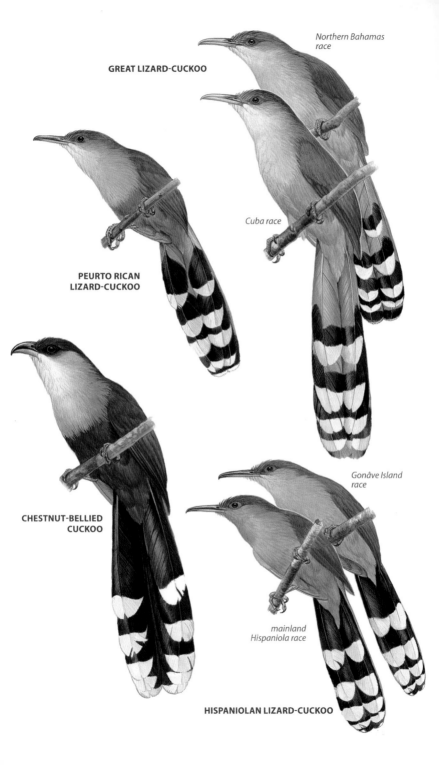

GREAT LIZARD-CUCKOO

Northern Bahamas race

Cuba race

PEURTO RICAN LIZARD-CUCKOO

CHESTNUT-BELLIED CUCKOO

Gonâve Island race

mainland Hispaniola race

HISPANIOLAN LIZARD-CUCKOO

BIRDS | CUCKOOS

JAMAICAN LIZARD-CUCKOO *Coccyzus vetula*

KEY FEATURES 38 cm (15 in.). A fairly large, long-tailed bird with a long, straightish bill. The lower underparts are pale reddish-brown, and it has a reddish-brown wing patch and red eye-ring. Voice is a rapid, low, trailing *cak-cak-cak-ka-ka-ka-k-k*.
STATUS AND RANGE Endemic to Jamaica, where it is common and widespread primarily in moist or wet mid-elevation forests, woodlands, and wooded ravines. This species moves slowly through the understory, peering here and there and feeding on a wide range of animal matter. It is more often heard than seen.

MANGROVE CUCKOO *Coccyzus minor*

KEY FEATURES 28–30 cm (11–12 in.). Note the black ear patch and buff-colored abdomen. The bird is slender, with a long, white-tipped tail and a long, down-curved bill that is yellow at the base. Voice is a nasal *ka-ka-ka-ka-ka-ka-ka-ka-low, kow, kow, kow* (or *kowp, kowp, kowp*) at the end.
STATUS AND RANGE Generally a fairly common resident throughout the Caribbean. In Cuba it occurs primarily in the east, where it is uncommon. The species frequents dry scrub, mangroves, and thickets, where it is inconspicuous and usually located by its call. In Puerto Rico it occurs into the mountains.

SMOOTH-BILLED ANI *Crotophaga ani*

KEY FEATURES 30–33 cm (12–13 in.). A large, entirely black bird with a parrotlike bill and long tail. It typically occurs in small, loose flocks. Voice is a loud, squawky whistle *a-leep*.
STATUS AND RANGE A common resident of the Bahamas, Greater Antilles, Virgin and Cayman Islands, Dominica, St. Vincent, and Grenada. It is uncommon in Martinique and Guadeloupe and rare or absent in the other Lesser Antilles. It frequents open lowlands with scattered scrub. Anis are unique birds in that various females lay several layers of eggs in a communal nest. Only the topmost layer is likely to hatch. These birds sometimes land on cattle and pick off parasites.

OWLS AND OTHER NOCTURNAL BIRDS

ANTILLEAN NIGHTHAWK *Chordeiles gundlachii*

KEY FEATURES 20–25 cm (8–10 in.). A dark, hawklike bird with slender, pointed wings and conspicuous white wing patches. Its flight is darting and erratic. Voice is a loud, raspy *que-re-be-bé*.
STATUS AND RANGE A common breeding resident of the Bahamas, Cuba, Cayman Islands, Jamaica, Hispaniola, and Puerto Rico, primarily from May through August. It is a locally common breeding bird in the Virgin Islands and Guadeloupe during these same months and is generally a rare migrant through the Lesser Antilles. The species is most active at dawn and dusk, when it often swoops over open fields, pastures, pine barrens, savannas, and coastal forest edges, scooping insects from the air with its large, bristled mouth.

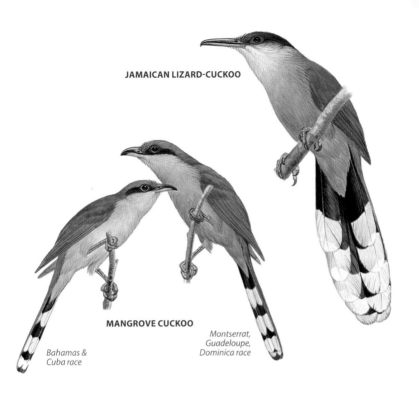

JAMAICAN LIZARD-CUCKOO

MANGROVE CUCKOO

*Montserrat,
Guadeloupe,
Dominica race*

*Bahamas &
Cuba race*

SMOOTH-BILLED ANI

ANTILLEAN NIGHTHAWK

CUBAN PYGMY-OWL *Glaucidium siju*

KEY FEATURES 17.5 cm (7 in.). A small owl with a big head and yellow eyes that is more active during the day than most other owls. It has short, feathered yellow feet; a short tail often twitched sideways; and two dark spots on the back of its head. Voice is a low, sporadically repeated *uh, uh, uh* …, syllables short and plaintive; also *hui-hui-chiii-chiii-chi-chi-chi* …, increasing in strength. It does not hoot.

STATUS AND RANGE Endemic to Cuba, where it is fairly common in woods and tree plantations. The species is active day and night. It often turns its head almost completely around, showing the spots that mimic eyes on the back of the head. Lizards and insects are its primary prey.

BURROWING OWL *Athene cunicularia*

KEY FEATURES 23 cm (9 in.). A small terrestrial owl with long legs that is active during the day when breeding. It often perches on fence posts and bobs when approached. Adult underparts are barred. Voice is a soft, high-pitched, two-note *coo-coooo;* also a clucking chatter when alarmed.

STATUS AND RANGE In the Bahamas it is generally a fairly common resident. In Cuba the species is locally common primarily in the west. In Hispaniola this owl is a common resident of Haiti and the western Dominican Republic. The Burrowing Owl occupies open scrub, sandy pine savannas, pastures, and golf courses. It nests in a deep burrow that it excavates in sandy soil.

SWIFTS

BLACK SWIFT *Cypseloides niger*

KEY FEATURES 15–18 cm (5.75–7 in.). A fairly large, black swift with a slightly forked tail. As with all swifts, it is highly aerial and occurs in flocks. Most similar swifts are smaller and have shorter tails, more darting flight, and quicker wing beats.

STATUS AND RANGE Widespread in the Caribbean, where it is a locally common resident of Jamaica and Hispaniola and a common breeding resident April through September in Puerto Rico, Guadeloupe, Dominica, and Martinique. It is uncommon to rare elsewhere. This swift primarily frequents mountains.

WHITE-COLLARED SWIFT *Streptoprocne zonaris*

KEY FEATURES 20–22 cm (8–8.5 in.). A large black swift with a distinctive white collar. All swifts have a distinctive manner of flying with rapid, shallow wing beats. All are extremely aerial and occur in flocks. Voice is a high-pitched *screee-screee* or rapid *chip-chip-chip-chip*.

STATUS AND RANGE A common resident of Jamaica and Hispaniola, though declining in Haiti. It is a fairly common but local resident of Cuba, primarily occurring in the eastern mountains and Sierra del Escambray. This swift occurs primarily over foothills, mountain valleys, and forests, including open areas. Like other swifts, this species is insectivorous.

CUBAN PYGMY-OWL

rear view

front view

adult

BURROWING OWL
Hispaniola race

BLACK SWIFT

WHITE-COLLARED SWIFT

LESSER ANTILLEAN SWIFT *Chaetura martinica*

KEY FEATURES 11 cm (4.25 in.). A small swift with dull brownish-gray upper parts, gray rump, dark gray underparts, and short gray tail. It is highly aerial and occurs in flocks.

STATUS AND RANGE A fairly common resident of Dominica, Martinique, St. Lucia, and St. Vincent. It is uncommon in Guadeloupe. These islands compose the entire range of the species. This swift occurs primarily over mountain forests but also over lowland forests and open areas. Like other swifts, it forages on flying insects. The nest is a half-cup of twigs glued with saliva to a vertical surface of a hollow tree or cave.

ANTILLEAN PALM-SWIFT *Tachornis phoenicobia*

KEY FEATURES 10–11 cm (4–4.25 in.). A small swift with a white rump and black breast band. It is highly aerial and occurs in flocks. Voice is a constantly emitted, high-pitched twitter typical of swifts. Also like other swifts, it has rapid, erratic, batlike flight, gliding between bursts of shallow flapping. Most swifts are not known to alight during the day. Even copulation occurs in flight.

STATUS AND RANGE A common resident of Cuba, Jamaica, and Hispaniola. These islands comprise the entire range of the species. This swift occurs over open cultivated areas, sugarcane plantations, edges of palm savannas, and urban zones. Like other swifts, it uses saliva in nest construction.

SWALLOWS

PURPLE MARTIN *Progne subis*

KEY FEATURES 20–22 cm (8–8.5 in.). Adult male is entirely bluish purple and is indistinguishable from the Cuban Martin. Adult female and immature: Note the scaled pattern on the grayish-brown breast, light gray patches on sides of the neck, and an indistinct border between the darker breast and whitish belly. The female Caribbean Martin has a brown wash on the breast, rather than a scaled pattern. Voice is gurgling, including a high *twick-twick*; also a high, melodious warble.

STATUS AND RANGE A common migrant in Cuba and on Grand Cayman in the Cayman Islands, it is uncommon in the Bahamas. This martin occurs primarily from mid-August through mid-October and frequents towns and open areas. The short, broad bill and long, pointed wings of the martins and swallows adapt these species for capturing flying insects on the wing.

LESSER ANTILLEAN SWIFT

ANTILLEAN PALM-SWIFT

♀ & imm.

PURPLE MARTIN

adult ♂

CUBAN MARTIN *Progne cryptoleuca*

KEY FEATURES 20–22 cm (8–8.5 in.). Male is bluish purple overall and indistinguishable from the male Purple Martin. Female's white belly and abdomen contrast sharply with the brown breast. In the female Purple Martin the brown breast blends gradually into the whitish belly. Both sexes of the Caribbean Martin are similar to the female Cuban Martin as to the pattern of their underparts, but the white is more restricted. Also, the female Caribbean Martin has less contrast between white and dark of its underparts. Voice is gurgling, including a high-pitched *twick-twick*, like a vibrating wire; also a strong, melodious warble.
STATUS AND RANGE A common breeding resident from February through October in Cuba, where it frequents cities and towns. It also occurs over swamp borders and open areas, particularly in lowlands. It is believed to migrate to South America outside the breeding season.

CARIBBEAN MARTIN *Progne dominicensis*

KEY FEATURES 20 cm (8 in.). Adult male is primarily blue with a white belly and abdomen. In female and immature the breast is brownish, blending into the white of the belly. Voice is gurgling, including a high *twick-twick*; also a melodious warble and gritty *churr*.
STATUS AND RANGE A fairly common breeding resident of much of the Caribbean from January to September, though extremely rare or absent in the Bahamas, Cayman Islands, and Cuba. The species occurs primarily over towns, open areas, freshwater bodies, and coastal rock promontories, where it is seen hawking for insects or perched on utility wires.

CAVE SWALLOW *Pterochelidon fulva*

KEY FEATURES 12.5–14 cm (5–5.5 in.). Note the dark reddish-brown rump and forehead, the pale reddish-brown ear patch, throat, breast, and sides, and the slightly notched tail. Voice is a chattering or twittering; also a rather musical *twit*.
STATUS AND RANGE A common breeding resident through the Greater Antilles where present year-round except Cuba where most birds depart September through February. It is a rare breeding resident on South Andros (Bahamas) and a rare migrant in the Cayman and Virgin Islands. Typical habitat is over fields, wetlands, cliffs, and towns. It usually occurs in large flocks, which often perch on utility wires. Its mud nests are often attached to buildings.

BARN SWALLOW *Hirundo rustica*

KEY FEATURES 15–19 cm (5.75–7.5 in.). Tail is deeply forked tail. The underparts are primarily tan and the throat dark reddish-brown. Voice is a thin, unmusical *chit*.
STATUS AND RANGE Generally a common migrant throughout the Caribbean primarily September through October and April through May, but occurs during every month. It frequents open areas over fields and swamps, primarily along the coast. Generally in flocks, swooping for insects or perched on wires.

CUBAN MARTIN

adult ♂

CARIBBEAN MARTIN

adult ♂

CAVE SWALLOW

BARN SWALLOW

adult

imm.

JAMAICAN MANGO *Anthracothorax mango*

KEY FEATURES 13 cm (5 in.). A large hummer distinguished by its black underparts and reddish-purple cheeks. Female is duller. Voice: Sharp, raspy *tics*.
STATUS AND RANGE Endemic to Jamaica, where it is widespread and common particularly in lowland forest edges, banana plantations, and gardens. It feeds on spiders and nectar. The only Jamaican hummer to frequent cactus flowers.

ANTILLEAN MANGO *Anthracothorax dominicus*

KEY FEATURES 11–12.5 cm (4.25–5 in.). A large hummer with a down-curved black bill. Adult male is primarily black below with a green throat. Female is whitish below and on the tail tips. Immature male has a black stripe down the center of its whitish underparts. Voice: An unmusical, thin trill, quite loud; also sharp, chipping notes.
STATUS AND RANGE The range is confined to only a few islands, the hummer being most abundant on Hispaniola, where it is common at all elevations. In Puerto Rico it is common along the southern coast and in the northern haystack hills. In the Virgin Islands this bird is increasingly rare. Throughout its range it inhabits clearings, scrub, gardens, and shade coffee plantations.

GREEN MANGO *Anthracothorax viridis*

KEY FEATURES 11.5 cm (4.5 in.). A large hummer with entirely emerald-green underparts, a black, down-curved bill, and a rounded tail. Voice: A trill-like twitter; loud, harsh rattling or chattering notes; a hard *tic*.
STATUS AND RANGE Endemic to Puerto Rico, where common in the mountains. It inhabits forests and coffee plantations, where it frequents flowers. Its delicate nest is bound together with spider webs and camouflaged with lichens.

GREEN-THROATED CARIB *Eulampis holosericeus*

KEY FEATURES 10.5–12 cm (4–4.75 in.). A large hummer with a green breast and slightly down-curved bill. The blue breast mark is visible only in good light. Voice: A sharp *chewp* and loud wing rattle.
STATUS AND RANGE A common resident throughout the Lesser Antilles, Virgin Islands, and northeastern Puerto Rico. It inhabits gardens and rain forests at all elevations in the Lesser Antilles, while in Puerto Rico it is primarily in the lowlands. Like most hummingbirds, its iridescent coloration appears black in poor light.

PURPLE-THROATED CARIB *Eulampis jugularis*

KEY FEATURES 11.5 cm (4.5 in.). A large hummer with a purplish-red throat and breast, emerald-green wings, and a down-curved bill. Female has a longer, more sharply down-curved bill than the male. Voice: A sharp *chewp*, repeated rapidly when agitated.
STATUS AND RANGE This species occurs only in the Lesser Antilles, where it is a fairly common resident on most islands. Its primary habitat is mountain forests and banana plantations.

JAMAICAN MANGO
adult ♂

adult ♂

adult ♀

imm. ♂

ANTILLEAN MANGO

GREEN MANGO

PURPLE-THROATED CARIB

GREEN-THROATED CARIB

RUFOUS-BREASTED HERMIT *Glaucis hirsutus*

KEY FEATURES 12.5 cm (5 in.). Large. with a long down-curved bill. Male upper parts are dull green. Voice: A high *sweep*, sometimes repeated.
STATUS AND RANGE A fairly common resident of Grenada in higher mountains. The species inhabits forests, forest edges, and plantations. It favors flowering Heliconia.

BAHAMA WOODSTAR *Calliphlox evelynae*

KEY FEATURES 9–9.5 cm (3.5–3.75 in.). Adult male: Note the deeply forked tail with reddish-brown inner feathers. Adult female: The throat is white and the tail rounded. Voice: A sharp *tit, titit, tit, tit, titit*, often speeding to a rapid rattle.
STATUS AND RANGE Endemic and common throughout the Bahamas. It occurs in gardens, scrub, woodlands, forest edges, clearings, and mixed pine forests. The tiny cup-shaped nest is bound with spider webs and camouflaged with bark and lichens.

CUBAN EMERALD *Chlorostilbon ricordii*

KEY FEATURES 9–10.5 cm (3.5–4 in.). A small hummer with a long, forked tail and long, thin bill, which is pinkish below. Voice: A short, squeaking twitter.
STATUS AND RANGE A common, widespread resident of Cuba and the Bahamas (Grand Bahama, Abaco, and Andros), which make up its entire range. This hummer occupies all habitats from the coast to mid-elevations. It feeds on nectar and small invertebrates, especially spiders and insects caught in their webs. Also like other hummers, it is very pugnacious and territorial.

HISPANIOLAN EMERALD *Chlorostilbon swainsonii*

KEY FEATURES 10.5 cm (4 in.). A small hummer with a straight bill. Male: Green overall, with a dull black breast spot, deeply forked tail, and pinkish lower mandible. Female: Dull grayish below, with metallic green sides and whitish outer tail tips. Voice: A sharp, metallic *tic*.
STATUS AND RANGE This hummer is endemic to Hispaniola where it is generally common in the mountains, but rare at low elevations. It is considered threatened in Haiti due to habitat destruction. It occurs in moist forests, shade coffee plantations, and clearings.

PUERTO RICAN EMERALD *Chlorostilbon maugaeus*

KEY FEATURES 9–10 cm (3.5–4 in.). A small hummer with a forked tail. Male: Green overall, with a black tail and pinkish lower bill. Female: Underparts are white, and the bill entirely black; outer tail feathers are tipped with white and may be forked, notched or even-edged. Voice: A series of *tics* and a trill with a buzz at the end.
STATUS AND RANGE Endemic to Puerto Rico, where common in the mountains and irregular on the coast, primarily the drier south coast. The species frequents flowering plants in forests, shade coffee, wooded areas, and forest edges.

RUFOUS-BREASTED HERMIT

♂ ♀

adult ♂ *adult* ♀

BAHAMA WOODSTAR

♂ ♀

CUBAN EMERALD

♂ ♀

HISPANIOLAN EMERALD

♂ ♀

PUERTO RICAN EMERALD

ANTILLEAN CRESTED HUMMINGBIRD *Orthorhyncus cristatus*

KEY FEATURES 8.5–9.5 cm (3.25–3.75 in.). The only crested hummer in the Caribbean. Voice: Emphatic notes.

STATUS AND RANGE A common resident throughout the Lesser Antilles, Virgin Islands, and Puerto Rico's northeastern coast. Primarily inhabits lowland openings, gardens, forest edges, and arid areas. It sometimes occurs in mountain forests.

BLUE-HEADED HUMMINGBIRD *Cyanophaia bicolor*

KEY FEATURES 9.5 cm (3.75 in.). Male: Note the violet-blue head, throat, upper breast, and tail. Female: Shiny green above and grayish white below, with flecks of green on the sides and a blackish ear patch. Voice: Shrill, metallic notes, rapidly descending.

STATUS AND RANGE Common resident of Dominica and Martinique, which make up its entire range. This hummer usually occurs at mid-elevations in moist open areas in mountain forests, along mountain streams, and in wooded edges of fields.

STREAMERTAIL *Trochilus polytmus*

KEY FEATURES Male (with tail plumes) 22–25 cm (8.5–10 in.); female 10.5 cm (4 in.). Male: Note the two long tail feathers. Female: The tail is short and the underparts white. Voice: A loud, metallic *ting* or *teet* and prolonged *twink-twink-twink* …, dropping in pitch. In flight, the male's streamers hum.

STATUS AND RANGE Endemic to Jamaica, where it is widespread and may be the most abundant bird. This hummer occurs primarily in middle- and high-elevation forests and gardens. It is seasonal along the coast. This is Jamaica's national bird.

VERVAIN HUMMINGBIRD *Mellisuga minima*

KEY FEATURES 6 cm (2.5 in.). A tiny hummer with a straight black bill. It is the second smallest bird in the world. The chin and throat are sometimes flecked, while the sides and flanks are dull green. Voice: Loud, rhythmic, high-pitched metallic squeaks; also a throaty buzz.

STATUS AND RANGE Common and widespread in Jamaica and Hispaniola, islands that make up its entire range. This hummer occurs in open areas, including open woodlands and shade coffee plantations. Its egg weighs 0.37 g (0.01 oz.).

BEE HUMMINGBIRD *Mellisuga helenae*

KEY FEATURES 5.5 cm (2.25 in.). This is the world's smallest bird. Its tail is very short and tipped with white. The male's iridescent red throat plumes appear differently colored, depending on the light. Voice: A twitter, long and quite high; also low warbling notes.

STATUS AND RANGE Endemic to Cuba, where rare and local. It occurs primarily in coastal forests and forest edges but also in swamplands, gardens, and interior mountain valleys and forests. The species is threatened apparently as a result of habitat alteration and destruction. Males often perch high on bare twigs.

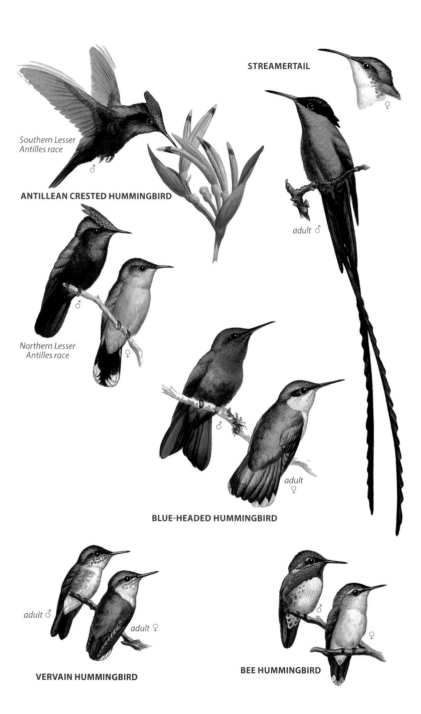

STREAMERTAIL

Southern Lesser Antilles race
♂

ANTILLEAN CRESTED HUMMINGBIRD

adult ♂

Northern Lesser Antilles race
♂
♀

♂
adult ♀

BLUE-HEADED HUMMINGBIRD

adult ♂
adult ♀

VERVAIN HUMMINGBIRD

♂
♀

BEE HUMMINGBIRD

CUBAN TROGON *Priotelus temnurus*

KEY FEATURES 25–28 cm (10–11 in.). Note the red belly, green back, blue crown, and long, peculiar tail with much white on its underside. Voice is very varied, but most commonly a repeated *toco-toco-tocoro-tocoro* … ; also a low, short, mournful call that is difficult to locate.

STATUS AND RANGE Endemic to Cuba, where it is widely distributed and common. It occurs in both wet and dry forests at all altitudes, primarily frequenting shady areas. This is Cuba's national bird. It feeds mainly on flowers but also buds and fruits. The flight is short and noisy, the bird sometimes hovering to feed. It is entirely arboreal and usually found in pairs.

HISPANIOLAN TROGON *Priotelus roseigaster*

KEY FEATURES 27–30 cm (10.5–12 in.). Note the glossy-green upper parts, red belly, yellow bill, and gray throat and breast. The bird has a long, dark-blue tail heavily marked with white below. Voice is a *toca-loro … coc, ca-rao* or *cockcraow*, repeated several times; also a cooing and puppy-like whimpering.

STATUS AND RANGE Endemic to Hispaniola, where it is locally common in undisturbed habitat. During the nonbreeding season, it descends to lower elevations. It occurs in mountain forests, including mature pine and broadleaf forests, and sometimes ranges to coastal mangroves. The species depends on large trees for nesting cavities. Insects, fruits, and lizards make up its diet. In Haiti it is declining and considered threatened due to habitat destruction.

BELTED KINGFISHER *Megaceryle alcyon*

KEY FEATURES 28–36 cm (11–14 in.). A distinctive bird with a large bill and crest and always associated with water. It characteristically hovers and dives for fish. The Ringed Kingfisher is larger and heavier billed and has more extensive reddish-brown underparts and reddish underwing coverts. Voice is a loud, harsh rattle.

STATUS AND RANGE Generally a fairly common nonbreeding resident throughout the Caribbean from September through April, though it is recorded from every month. The species frequents conspicuous perches around calm bodies of water, both saline and fresh.

RINGED KINGFISHER *Megaceryle torquata*

KEY FEATURES 38–41 cm (15–16 in.). A large bird with a noticeable crest and large bill. Its underparts are primarily reddish brown. In flight, the Ringed Kingfisher displays distinctive reddish underwing coverts. It characteristically hovers and dives for fish. The Belted Kingfisher is smaller, with a white lower belly and underwing-coverts. Voice is a very distinctive loud, harsh rattle.

STATUS AND RANGE A fairly common resident of Dominica and Martinique, it is uncommon and local in Guadeloupe. The species occurs along the edges of large streams, lakes, and reservoirs. Breeding is sometimes colonial, the nest consisting of a burrow excavated in a clay bank. The nest tunnel may be 2 m (7 ft.) long.

CUBAN TROGON

HISPANIOLAN TROGON

♀ hovering

BELTED KINGFISHER

RINGED KINGFISHER

PUERTO RICAN TODY *Todus mexicanus*

KEY FEATURES 11 cm (4.25 in.). See Cuban Tody. The abdomen is yellow. Voice is a loud, nasal *beep* or *bee-beep*. The tody sometimes rattles its wings in flight.
STATUS AND RANGE Endemic to Puerto Rico, where it is common and widespread from the coast to the mountains. It occurs in forested habitats and dense thickets. Typically todies perch on a twig low to the ground, from which they sally to snatch insects from the air or from the bottom of a leaf.

CUBAN TODY *Todus multicolor*

KEY FEATURES 11 cm (4.25 in.). A tiny, chunky bird, bright green above with a red throat and long, broad, reddish bill. The flanks are pink and sides of the throat blue. Voice is typically a soft *pprreeee-pprreeee*, sometimes a peculiar short *tot-tot-tot-tot*. It also has a characteristic wing rattle.
STATUS AND RANGE Endemic to Cuba, where common and widespread. This tody occurs at all elevations in wooded and semiwooded areas, forests, stream edges, and areas with earthen embankments. Todies feed voraciously on insects.

BROAD-BILLED TODY *Todus subulatus*

KEY FEATURES 11–12 cm (4.25–4.75 in.). See Cuban Tody. The underparts are tinted yellow with pink sides. The lower mandible is entirely reddish. The Narrow-billed Tody is whiter below and usually has a black-tipped bill. Both species are best distinguished by voice. Voice is a monotonous, often-repeated whistle, *terp*, *terp*, *terp*, in a complaining tone. A single-note call of the same tone contrasts with the Narrow-billed Tody's two-note call.
STATUS AND RANGE Endemic to Hispaniola, where it is common in semiarid areas from the lowlands to 1,700 m (5,600 ft.) in forests, scrub, shade coffee plantations, and some mangroves. It regularly frequents vegetated ravines.

NARROW-BILLED TODY *Todus angustirostris*

KEY FEATURES 11 cm (4.25 in.). See Broad-billed Tody. It is best distinguished by voice—a frequently repeated, two-part *chip-chee*, accented on the second syllable; also a chattering, trilly *chippy-chippy-chippy-chip*, dropping in pitch but not in tone.
STATUS AND RANGE Endemic to Hispaniola, where it is common at higher elevations. It occurs in dense, wet forests and regularly frequents vegetated ravines with earthen embankments. The species is threatened in Haiti due to habitat destruction.

JAMAICAN TODY *Todus todus*

KEY FEATURES 9 cm (3.5 in.). See Cuban Tody. The flanks are pink and the abdomen yellow. Calls include a loud *beep* and a rapid guttural rattling.
STATUS AND RANGE Endemic to Jamaica, where widespread and common from the coast to the mountains in all forest types. Like other todies, excavates a burrow in an earthen bank or rotten tree trunk, generally laying three to four eggs.

PUERTO RICAN TODY

adult

imm.

CUBAN TODY

BROAD-BILLED TODY

NARROW-BILLED TODY

JAMAICAN TODY

GUADELOUPE WOODPECKER *Melanerpes herminieri*

KEY FEATURES 25–29 cm (10–11.5 in.). Black overall, with a reddish wash on the throat and belly, most noticeable in the breeding season. Male's bill is about 20 percent longer than the female's. Flight is direct, unlike most other woodpeckers. Voice is a *wa-uh*, or *wa-ah*, and staccato *cht-cht-cht-cht-cht-cht-cht-cht*.
STATUS AND RANGE Endemic to Guadeloupe, where it is common and widespread. The species occurs from sea level to the tree line at 1,000 m (3,300 ft.) in every forest type, including semideciduous and evergreen forests, coconut palms, and mangroves. This is a shy and retiring species. In addition to feeding on insect larvae pecked from dead trees, it also feeds on fruits and sometimes treefrogs. Clear-cutting and tree removal, along with introduced rats, are the primary threats to the species. This woodpecker is Guadeloupe's only endemic bird.

PUERTO RICAN WOODPECKER *Melanerpes portoricensis*

KEY FEATURES 23–27 cm (9–10.5 in.). Note the red throat and breast, white rump and forehead, and blackish upper parts. In the adult male, the underparts are primarily red with buffy sides; adult female and immature, less red on the underparts. Flight is undulating. Voice consists of a wide variety of calls, most commonly *wek*, *wek*, *wek-wek-wekwek-wek* … becoming louder and faster.
STATUS AND RANGE Endemic to Puerto Rico, where it is common and widespread. The species occurs from coastal plantations to mountain forests, but it primarily frequents hills and lower mountains, including shade coffee. It regularly forms small groupings of two to five birds. Like other woodpeckers, it excavates a nest cavity high in a tree.

WEST INDIAN WOODPECKER *Melanerpes superciliaris*

KEY FEATURES 26 cm (10 in.). The upper parts and wings are barred black and white, the underparts buff cinnamon to brownish gray, and the abdomen is red. In the adult male, the crown to hindneck is red. The top of the head in the adult female is black or tan, and only the back of the crown and hindneck is red. Voice is a distinctive loud, high-pitched *krruuu-krruu-kruu* …, frequently repeated.
STATUS AND RANGE The species is known only from the Bahamas, Cuba, and Cayman Islands. In Cuba it is common and widespread, while in the Bahamas it is common on Abaco, uncommon on San Salvador, and nearly extirpated from Grand Bahama. This woodpecker, in the Cayman Islands, is fairly common on Grand Cayman and absent from the other islands. It occurs primarily in dry forest, scrub, coastal forests, and palm groves. On Abaco it also frequents settlements.

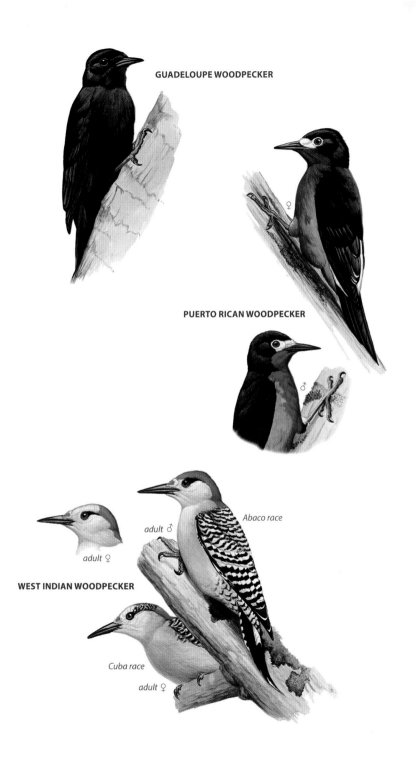

GUADELOUPE WOODPECKER

♀

PUERTO RICAN WOODPECKER

♂

adult ♀

adult ♂　　*Abaco race*

WEST INDIAN WOODPECKER

Cuba race

adult ♀

JAMAICAN WOODPECKER *Melanerpes radiolatus*

KEY FEATURES 24 cm (9.5 in.). Note the red hindcrown and hindneck, whitish face, black upper parts, and the wings finely streaked with white. Male's crown is entirely red; female's, brownish olive. Voice is a loud, rollicking *chee-ee-urp* cry, similar to the Olive-throated Parakeet. The call is variable, sometimes a single note or a rapid series of three or more *churp-chur-churp* notes.

STATUS AND RANGE Endemic to Jamaica, where it is common and widespread. This is the only woodpecker in Jamaica, except for the uncommon Yellow-bellied Sapsucker. The species occurs from coastal coconut groves to forested mountain summits, including dry and wet forests, forest edges, woodlands, shade coffee plantations, and gardens. Like most other woodpeckers, it chips away rotten wood in search of insects and larvae.

HISPANIOLAN WOODPECKER *Melanerpes striatus*

KEY FEATURES 22–25 cm (8.5–10 in.). A medium-size woodpecker with white and black patches on the hindneck, a red hindcrown and uppertail coverts, and a whitish to yellow eye. Male is larger and longer billed. Voice is strong and variable, including a loud, rolling call interrupted with throaty noises. The call notes include a *wup* and *ta-a* and a short *bdddt* with three to five distinct notes.

STATUS AND RANGE Endemic to Hispaniola, where it is common and widespread. It occurs from the coast to humid mountain forests but primarily in hilly, partly cultivated, and partly wooded areas, and in palms scattered among cultivated fields. This may be the most widespread of Hispaniola's endemic birds. Unusual traits of this woodpecker include its tendency to form noisy social groups and to nest colonially with up to a dozen pairs in a single tree.

CUBAN GREEN WOODPECKER *Xiphidiopicus percussus*

KEY FEATURES 21–25 cm (8–10 in.). A medium-size woodpecker with a noticeable crest. Also note the green upper parts, yellowish underparts streaked and barred with black, the white face with a black stripe behind the eye, and a red patch on the breast. Male has a red crown, female a black crown. Voice is a short, low, and harsh *jorr-jorr-jorr*; also a higher-pitched, shorter *eh-eh-eh*.

STATUS AND RANGE Endemic to Cuba, where it is common and widespread. It occurs in many forest types, including wet and dry, open and dense, mountains and lowlands, including mangroves. The nest cavity is drilled either in a live or dead tree or termitarium. The species feeds on insects and larvae under bark and in tree crevices. Like other woodpeckers, this species has a long tongue for extracting prey from crevices.

JAMAICAN WOODPECKER

HISPANIOLAN WOODPECKER

CUBAN GREEN WOODPECKER

LESSER ANTILLEAN FLYCATCHER *Myiarchus oberi*

KEY FEATURES 19–22 cm (7.5–8.5 in.). This medium-size flycatcher has mostly yellow underparts from the upper belly to the undertail coverts. The tail feathers possess reddish inner webs. Voice is a loud, plaintive whistle, *peeu-wheeet*; also short whistles, *oo-ee*, *ooee* or *e-oo-ee*.

STATUS AND RANGE A common resident on Barbuda, St. Kitts, Nevis, Dominica, Martinique, and St. Lucia, it is rare on Guadeloupe. These islands comprise the entire range of the species. It occurs primarily along edges of dense woodlands, forests, and tree plantations at or above 100 m (330 ft.), though it sometimes frequents second growth or scrub at lower altitudes.

GRAY KINGBIRD *Tyrannus dominicensis*

KEY FEATURES 22–25 cm (8.5–10 in.). Gray above and pale gray-white below, with a distinct dark mask extending under the eye. The tail is slightly notched, and the yellow-orange crown patch is rarely visible. Voice is an emphatic *pi-tirr-ri*.

STATUS AND RANGE A conspicuous and common bird throughout the Caribbean, where it is resident from Hispaniola east through the Lesser Antilles. Most breeding birds from the Bahamas, Cuba, Jamaica, and Cayman Islands migrate off-island from November through March. Some leave the Lesser Antilles as well. Kingbirds frequent exposed perches in open areas with scattered trees both in the lowlands and mountains. They sally from these to capture insects in flight and then return to the same or a nearby perch to swallow their prey.

LOGGERHEAD KINGBIRD *Tyrannus caudifasciatus*

KEY FEATURES 24–26 cm (9.5–10 in.). A distinctively two-toned flycatcher— dark above and white below. The crown is blackish, with a rarely seen yellow or orangish patch. The bill is large, and the square tail has a white trailing edge, except in Hispaniola and Puerto Rico. Voice is variable; it is usually a loud, mallet-like chattering, with *bzze-beep* or *bee-beep* elements. The song is bubbling, with a repeated *p-p-q*.

STATUS AND RANGE A common and widespread resident through the northern Bahamas, Greater Antilles, and Cayman Islands. These islands comprise the entire range of the species. This kingbird occurs in woodlands, pine, and broadleaf forests, shade coffee plantations, mangrove swamps, and open areas with scattered trees from lowlands to mid-elevations. Like other flycatchers it frequents exposed perches, from which it takes short flights to capture insects.

LESSER ANTILLEAN FLYCATCHER

GRAY KINGBIRD

Puerto Rico race

Cuba race

LOGGERHEAD KINGBIRD

COCOA THRUSH *Turdus fumigatus*

KEY FEATURES 23 cm (9 in.). A fairly large thrush, brown overall, with rich-brown underparts. The throat is whitish with brown streaks, and the bill is dark. Voice is a series of loud, musical phrases, each short and differing from one another, with a brief pause between each. Sometimes a plaintive, four-note call, the first two notes higher, the last two lower. Also a *weeo, weeo, weeo.*

STATUS AND RANGE A fairly common resident of St. Vincent and Grenada, where it occurs in forests, cacao plantations, and croplands with scattered trees. The species is more frequent at higher elevations. This thrush primarily forages on the ground for invertebrates, especially ants, and berries.

SPECTACLED THRUSH *Turdus nudigenis*

KEY FEATURES 23 cm (9 in.). A fairly large thrush of plain olive-gray coloration, with a broad, pale yellow eye-ring and a white throat with brown streaks. Voice is a loud, liquid, variable *cheerily cheer-up cheerio,* especially at dawn; also a squeaky *miter-ee.*

STATUS AND RANGE A fairly common resident of Martinique, St. Lucia, St. Vincent, the Grenadines, and Grenada. It is uncommon on Guadeloupe. The species is expanding its range northward through the Lesser Antilles, where it occurs primarily in lowlands in dry and moderately moist open woodlands, plantations, second growth, and forest borders. Typically arboreal, it also forages on the ground, often along road edges. It is very aggressive towards other thrushes.

WHITE-EYED THRUSH *Turdus jamaicensis*

KEY FEATURES 23 cm (9 in.). Adult is distinguished by its reddish-brown head, conspicuous whitish eye, and white breast bar. Voice consists of repeated phrases like the Northern Mockingbird, but louder and less variable. A whistled *hee-haw* is often included in the song. The bird also issues other high-pitched, harsh call notes.

STATUS AND RANGE Endemic to Jamaica, where fairly common in wet forests from the hills to mountain summits. It also frequents shade coffee plantations and other wooded areas at moderate elevations. This thrush is secretive, often foraging among dense vegetation for fruits and invertebrates from the forest floor to treetops.

WHITE-CHINNED THRUSH *Turdus aurantius*

KEY FEATURES 24 cm (9.5 in.). A fairly large, highly terrestrial thrush. It displays a conspicuous white diagonal bar on the wing, a white chin, and an orange bill and legs, and it cocks its tail upward. Voice is variable, including a musical song, a shrill whistle—*p'lice, p'lice*—and repeated chickenlike clucking.

STATUS AND RANGE Endemic to Jamaica, where it is common and widespread. This thrush primarily inhabits forests, woodlands, road edges, cultivated areas, and gardens, in mountains at middle and high elevations. It is less frequent in lowlands. Foraging occurs principally on the ground for a wide variety of prey, including slugs, lizards, insects, berries and even frogs, mice, and small birds.

COCOA THRUSH

SPECTACLED THRUSH

WHITE-EYED THRUSH

WHITE-CHINNED THRUSH

RED-LEGGED THRUSH *Turdus plumbeus*

KEY FEATURES 25–28 cm (10–11 in.). Large, primarily gray with reddish legs, bill, and eye-ring. Its tail is white-tipped. The underparts vary greatly in color. Voice is a low *wéecha*, a rapid, high-pitched *chu-wéek, chu-wéek, chu-wéek*, and a loud *wheet-wheet*. The song is melodious but monotonous; similar to Pearly-eyed Thrasher.
STATUS AND RANGE A common and widespread resident of the northern Bahamas, Cuba, Hispaniola, Puerto Rico, and Dominica. It is fairly common on Cayman Brac (Cayman Islands). These islands comprise its entire range. It inhabitats woodlands and forests at all elevations, scrub, thick undergrowth, and gardens. It forages primarily on the ground for invertebrates among leaf litter.

PEARLY-EYED THRASHER *Margarops fuscatus*

KEY FEATURES 28–30 cm (11–12 in.). Large, with streaked underparts, a white eye, large yellowish bill, and large white tail patches. The similar Scaly-breasted Thrasher has a black bill and little white on the tail. Voice is a series of one- to three-syllable phrases with lengthy pauses between; also raucous call notes.
STATUS AND RANGE A common resident in most of the Bahamas, northeastern Hispaniola, Puerto Rico, the Virgin Islands, and Lesser Antilles south to St. Lucia. On Martinique it is uncommon. Its range is confined to the Caribbean and Bonaire. It frequents thickets, woodlands, forests at all elevations, and urban areas. This aggressive bird has detrimentally affected other species.

SCALY-BREASTED THRASHER *Allenia fusca*

KEY FEATURES 23 cm (9 in.). Fairly large with heavily scaled underparts, a black bill, yellow-brown eye, one whitish wing bar, and a white-tipped tail. (See the Pearly-eyed Thrasher.) Vocally it repeats phrases similar to the Tropical Mockingbird, but with less vigor.
STATUS AND RANGE Generally a fairly common resident from Saba and St. Bartholomew south to St. Vincent. It is rare and local on Grenada and possibly extirpated on St. Eustatius, Barbuda, and Barbados. These islands comprise its entire range. The species frequents moist and semiarid forests and woodlands, where it is arboreal and feeds primarily on fruits.

BROWN TREMBLER *Cinclocerthia ruficauda*

KEY FEATURES 23–26 cm (9–10 in.). Fairly large, identified by its dark reddish-olive upper parts, buffish-brown underparts, yellow eye, and long curved bill. This bird often droops its wings and trembles. It also cocks its tail over its back. Voice is a series of semimelodic phrases and harsh alarm notes.
STATUS AND RANGE A fairly common resident on Saba, Guadeloupe, and Dominica; uncommon on St. Kitts, Nevis, Montserrat, St. Lucia, and St. Vincent; and rare on Martinique and Grenada. These islands comprise the entire range. It primarily inhabits wet forests but also drier woodlands. On St. Lucia it occurs only in dry forests and scrub. Tremblers toss vegetation aside as they search for prey.

Hispaniola & Puerto Rico race

Cuba race

RED-LEGGED THRUSH

PEARLY-EYED THRASHER

SCALY-BREASTED THRASHER
Dominica race

BROWN TREMBLER

NORTHERN MOCKINGBIRD *Mimus polyglottos*

KEY FEATURES 23–28 cm (9–11 in.). A slender, fairly large gray-and-white bird, the wings and tail are conspicuously marked with white and its long tail is often cocked upward. Voice is clear, melodious phrases, each repeated several times. It sometimes incorporates songs of other birds in its repertoire. The call note is a loud *tchack*.
STATUS AND RANGE A common resident throughout the Bahamas, Greater Antilles, and Virgin and Cayman Islands. The species occupies open country with scattered bushes or trees, including semiarid scrub, open mangrove forests, gardens, parks, and settled areas primarily in the lowlands. It is not shy.

TROPICAL MOCKINGBIRD *Mimus gilvus*

KEY FEATURES 23–24 cm (9–9.5 in.). A slender, fairly large gray-and-white bird, very similar to the Northern Mockingbird, but they do not overlap in range. Voice consists of repeated couplets of musical whistles and phrases. Also a harsh *chuck*.
STATUS AND RANGE A fairly common resident on Guiana Island (Antigua), Guadeloupe, Dominica, Martinique, St. Lucia, St. Vincent, the Grenadines, and Grenada. It is very local in eastern Guadeloupe. The species frequents open areas around human dwellings, dry lowland scrub, and agricultural lands. This mocker is expanding northward, likely due to human alterations creating more favorable conditions.

BAHAMA MOCKINGBIRD *Mimus gundlachii*

KEY FEATURES 28 cm (11 in.). A large bird, its upper parts are brownish gray with fine streaks, the underparts whitish with dark side streaks, and the tail long and white-tipped. The species has two white wing bars not conspicuous in flight. Voice consists of a series of phrases, each repeated several times.
STATUS AND RANGE Generally a common resident of the Bahamas, Cuba's northern cays, and the Hellshire Hills of southern Jamaica. These islands comprise the entire range. This mocker occurs in semiarid scrub, woodlands, and around human habitation.

PALMCHAT

PALMCHAT *Dulus dominicus*

KEY FEATURES 20 cm (8 in.). A conspicuous flocking bird of the treetops, it is dark brown above and has white underparts heavily streaked with brown. Voice is noisy, particularly around the nest, producing an array of strange call notes.
STATUS AND RANGE Endemic to Hispaniola, where it is common, conspicuous, and widespread from the lowlands to mid-elevations. The species primarily inhabits royal palm savannas, but it also occurs in other types of open areas with scattered trees. A large communal nest with separate chambers for each pair is built high in a palm tree. The Palmchat is the national bird of the Dominican Republic and along with the todies is one of the Caribbean's two endemic families of birds.

TROPICAL MOCKINGBIRD

imm.

adult

*Southern Lesser
Antilles race*

adult

adult

NORTHERN MOCKINGBIRD

San Andrés race

BAHAMA MOCKINGBIRD

PALMCHAT

SHINY COWBIRD *Molothrus bonariensis*

KEY FEATURES 18–20 cm (7–8 in.). A medium-size dark bird with a conical bill. It often flocks. Adult male is glossy black with a purplish sheen. (The female Red-shouldered Blackbird has a finer bill and lacks a purplish sheen.) Adult female is drab grayish brown with a faint eyebrow stripe. Voice consists of whistles followed by a melodious trill; also a variety of short call notes.

STATUS AND RANGE A common resident through much of the Caribbean, its range continuingly expanding. This cowbird occurs primarily in open country and along edges in lowlands. It favors dairies and areas where grains are available. The female lays its eggs in nests of other species for their care. This *brood parasitism* has caused the decline of several Caribbean birds (see Invasive Species, p.22).

EASTERN MEADOWLARK *Sturnella magna*

KEY FEATURES 23 cm (9 in.). A medium-size bird with conspicuous yellow underparts and a distinctive black V on the breast. The outer tail feathers are white. The walk is a peculiar strut. Voice is a distinctive, high call on three tones; also a peculiar harsh, loud alarm note.

STATUS AND RANGE A common resident of Cuba, where it occurs in open grasslands, savannas, marshes, and pastures with only scattered trees or bushes primarily in lowlands. This bird often perches on fence posts or wires. Usually in pairs, it feeds on the ground, its prey consisting mainly of insects, worms, seeds, lizards, and frogs, as well as small fruits.

TAWNY-SHOULDERED BLACKBIRD *Agelaius humeralis*

KEY FEATURES 19–22 cm (7.5–8.5 in.). A medium-size, black bird with a tawny shoulder patch most conspicuous in flight. Sometimes the shoulder patch is not visible, giving the appearance of a female Red-shouldered Blackbird. It typically flocks. Voice is a strong, short *chic-chic*; also a harsh call.

STATUS AND RANGE Known only from Cuba, where it is common, and Haiti, where it is uncommon and local. This blackbird inhabits woodlands, gardens, farms, swamp edges, pastures, and rice fields in the lowlands. It is threatened in Haiti. The species feeds primarily on seeds but also fruits, pollen, nectar, flowers, small lizards, and domestic animal feed. In Cuba it sometimes enters restaurants for food scraps.

YELLOW-SHOULDERED BLACKBIRD *Agelaius xanthomus*

KEY FEATURES 20–23 cm (8–9 in.). A medium-size, black bird with a yellow shoulder patch. Voice consists of a wide variety of calls, including a raspy *tnaaa*, a whistled *tsuu* descending the scale, a melodious *eh-up*, the second syllable lower and accented, and also a *chuck*.

STATUS AND RANGE Endemic to Puerto Rico, where it is local along the southwestern coast and on Mona Island. The species is critically endangered. This blackbird occurs primarily in mangroves and arid scrublands, where it forages both in trees and on the ground. Moths and crickets are a major food.

adult ♀

adult ♂

SHINY COWBIRD

EASTERN MEADOWLARK

non-br. adult

br. adult

adult

TAWNY-SHOULDERED BLACKBIRD

imm.

adult

YELLOW-SHOULDERED BLACKBIRD

HISPANIOLAN ORIOLE *Icterus dominicensis*

KEY FEATURES 20–22 cm (8–8.5 in.). The adult has distinctive yellow shoulders, rump, and undertail coverts. The immature has mainly olive upper parts and dull yellow underparts. Voice is a hard, sharp *keek* or *check*.

STATUS AND RANGE Endemic to Hispaniola, where it is fairly common. The species inhabits forests, forest edges, woodlands, and gardens from the coast to mid-elevations, particularly near palms. Fruits, insects, flowers, and nectar are its primary foods. The bird often searches for prey on the undersides of palm fronds. Similar species, each endemic, occur in Cuba, Puerto Rico, and the Bahamas.

ST. LUCIA ORIOLE *Icterus laudabilis*

KEY FEATURES 20–22 cm (8–8.5 in.). Adult male is primarily black, but with substantial orange or orange-yellow markings on the lower back, rump, shoulder, and lower belly. Adult female is duller, immature mostly greenish, with a blackish throat. Voice consists of drawn-out melodic whistles.

STATUS AND RANGE Endemic to St. Lucia, where it is uncommon and declining. The species inhabits woodlands, including moderately dry and moist forests from near sea level to about 700 m (2,300 ft.). It lives in association with palms, which provide nest sites. The St. Lucia Oriole is threatened. Related orioles on Martinique and Montserrat are also uncommon and becoming rare. The nest, constructed well above the ground, is usually sewn to the bottom of a leaf or palm frond from which it hangs. This unusual habit is typical of most Caribbean orioles.

JAMAICAN ORIOLE *Icterus leucopteryx*

KEY FEATURES 21 cm (8 in.). Distinguished by its bright-yellow to dull greenish-yellow plumage, black throat, and large white wing patch. In the immature the white in the wing is less extensive. Voice is a whistled *you cheat* or *cheat-you*.

STATUS AND RANGE A common resident of Jamaica and San Andrés. These islands comprise its entire range. The species formerly occurred in the Cayman Islands. This oriole inhabits nearly all forest types, woodlands, and areas with trees, including gardens. It does not occur in mangroves. Insects are its primary food, which it searches for by prying away bark, a behavior not shared by other Caribbean orioles.

CUBAN BLACKBIRD *Dives atroviolaceus*

KEY FEATURES 25–28 cm (10–11 in.). A large, grackle-size, black bird with glossy purplish iridescence, a dark eye, and square tail. It typically forms flocks. The male Shiny Cowbird is smaller, with a more conspicuous sheen. Voice consists of a vast variety of calls, the most typical a loud, repetitive *ti-o*, with a metallic tone.

STATUS AND RANGE Endemic to Cuba, where common and widespread. It occurs primarily in gardens in urban and rural areas but also woodlands from the lowlands to mid-elevations. The species regularly walks on the ground and sometimes mixes with grackles and other blackbirds. This bird sometimes enters barns and pierces grain sacs to feed on the contents. It also perches atop cattle to extract parasites.

ST. LUCIA ORIOLE

HISPANIOLAN ORIOLE

adult

adult ♂

imm.

adult

imm.

JAMAICAN ORIOLE

CUBAN BLACKBIRD

GREATER ANTILLEAN GRACKLE *Quiscalus niger*

KEY FEATURES 25–30 cm (10–12 in.). A large bird with dark plumage, a long tail, and pointed bill. The species typically flocks. Adult male has glossy, metallic blue to violet-black plumage, with a yellow eye and a long, distinctive V-shaped tail. Adult female is duller and the tail has a smaller V. All other black birds within this bird's range lack a V-shaped tail. The smaller Carib Grackle replaces it in the Lesser Antilles. Voice is highly variable; it includes a high *cling, cling, cling.*

STATUS AND RANGE A common resident of Cuba, Jamaica, Hispaniola, Puerto Rico, and the Cayman Islands. These islands comprise the entire range of the species. It occurs primarily in many types of lowland open areas, including parks and gardens. Often very tame, it may scavenge for food scraps from humans.

CARIB GRACKLE *Quiscalus lugubris*

KEY FEATURES 24–28 cm (9.5–11 in.). A large bird with dark plumage, a long tail, and pointed bill. It typically flocks. Adult male is black with a violet, green, or steel-blue sheen, a yellowish-white eye, and a long, V-shaped tail. Adult female is smaller and variable in coloration from relatively dark to quite pale; the tail is shorter and less V-shaped. Voice is a squeaky pattern of three to seven syllables, with a rising inflection; also a variety of whistles and chucks.

STATUS AND RANGE A common year-round resident on most of the Lesser Antilles from Anguilla to Grenada, though possibly introduced into the islands north of Montserrat. It occurs primarily in lowland open areas, including pastures, scrublands, agricultural fields, and residential zones. This grackle is quite diverse in its feeding habits. Being very tame, it frequently takes food scraps from humans.

TANAGERS

BLACK-CROWNED PALM-TANAGER *Phaenicophilus palmarum*

KEY FEATURES 18 cm (7 in.). In the adult, note its black crown and white throat blending into the gray of the breast and abdomen. Voice includes a nasal *pi-au,* a pleasant dawn song, and a low *chep.*

STATUS AND RANGE Endemic to Hispaniola where it is common in the lowlands, occurring less frequently well into the mountains. In Haiti it is generally common, but rare west of Port-au-Prince. The species primarily inhabits thickets, both wet and dry, but occurs wherever there are trees, from towns to dense forests. It feeds on seeds, fruits, and insects. Generally the bird is found moving slowly and deliberately through dense cover, occasionally twitching its tail. It is often part of mixed feeding flocks. Its Spanish name, Cuatro Ojos, means "four eyes," referring to the four white facial markings.

GREATER ANTILLEAN GRACKLE

adult ♂

CARIB GRACKLE

adult ♀

adult ♂

imm.

BLACK-CROWNED PALM-TANAGER
adult

PUERTO RICAN SPINDALIS *Spindalis portoricensis*

KEY FEATURES 16.5 cm (6.5 in.). In the male, the black head striped with white is diagnostic; the underparts are primarily yellow, with a reddish-orange wash on the breast and hindneck. Female has a whitish mustache stripe, a faint eyebrow stripe, and striped underparts. Voice is a variable thin, high-pitched whistle, *zeé-tit-zeé-tittit-zeé*; also a soft *teweep*.

STATUS AND RANGE Endemic to Puerto Rico, where common and widespread in woodlands and forests at all elevations. The species is arboreal and feeds primarily on small fruit and flower buds. The four spindalis, each endemic to a different island, used to be considered one species, but research demonstrated each is distinct.

JAMAICAN SPINDALIS *Spindalis nigricephala*

KEY FEATURES 18 cm (7 in.). Male has distinctive black head striped with white; the underparts are primarily yellow, blending to reddish orange on the breast. Female is somewhat similar, but the head is gray and unstriped. Voice is a soft *seep* and high, fast notes.

STATUS AND RANGE Endemic to Jamaica, where it is common and widespread, particularly in the hills and mountains. This arboreal bird inhabits forests, woodlands, and brushy areas. It is frequently found in pairs or family groups.

HISPANIOLAN SPINDALIS *Spindalis dominicensis*

KEY FEATURES 16.5 cm (6.5 in.). In the male the black head striped with white is diagnostic; the underparts are primarily yellow, with a reddish-orange wash on the breast. Female has a whitish mustache stripe and finely striped underparts. Voice is a weak, high-pitched *thseep*; also a thin, high-pitched whistle.

STATUS AND RANGE Endemic to Hispaniola, where it is common in the mountains and less so on the coast. The species occurs in many forest types, from coastal mangroves to high-elevation pines. Like most other tanagers, it is arboreal and feeds on fruits. Deforestation has reduced its habitat.

WESTERN SPINDALIS *Spindalis zena*

KEY FEATURES 15 cm (5.75 in.). In the male the black head striped with white is diagnostic; the underparts are primarily yellow, with a reddish-brown wash on the breast and hindneck. Female: Note the two distinctive facial stripes. Voice is variable, but generally a very high-pitched, thin, ventriloquial whistle.

STATUS AND RANGE A common resident throughout Cuba and the Bahamas and fairly common on Grand Cayman (Cayman Islands). These islands are the entire range of the species. In the Bahamas it primarily frequents native and Australian pines during the breeding season and ranges to other habitats, especially coppice, when not breeding. Cayman Islands' birds breed in brush and woodlands but forage in a broad range of habitats. The species occurs at all elevations in Cuba, where it frequents open woods, brush, and mangroves. It is less common on the coast and is generally absent from dense forests.

PUERTO RICAN SPINDALIS

♀

♂

JAMAICAN SPINDALIS

♀

♂

HISPANIOLAN SPINDALIS

♂

♀

Cuba race

♂

Bahamas race

♂

WESTERN SPINDALIS

CUBAN GNATCATCHER *Polioptila lembeyei*

KEY FEATURES 10.5 cm (4 in.). Small, and slender with a long tail displaying white outer feathers, often cocked upward. Body is gray above, grayish white below. Note the white eye-ring and black facial crescent. The similar Blue-gray Gnatcatcher lacks the facial crescent. Female is paler. Voice is a loud and melodious song that begins with four whistles, followed by a trill and thin, varied whisper.
STATUS AND RANGE Endemic to Cuba, where common in the east and absent in the west. The species inhabits fairly dense coastal thorn-scrub, sometimes ranging inland. It is tame and active, foraging incessantly for insects.

BLACK-WHISKERED VIREO *Vireo altiloquus*

KEY FEATURES 15–16.5 cm (5.75–6.5 in.). Best identified by its song. However, the whitish eyebrow stripe, dark eye-line, black mustache stripe, and absence of wing bars distinguish it. All other vireos in the Caribbean lack the mustache stripe. Voice is a monotonous song, sung throughout the day and consisting of short, melodious two- to three-syllable phrases, each different, separated by pauses.
STATUS AND RANGE A common breeding resident nearly throughout the Caribbean. It is resident in Hispaniola and the Lesser Antilles year-round, but in the Bahamas, Cuba, Jamaica, Puerto Rico, and Cayman Islands it is absent September to January. This vireo frequents all forest types at all elevations as well as tall undergrowth and gardens. The bird typically remains nearly motionless in dense canopy foliage, where it goes unnoticed except when singing.

YELLOW WARBLER *Setophaga petechia*

KEY FEATURES 11.5–13.5 cm (4.5–5.25 in.). Adult male is yellow with reddish streaks on the breast and sides; the head varies dramatically among islands from yellow to entirely reddish brown. Adult female and immature are paler. The song is variable, but typically a loud, clear, and rapid *sweetsweet-sweet-ti-ti-ti-weet*.
STATUS AND RANGE A common resident widely in the Caribbean, it is uncommon in the northern Bahamas and may not breed on Saba, Grenada, St. Vincent, and some of the Grenadines. The species occurs primarily in mangroves, but on some islands also in coastal scrub. In Martinique, peculiarly, it ranges into mountain forests. Several populations have declined due to the Shiny Cowbird.

BANANAQUIT *Coereba flaveola*

KEY FEATURES 10–12.5 cm (4–5 in.). Small, active bird with very variable plumage. All have a noticeably curved bill, and most have a white eyebrow stripe and wing spot along with a yellow breast, belly, and rump. The black color phase in Grenada and St. Vincent lacks the white eyebrow stripe and wing spot. Immature is duller. Voice is variable, generally thin, high-pitched ticks, clicks, and insectlike buzzes.
STATUS AND RANGE A very common resident throughout the Caribbean except in Cuba where a vagrant. The Bananaquit occurs in all habitats, except on the highest peaks and in the driest lowlands. The primary food is nectar.

CUBAN GNATCATCHER

♂

BLACK-WHISKERED VIREO

adult ♂

YELLOW WARBLER

Martinique race

adult ♂

Bahamas & Cuba race

adult ♂

Anegada & most Lesser Antilles race

adult ♂

adult

Bahamas race

imm.

adult

Puerto Rico race

adult St. Vincent race

BANANAQUIT

SAFFRON FINCH *Sicalis flaveola*

KEY FEATURES 14 cm (5.5 in.). A medium-size finch. Adult is entirely yellow, with an orange crown. Voice is a sharp *pink*, a whistled *wheat* on one pitch, and a fairly loud, melodious but slightly harsh *chit, chit, chit, chi-chit*, of differing length.
STATUS AND RANGE Introduced in the Caribbean. On Jamaica it is widespread and common. In Puerto Rico it is fairly common but local to San Juan. The species frequents lawns in Puerto Rico, but in Jamaica it also occurs along roadsides and in farmlands. It forages for seeds primarily on the ground, but often retires to a tree. It is native to South America.

INDIGO BUNTING *Passerina cyanea*

KEY FEATURES 14 cm (5.5 in.). The male is seen in its spectacular blue breeding plumage only shortly before migrating north. Most of the time in the Caribbean the male is dull brown overall with faint breast stripes and traces of blue in the wings and tail. Female is similar but lacks traces of blue. The species typically flocks. Voice is an emphatic *twit*. This bird sometimes sings thin paired phrases.
STATUS AND RANGE A visitor to the region from October to early May; common in the Bahamas, Cuba, and the larger Virgin Islands; uncommon in Jamaica, Hispaniola, Puerto Rico, and the Cayman Islands. This bunting occurs in rice fields, grassy areas bounded by heavy thickets, woodlands, pasture edges, and scrub.

ANTILLEAN SISKIN *Spinus dominicensis*

KEY FEATURES 11 cm (4.25 in.). A small, chunky bird with a light yellow bill, it typically forms flocks. Male is distinctive with its black head and yellowish body; the tail is black with two yellow patches. Female is olive green above and yellowish white below, with faint breast streaks, two yellow wing bars, and a pale-yellowish rump. Voice is a soft *chutchut* and a higher-pitched *swee-ee*; also a low, bubbling trill.
STATUS AND RANGE Endemic to Hispaniola, where it is common and widespread in the western Dominican Republic. In Haiti it is uncommon, but increasing on the Massif de la Hotte. This species frequents pine forests and associated grassy clearings and forest edges in the mountains, but sometimes wanders to lower altitudes, including agricultural areas bordered by dry scrub forest. Large flocks forage among trees, bushes, or grasses. The species is declining.

LESSER ANTILLEAN SALTATOR *Saltator albicollis*

KEY FEATURES 22 cm (8.5 in.). A fairly large bird with dull olive upper parts. Note the whitish eyebrow stripe, black mustache stripe, and black bill with an orange-white tip. The underparts are finely streaked. Voice is a series of harsh, loud notes that rise and fall.
STATUS AND RANGE A common resident of Guadeloupe, Dominica, Martinique, and St. Lucia. These islands comprise the entire range. It occurs in thickets, second growth, dry scrub, and forest-edge undergrowth. The name *saltator* derives from the manner in which the bird hops around.

SAFFRON FINCH

♂

imm.

INDIGO BUNTING

♀

br. ♂

ANTILLEAN SISKIN

♀

♂

LESSER ANTILLEAN SALTATOR

adult

CUBAN BULLFINCH *Melopyrrha nigra*

KEY FEATURES 14–15 cm (5.5–5.75 in.). A small, dark bird with a thick, curved bill and a white band on the wing edge. Male primarily black. Female in Cuba is grayish black; in Grand Cayman olive-gray. Voice is a buzzing *chip* with a ventriloquial quality; also a thin, long, melodious trill, descending then ascending, *ti, ti, ti, ti-si-sssiiittt-sssiii.*

STATUS AND RANGE Known only from Cuba and Grand Cayman (Cayman Islands). In Cuba it is common and widespread. On Grand Cayman it is most abundant at North Side, North Sound Estates, and South Sound Swamp. This bullfinch inhabits forests, including mangroves, woodlands, brushy areas, and undergrowth in pine country. It occurs at all elevations usually in small flocks. Foraging occurs from the upper canopy to the ground, on seeds, buds, and fruits.

PUERTO RICAN BULLFINCH *Loxigilla portoricensis*

KEY FEATURES 16.5–19 cm (6.5–7.5 in.). Adult is black with a reddish-brown throat, undertail coverts, and crown band. Voice is two to ten distinctive rising whistles then a buzz; also a whistled *coochi, coochi, coochi* and medium-strength *check.*

STATUS AND RANGE Endemic to Puerto Rico, where it is common though curiously rare on the eastern tip. It inhabits dense forests and thickets of all types and at all elevations. This bird formerly inhabited St. Kitts where now extirpated. (See Environmental Threats, p.17.)

GREATER ANTILLEAN BULLFINCH *Loxigilla violacea*

KEY FEATURES 15–18 cm (5.75–7 in.). A chunky bird with a thick bill and a reddish-brown eyebrow stripe, throat, and undertail coverts. Voice is a shrill, insectlike *t'zeet, t'seet, t'seet, tseet, seet, seet,* etc.

STATUS AND RANGE A common resident on the larger islands of the Bahamas, Hispaniola and Jamaica, which comprise its entire range. The species inhabits dense thickets and undergrowth at all elevations, from dry coastal scrub to wet mountain forests. It also occurs in gardens. Fruits and seeds are its primary foods, but it also takes flower parts and snails.

LESSER ANTILLEAN BULLFINCH *Loxigilla noctis*

KEY FEATURES 14–15.5 cm (5.5–6 in.). Male is black, with a reddish-brown chin, throat, and mark in front of the eye. Some have red undertail coverts. Female and immature are brownish olive above and gray below, with orangish undertail coverts. Voice is a short, crisp trill; a harsh *chuk*; a thin, wiry *tseep, tseep*; and a lengthy twitter.

STATUS AND RANGE A common resident, endemic through the Lesser Antilles to the Virgin Islands (St. John, St. Croix). Absent from Barbados. This bullfinch occurs in shrubbery, gardens, thickets, and forest understory at all elevations. Formerly considered to occur on Barbados, the bird there is now believed to be so distinct as to be considered a separate species—the Barbados Bullfinch. The male of that species looks identical to a female Lesser Antillean Bullfinch.

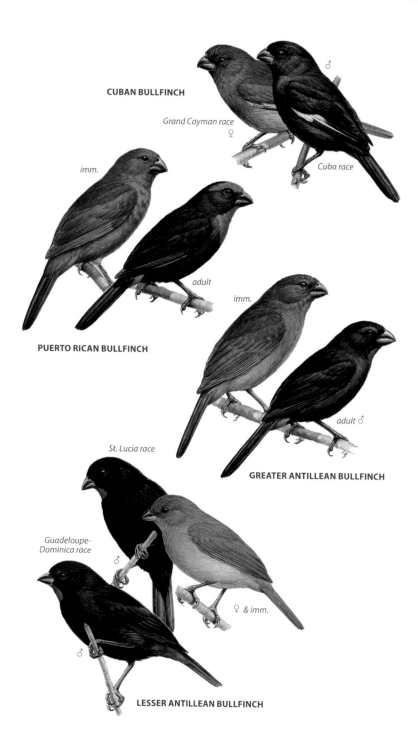

CUBAN BULLFINCH

Grand Cayman race
♀

♂

Cuba race

imm.

adult

PUERTO RICAN BULLFINCH

imm.

adult ♂

GREATER ANTILLEAN BULLFINCH

St. Lucia race

Guadeloupe-Dominica race
♂

♂

♀ & *imm.*

LESSER ANTILLEAN BULLFINCH

CUBAN GRASSQUIT *Tiaris canora*

KEY FEATURES 11.5 cm (4.5 in.). A small bird with olive upper parts. A conspicuous yellow crescent divides the face and breast. This grassquit usually forms flocks. Male has a black face and breast; in the female the yellow is paler and the face is a dark reddish-brown. Voice is a shrill, raspy *chiri-wichiwichi,chibiri-wichi-wichi*, resembling the Bee Hummingbird. Also a frequent *chip*.
STATUS AND RANGE Endemic to Cuba, where it is common. The bird was introduced into New Providence (Bahamas), where it is fairly common. The species primarily inhabits semiarid country, but also pine undergrowth, edges of woods, bushy areas, shade coffee and citrus plantations, and farms with much shrubbery. It occurs from the coast to mid-elevations. This grassquit has declined in Cuba.

YELLOW-FACED GRASSQUIT *Tiaris olivacea*

KEY FEATURES 11.5 cm (4.5 in.). In the male, note the distinctive yellow throat and eyebrow stripe; the breast is black. Female is yellowish olive overall and usually with a faint, yellowish eyebrow stripe, eye-ring, and chin. Voice is a thin trill, sometimes sequentially at different pitches. Also a soft *tek*.
STATUS AND RANGE A common resident of Cuba, Jamaica, Hispaniola, Puerto Rico, and the Cayman Islands, where it occurs primarily in open grassy areas from the lowlands to moderate elevations and sometimes high mountains. Generally singly or in small groups, it forages on seeds, usually from grass heads but sometimes the ground.

BLACK-FACED GRASSQUIT *Tiaris bicolor*

KEY FEATURES 11.5 cm (4.5 in.). Male: Note the black head and underparts. Very nondescript, the female is a drab brownish olive overall. Voice is an emphatic buzz, often followed by a second, louder effort.
STATUS AND RANGE Generally a common resident throughout the Caribbean, though rare and very local in Cuba. It occurs in open areas of grasses and shrubs, including forest clearings, road edges, sugarcane plantations, and gardens. The species occurs singly or in small numbers and is quite tame.

YELLOW-SHOULDERED GRASSQUIT *Loxipasser anoxanthus*

KEY FEATURES 10 cm (4 in.). Male is a small, two-toned bird with a black head and underparts contrasting with the yellowish-olive wings and back; the undertail coverts are reddish brown. Female is gray below and yellowish olive above, with a yellow patch on the bend of the wing. The undertail coverts are pale reddish brown. Voice is five notes, descending with an echolike quality.
STATUS AND RANGE Endemic to Jamaica, where it is fairly common and widespread. It occurs along forest edges from wet to dry habitats and at all elevations. The species also inhabits woodlands and gardens near wooded areas. It is often seen in small groups, foraging in bushes and low trees for fruits and seeds.

CUBAN GRASSQUIT

♂

♀

YELLOW-FACED GRASSQUIT

♂

♀ & imm.

♂

BLACK-FACED GRASSQUIT

♀ & imm.

adult ♂

YELLOW-SHOULDERED GRASSQUIT

adult ♀

HOUSE SPARROW *Passer domesticus*

KEY FEATURES 15 cm (5.75 in.). A chunky, heavy-billed sparrow, typically in flocks, easily distinguished by its preferred habitat—city streets. Note the male's black bib, gray crown, and pale cheek. The female and immature have a buff-colored eyebrow stripe and underparts and brown upper parts streaked with black. Voice is a distinctive *chirp*.

STATUS AND RANGE Introduced into the Caribbean, it is very common and widespread in Cuba and Puerto Rico and locally common in the Bahamas (Northern Bahamas and Great Inagua), Dominican Republic, Virgin Islands (St. Thomas and St. John), St. Martin, and Guadeloupe. The bird's range continues to expand. The species frequents urban areas. Native to Eurasia and Africa, this sparrow now ranges globally. It feeds on the ground and is extremely tame.

JAVA SPARROW *Padda oryzivora*

KEY FEATURES 15–16.5 cm (5.75–6.5 in.). Primarily gray, with a distinctive white cheek patch and broad, pinkish-red bill. Voice is a hard, metallic *chink*.

STATUS AND RANGE Introduced into the Caribbean, where it is fairly common around San Juan (Puerto Rico). There are recent reports from Jamaica. Primarily of urban areas, it occurs in short grass. The species typically flocks, is quite tame, and eats seeds. It is native to Indonesia.

VILLAGE WEAVER *Ploceus cucullatus*

KEY FEATURES 17 cm (6.75 in.). A chunky bird with a heavy bill, it often occurs in flocks. Male is orange yellow overall, with a black hood and red eye. Female has a yellowish-green face and breast, with yellow wing bars. Voice is a steady, high-pitched chatter, with musical whistling calls.

STATUS AND RANGE Introduced into the Caribbean, it is common and widespread in Hispaniola and is common but very local on the northern end of Martinique. It occurs primarily in the lowlands in rice fields, vegetation near water, open woodlands, scrub, and also gardens. During breeding the male performs a spread-wing flapping display, sometimes hanging upside down. Nesting is in noisy colonies. The species can cause major damage to rice crops. It is native to Africa.

ORANGE BISHOP *Euplectes franciscanus*

KEY FEATURES 12.5 cm (5 in.). The male in breeding plumage is a dramatic orange-red, with a black belly and crown. Female and nonbreeding male are mottled brown above and buff colored below, with a buff-colored eyebrow stripe. The breast and crown are finely striped. Breeding males sing a sputtering song.

STATUS AND RANGE Native to Africa and introduced into Puerto Rico, Martinique, and Guadeloupe, where it is uncommon and local on each island. In Puerto Rico it occurs most frequently from San Juan to Arecibo. There are recent records from other islands. It frequents grassy borders of sugarcane fields and other habitats with adequate cover combined with seeding grasses.

adult ♂

HOUSE SPARROW

♀ & imm.

JAVA SPARROW

imm.

adult

♀

VILLAGE WEAVER

br. ♂

ORANGE BISHOP

♂

♀ & non-br. ♂

PIN-TAILED WHYDAH *Vidua macroura*

KEY FEATURES Breeding male is 30–33 cm (12–13 in.); female and nonbreeding male, 11.5 cm (4.5 in.). The long, trailing tail plumes of the breeding male make it unmistakable. Female and nonbreeding male are mottled reddish brown above, with a red bill and black-and-white facial stripes. Voice consists of twittering, sometimes with loud chattering and whistles.
STATUS AND RANGE Introduced into Puerto Rico, where it is uncommon and local on the coast. This species feeds in flocks on lawns and fields with short grass. Native to Africa, the whydah lays its eggs in nests of waxbills.

ORANGE-CHEEKED WAXBILL *Estrilda melpoda*

KEY FEATURES 10 cm (4 in.). A small bird typically in flocks. Note the distinctive orange cheek patch and the reddish bill and uppertail coverts. Voice is a clear *pee*, singly or in series. Flocks have a characteristic twitter.
STATUS AND RANGE Introduced into Puerto Rico, where it is common and widespread. There are recent records from Guadeloupe and Martinique. The species frequents tall seeding grass. It is native to central West Africa.

BRONZE MANNIKIN *Lonchura cucullata*

KEY FEATURES 10 cm (4 in.). A small bird, typically in flocks. Identified by its black hood, dark grayish-brown back, and white belly with a scalloped pattern on the sides. Voice is a coarse *crrit*. Flocks chatter.
STATUS AND RANGE Introduced into Puerto Rico, where it is common and widespread. The species occurs in grassy areas. It is native to Africa.

NUTMEG MANNIKIN *Lonchura punctulata*

KEY FEATURES 11.5 cm (4.5 in.). A small bird, typically in flocks. The cinnamon-colored hood and scalloped underparts are diagnostic. Voice is a soft, plaintive whistle, *peet*, dropping in pitch and fading at the end.
STATUS AND RANGE Introduced into Puerto Rico, where it is common and widespread. It is locally common in the Dominican Republic and Guadeloupe, while decidedly uncommon and local in Cuba, Jamaica, and Martinique. The species occurs in lowland open areas such as sugarcane borders, road edges, and urban parks, where it forages for seeds. This bird is native to India and southeastern Asia.

TRICOLORED MUNIA *Lonchura malacca*

KEY FEATURES 11.5 cm (4.5 in.). A small bird typically in flocks. Note the black hood and belly and the cinnamon-colored back. Voice is a thin, nasal *honk*.
STATUS AND RANGE Introduced into the Caribbean, where it is locally common in Cuba and Hispaniola, uncommon in Puerto Rico, and uncommon and very local in Jamaica and Martinique. The species frequents high grasses bordering sugarcane, swampy areas, croplands, and canal edges. It is native from India through southeastern Asia.

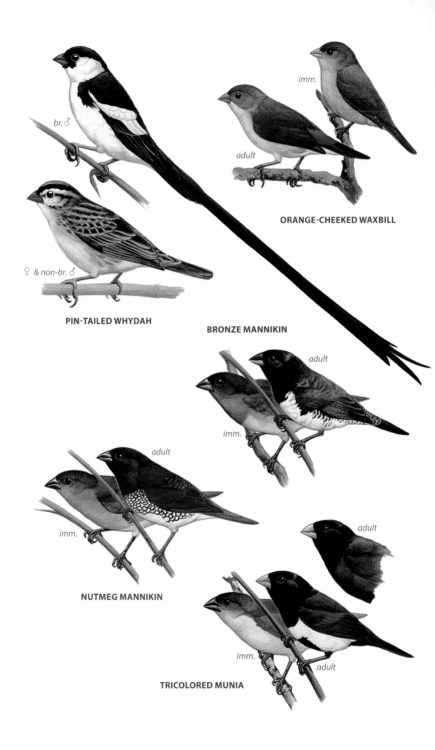

PIN-TAILED WHYDAH

br. ♂

♀ & non-br. ♂

ORANGE-CHEEKED WAXBILL

adult

imm.

BRONZE MANNIKIN

adult

imm.

NUTMEG MANNIKIN

adult

imm.

TRICOLORED MUNIA

adult

imm.

adult

TERRESTRIAL REPTILES | TURTLES

ANTILLEAN SLIDER *Trachemys stejnegeri*

KEY FEATURES Shell length to 28 cm (11 in.). A moderate-size turtle, the adult's upper shell is olive brown or blackish, smooth, and usually unmarked. The lower shell is yellowish with grayish markings, which may form confluent rings or irregular figures, with dark edges and yellowish interiors. The face, neck, and legs are streaked with yellow.

STATUS AND RANGE The Bahamas (Great Inagua Island), Hispaniola, and Puerto Rico account for the entire natural range of this species. It has been introduced into Marie-Galante (Guadeloupe). The species occurs in lowland freshwater lagoons, pools, and rivulets. It has declined due to destruction of wetlands, pollution, and hunting for food. Its diet includes insects, fish, and vegetation.

LIZARDS

GECKOS

Geckos of the genus *Sphaerodactylus* occur throughout the Caribbean, the larger islands supporting many species, there being at least nine in Puerto Rico alone. These tiny, ground-dwelling lizards generally occur under leaf litter, logs, and rocks, thus going unnoticed unless one searches for them. Only a few are presented here to give a sample of the group, since distinguishing among species, particularly where several may occur, is better left to experts.

JAMAICAN STIPPLED SPHAERO *Sphaerodactylus argus*

KEY FEATURES Snout to vent 3 cm (1.2 in.). A medium-size lizard, the upper parts have a gray, tan, or yellowish-brown background with a variable dorsal pattern of light, longitudinal stripes. The underparts range from unmarked to heavily spotted, and the tail underside is orange.

STATUS AND RANGE This gecko is native to Cuba, Jamaica, Bahamas (Bimini Islands, New Providence), and St. Andrew. It occurs on ridges, along beaches, in limestone dry scrub, in houses, hotel rooms, pastures, leaf litter, and trash.

BROWN-SPECKLED SPHAERO *Sphaerodactylus notatus*

KEY FEATURES Snout to vent 3 cm (1.2 in.). A medium-size lizard, the male's upper parts are tan to brown, unpatterned or with scattered darker scales. The head is tan to yellow, with or without heavy spotting. The female's upper parts are like the male's, but the head is marked with three brown lines on pale brown to tan ground color. Note the dark shoulder patch with one or two pale eye-like markings. The underside of the tail is reddish.

STATUS AND RANGE Native to Cuba and the Bahamas (Little and Great Bahama Banks, Great Inagua, Little San Salvador), it has been introduced into Morant and Pedro Cays (Jamaica). The species occurs in leaf litter and under rocks, logs, coppice, and hammocks. It is uncommon in occupied buildings but often associated with human debris and abandoned buildings.

ANTILLEAN SLIDER

JAMAICAN STIPPLED SPHAERO

BROWN-SPECKLED SPHAERO

BROOK'S HOUSE GECKO *Hemidactylus angulatus*

KEY FEATURES 7 cm (2.8 in.). A medium-size lizard with a flattened body and large eyes that lack eyelids. Its vertical pupil and broad toe pads distinguish all geckos, of which there are over two thousand species worldwide. The upper parts are brownish white to dark brown, with three to six light- to dark-brown butterfly-shaped marks (sometimes absent).

STATUS AND RANGE Introduced into Cuba, Hispaniola, and Puerto Rico, it primarily inhabits buildings but also rock and debris piles. It can walk upside down over smooth surfaces due to its Velcro-like toe pads. This gecko is primarily nocturnal. Native to Africa, it is probably a recent arrival in the Caribbean. Other *Hemidactylus* species have been introduced into the Caribbean.

ANOLES

Scores of anole species occur in the Caribbean. These small to medium-size lizards may occur in grass, bushes, or trees. Many have cryptic coloration, but some are colorful. Males often have a colorful dewlap or throat sac, which they extend to display for a number of purposes, including courtship and territorial defense. While performing this display, the anoles often do push-ups. Anoles are ambush predators on insects, waiting motionless until unwary prey pass near them, at which point the lizard makes a dash and snaps up the prey in its jaws. When being attacked by a larger predator, anoles, like a number of other lizards, have the capacity to sacrifice to the attacker their tail, which continues to wriggle as the anole escapes.

CUBAN BLUE ANOLE *Anolis allisoni*

KEY FEATURES Snout to vent 7.5 cm (3 in.). A medium-size lizard, the upper parts are dark brown to bright green. When breeding, the head and thorax of males is a vivid electric blue. Females have a light mid-dorsal stripe, dark patch above the forelimbs, white stripe from the ventral border of the eye to the ear, reddish to mauve throat sac, and whitish underparts.

STATUS AND RANGE Native to Cuba, it is common in the vicinity of human dwellings, gardens, on fence posts, and coconut and royal palms, where it is active by day. This anole also occurs on a few islands off the coast of Central America.

JAMAICAN TURQUOISE ANOLE *Anolis grahami*

KEY FEATURES Snout to vent 8 cm (3.2 in.). A medium-size lizard, this is one of the most beautiful of all anoles. The upper body is usually bluish green on the head and upper back shading to a deep blue on the lower back and tail. This lizard can vary its coloration to various browns or nearly black when agitated. In this state it may also raise its head crest.

STATUS AND RANGE Endemic to Jamaica, where it is widespread and common. It occurs from the lowlands into the mountains. Highly arboreal, this anole is found in a wide range of habitats, including dry forests and scrubland, pastures, gardens, and in human dwellings. Eggs are laid inside decomposing logs or tree cavities.

BROOK'S HOUSE GECKO

CUBAN BLUE ANOLE

JAMAICAN TURQUOISE ANOLE

PUERTO RICAN CRESTED ANOLE *Anolis cristatellus*

KEY FEATURES Snout to vent 7.5 cm (3 in.). Medium-sized, the upper parts vary, bronze or greenish gray, with variable markings. The tail has mid-dorsal dusky spots, the underparts are white or greenish yellow, and the throat sac greenish centrally, reddish orange peripherally, or completely yellow, tan or orange.

STATUS AND RANGE Native to Puerto Rico and the Virgin Islands, it was introduced into eastern Hispaniola. This anole occurs from sea level to 850 m (2,800 ft.) in open forests, fields, along roadsides, on fence posts, and in deforested areas. It is common in towns and cities where it frequently enters houses. Active by day, it favors sunny sites.

HISPANIOLAN GRACILE ANOLE *Anolis distichus*

KEY FEATURES Snout to vent 6 cm (2.4 in.). A small lizard, the upper parts are tan, brown, or gray, sometimes with a greenish or yellowish cast, at times with a bold, wide lateral stripe or four dark dorsal chevrons. There is a dark bar between the eyes and a dark U or V on the upper neck. The underside of the tail is orange to yellow. The throat sac is variable—yellow, orange, or reddish.

STATUS AND RANGE Endemic to the northern Bahamas, it has been introduced elsewhere in the Bahamas and Hispaniola. It occurs in humid localities in otherwise extremely dry regions from sea level to 1,830 m (6,000 ft.). The species frequents trees and fence posts, in open agricultural areas, plantations, and forest edges, including rain forests. It is active by day.

PUERTO RICAN BUSH ANOLE *Anolis pulchellus*

KEY FEATURES Snout to vent 5 cm (2 in.). A small lizard with upper parts yellowish brown or brownish gray, more dusky along the midline. The head is darker, a brown line extending from eye to shoulder and a conspicuous cream-colored line from the snout to the groin or tail. The flanks and underside are yellow, the throat sac is bluish pink or purplish near the throat, merging to bright crimson, with yellow scales toward the edge.

STATUS AND RANGE Endemic to Puerto Rico and the Virgin Islands, it occurs from sea level to 630 m (2,080 ft.) in open grassy areas. It rests on branches and occasionally fence posts and is active by day.

CUBAN BROWN ANOLE *Anolis sagrei*

KEY FEATURES Snout to vent 7 cm (2.75 in.). Medium-sized, with upper parts highly variable: grayish or brown with spots, bars, or V-shaped markings, with vertical yellow stripes and dots on the flanks. Some females have a light stripe down the back. The tail is laterally compressed. The male's throat sac is orange, red, or brown.

STATUS AND RANGE Native to Cuba, Jamaica, the Bahamas, Cayman Islands, and Swan Island; introduced into Grenada, the Grenadines, and St. Vincent. It is widespread, occupying sunny habitats at low to moderate elevations. It is found on the ground, fences, rock walls, and buildings where active by day.

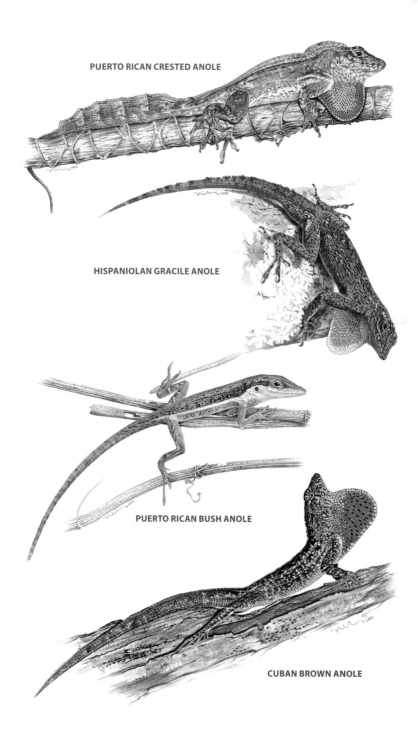

PUERTO RICAN CRESTED ANOLE

HISPANIOLAN GRACILE ANOLE

PUERTO RICAN BUSH ANOLE

CUBAN BROWN ANOLE

ROCK IGUANAS

These large, robust, prehistoric-looking lizards are of special stature among Caribbean wildlife, not only for their impressive size and appearance, but also because they represent a relic taxon, a group of species that formerly occurred more widely, including continental areas, but that now is confined to a small suite of islands represented by portions of the Greater Antilles and Bahamas Bank. All eight species that make up this group are endangered. In fact, the rock iguanas are considered the most endangered group of reptiles in the world. Their endangerment is due primarily to predation of the young by introduced mammals, as well as destruction of nests and eggs by feral pigs. Habitat loss is also a serious problem, as is susceptibility of these lizards to food resource competition by plant-eating feral mammals. Rock Iguanas are also subject to illegal hunting and exportation as pets. These iguanas are herbivorous. Some seeds on which they feed actually grow more successfully having passed through their gut.

RHINOCEROS IGUANA *Cyclura cornuta*

KEY FEATURES Snout to vent 51 cm (20 in.). A very large lizard, it has a heavy body, large head, a stout compressed tail, a small horn on the snout just in front of the eyes, a dorsal crest of spinelike scales extending from head to tail, and large jowls under the angle of the jaw, especially in large individuals. The upper parts are a patternless olive or olive gray, sometimes with brownish hues.
STATUS AND RANGE Native only to Hispaniola, Mona Island off Puerto Rico, and Navassa Island off Haiti. It occurs on rocky coasts near cliffs and caves as well as inland. Active by day, it sun bathes primarily in morning and late afternoon, basking on exposed "lookouts." Rock iguanas often remain still for long periods, and movements are usually slow, but they are capable of sudden dashes for short distances. Generally shy, they retreat into caves and rock crevices when disturbed. Eggs are laid in cavities dug in the soil. This species is considered vulnerable, but most other species of rock iguanas are critically endangered.

GREEN IGUANA *Iguana iguana*

KEY FEATURES Snout to vent 50 cm (16 in.) and 1.5m (5 ft.) in total length. A very large lizard, greenish, brown, or gray, with dark bands on its lengthy tail. A crest of long spines runs from neck to tail. It has a large throat sac.
STATUS AND RANGE Native to Saba, Montserrat, Guadeloupe, Les Saintes, St. Lucia, St. Vincent, the Grenadines, Grenada, Swan Island, St. Andrew, and Providence, the species was introduced into the Cayman Islands, Puerto Rico, and Virgin Islands. It occurs in forests and forest edges from sea level to moderate elevations. The species is found on the ground and in trees, often along streams, rivers, and lakes. Active during the day, it is commonly seen sunning and foraging. It feeds on vegetation and often dives into the water to escape a threat. This iguana is a popular food source in Central and South America, from whence Amerindians may have brought it to the Caribbean.

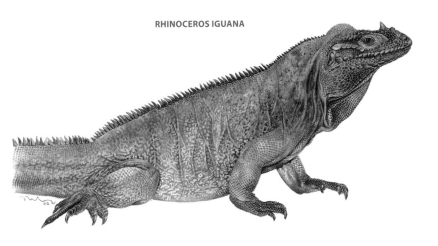

RHINOCEROS IGUANA

GREEN IGUANA

AMEIVAS OR GROUND LIZARDS

Various species of ameivas occur throughout the Caribbean, there being several species on each of the larger islands. They are commonly seen, due to being terrestrial, active by day, and prone to searching in the open for food. Their diet consists of a wide range of plant and animal matter, including smaller lizards. They often dig burrows in soft soil for shelter.

PUERTO RICAN GIANT AMEIVA *Ameiva exsul*

KEY FEATURES Snout to vent 20 cm (8 in.). A large lizard, its upper parts are olive to olive brown, with scattered whitish spots as far forward as the shoulders. The lower flanks usually have a checkerboard pattern of white or bluish spots on a darker background, and the underparts are whitish to pearly gray with a bluish tinge.

STATUS AND RANGE Endemic to Puerto Rico and the Virgin Islands, it occurs from sea level to about 150 m (500 ft.). The species is most common on sandy soil, particularly on beaches above the tidal zone, but it also occurs in arid areas, on lawns, in vacant lots, roadsides, city parks and plazas, around houses, and along mangrove borders. It is very active during the day.

JAMAICAN AMEIVA *Ameiva dorsalis*

KEY FEATURES Snout to vent 12 cm (4.7 in.). A medium-size lizard, its upper parts are brown, with a central flash of pointed white from the lower neck widening out to the tail. White and brown spots lie alongside this, and aqua spots line the flanks to the upper part of the tail. Underparts are lighter colored.

STATUS AND RANGE Endemic to Jamaica, it has a scattered distribution along the coast in highly disturbed areas, primarily in the south. This includes offshore cays, which provide a refuge from the mongoose, to which it is highly vulnerable. It is fairly common in parts of Kingston due to its adaptation to gardens around houses and to vacant lots. An active forager during the day, it goes underground when disturbed. Locally it is known as the Ground Lizard.

HISPANIOLAN SMOOTH GALLIWASP *Celestus costatus*

KEY FEATURES Snout to vent 13 cm (5 in.). A medium-size lizard with relatively long limbs, the upper parts tan to brown, often metallic. Coloration is variable from uniform to a series of fine, dorsal stripes of adjacently placed dots.

STATUS AND RANGE Endemic to Hispaniola, this lizard occurs most often in broadleaf forests but also in pine forest from sea level to 2,300 m (7,600 ft.). It is found under logs, stones, human trash, and piles of wood, in leaf litter, and occasionally above the ground in bromeliads. Related species inhabit other Caribbean islands.

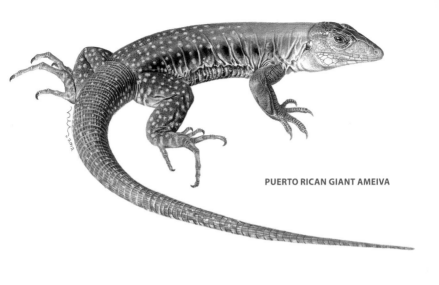

PUERTO RICAN GIANT AMEIVA

JAMAICAN AMEIVA

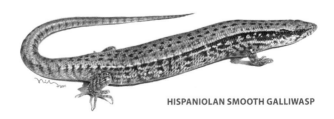

HISPANIOLAN SMOOTH GALLIWASP

SAW-SCALED CURLYTAIL *Leiocephalus carinatus*

KEY FEATURES Snout to vent 13 cm (5 in.). A large lizard, its body color is quite variable among populations but is generally gray to brown, with darker spotting or bands on its head and sides. The throat is typically speckled. Large keeled and pointed scales on the back form a raised crest on the faintly banded tail. Males curl their tail over the back in displays to attract females and drive away other males.

STATUS AND RANGE Native to Cuba, the Bahamas, and Cayman Islands, the species has been introduced into southern Florida. Its habitats include coastal beaches, open woods, coconut stands, as well as lawns and gardens. This lizard is active by day, when it is often seen perched on loose coral rubble, rocks, or logs. It retreats within a burrow or cavity when frightened.

CROCODILES

AMERICAN CROCODILE *Crocodylus acutus*

KEY FEATURES Adults to 7 m (23 ft.); average 3–4 m (10–13 ft.) in total length. A large crocodile, it is grayish, brown, or olive above, appearing nearly black. The undersides are white or yellow white. Younger animals have dark cross bands on the back and tail.

STATUS AND RANGE Native to Cuba, Hispaniola, and Jamaica, this crocodile occurs in coastal lowlands, where it is found in brackish or freshwater swamps, mangroves, estuaries, and large rivers. Habitat destruction and illegal hunting have dramatically reduced its numbers, and the species is now considered endangered. This is the most widespread croc in the Americas, occurring from Mexico to northern South America. Like other crocs, the female builds a mound of soil and vegetation; here she lays her eggs, which she aggressively defends.

CUBAN CROCODILE *Crocodylus rhombifer*

KEY FEATURES Adults to 3.5 m (11.5 ft.) in total length; average length 2–2.5 m (6.5–8 ft.). Medium-size for a crocodile, adults are yellowish green or green above, with dense, dark-green or black speckling on the head, body, and tail. The sides and tail are blotched with yellow and black, the undersides are white, and the edges of the eyelids are usually white, giving a "spectacled" appearance.

STATUS AND RANGE Endemic to Cuba, this croc is now uncommon and local, its estimated wild population being approximately three thousand individuals. Inhabiting primarily freshwater swamps, it has declined due to illegal hunting and hybridization, resulting in it being considered critically endangered. The species was formerly much more widespread and included a few of the Bahamas and Cayman Islands. It is the most terrestrial of the crocodiles and reputedly has exhibited pack hunting behavior. Small mammals, fish, and turtles are its primary prey.

SAW-SCALED CURLYTAIL

AMERICAN CROCODILE

CUBAN CROCODILE

TERRESTRIAL REPTILES |

Most of the Caribbean's snakes are quite harmless, with the notable exceptions of the St. Lucian and Martinique vipers. Even these species would like nothing better than to be left undisturbed. Nevertheless, like many other regions, the Caribbean has developed an impressive folklore regarding its snakes. For that reason it is all the more important to recognize the uniqueness of the region's snakes as well as the important role they play in controlling noxious rodents and other pests.

BOAS

Boas of the genus *Epicrates* occur widely in the Caribbean, and Hispaniola supports the most species—three. Their coloration varies substantially, some specimens being quite red or yellowish, whereas others are nearly black. They eat only animal matter, which they asphyxiate using their powerful coils. Puerto Rican boas are known to congregate at the mouths of bat caves and capture these flying mammals as they emerge for the night.

HISPANIOLAN BOA *Epicrates striatus*

KEY FEATURES Snout to vent 2.3 m (7.5 ft.). A large snake, the upper parts are brown, gray, or reddish brown, often without markings or with many darker gray, tan, or brown blotches. The underparts are cream, gray, or brown, with scattered to regular dark-brown to dark-gray markings.
STATUS AND RANGE Native only to the Bahamas and Hispaniola, this boa occurs most often in humid habitats from sea level to 370 m (1,220 m). It usually occurs in forests, including pinewoods and mangroves. Active at night, this snake forages on the ground and in trees. During the day it is found in rotten, dry, or hollow logs, tree stumps, limestone crevices, and clumps of vegetation growing on broad, horizontal branches. Large individuals frequently bask coiled high in trees. The Bahamas population is considered endangered.

BOA CONSTRICTOR *Boa constrictor*

KEY FEATURES Adults to 3 m (10 ft.) in total length. A large snake, its background color is a rich brown to dark, clouded gray-brown above patterned with rectangular or irregular crosswise markings. The underside is white to light gray, with contrasting black or gray mottling. There is a dark streak down the middle of the head, sometimes with a distinct stripe below the eye.
STATUS AND RANGE Native to Dominica, St. Lucia, St. Andrew, and Providence, this boa prefers humid conditions but may occur in wet ravines in dry country. It is found in trees or on the ground in woods, disturbed forest, plantations, and coconut husk debris, from sea level to 350 m (1,150 ft.) elevation. The species is active day and night and feeds on rats, agoutis, and bats. This boa also occurs from Mexico to northwestern South America.

HISPANIOLAN BOA

BOA CONSTRICTOR

PUERTO RICAN RACER *Borikenophis portoricensis*

KEY FEATURES Snout to vent 90 cm (3 ft.). A medium-size snake, whose dorsal and ventral patterns are quite variable but usually brown. The underparts are paler than the upper parts. The scales of the upper and lower parts are edged in darker brown, and the head is generally without markings.

STATUS AND RANGE Endemic to Puerto Rico and the Virgin Islands, this racer occurs in dry scrub, gardens, leaf litter under coconut palms, rain forest, open pasture, and rock piles. It is active during the day although seldom seen after mid-morning. Primarily terrestrial, it is sometimes found in trees to 23 m (75 ft.) in rain forests. An active forager, it is quite aggressive, not hesitating to bite when cornered. Various species of this genus occur throughout the Caribbean, a number of which are threatened or endangered.

CAUTION The saliva of this snake is mildly poisonous.

ST. LUCIA VIPER *Bothrops caribbaeus*

KEY FEATURES Snout to vent 1.3 m (4 ft. 4 in.). A large snake, it has a fairly slender body with a triangular head. The upper parts are usually gray to gray brown with slate-gray to chocolate-brown markings. This pattern is best developed along the middle of the back but is vague or absent along the sides. The underparts are yellow to cream colored, sometimes finely speckled with gray toward the sides. The side of the head has a dull, irregular stripe.

STATUS AND RANGE Endemic to St. Lucia, this snake occurs in coastal and lowland areas to 200 m (650 ft.) elevation. It frequents disturbed areas such as rock piles and stacks of coconut husks. The species is also found among rocks along rivers and is semiarboreal.

CAUTION This snake and the Martinique Viper (*Bothrops lanceolatus*) are the only dangerously poisonous snakes in the Caribbean.

PUERTO RICAN RACER

ST. LUCIA VIPER

One of the most noticeable elements of the Caribbean's fauna is the calling of its numerous treefrogs. Over one hundred and fifty species occur in the region, most being endemic to one particular island. In fact, even among those endemic species many are further restricted to one limited locality or microhabitat. Though very vocal and widely heard, these treefrogs are infrequently seen, due to their small size, cryptic coloration, and tendency to hide in dense vegetation. For that reason few are presented in the text. This group of treefrogs is renowned for not possessing a tadpole stage, each tiny frog emerging directly from an egg. Bypassing the tadpole stage enables these frogs to be less dependent upon water and thus occupy drier habitats than would be possible by most frogs. In a number of species either the male or female guards the eggs and, sometimes, the recently hatched young. The Golden Coqui of Puerto Rico, now believed extinct, was one of the few frogs anywhere in the world in which the female retained the eggs within her body and gave birth to live young. *Eleutherodactylus*, like other frogs, feed heavily on small insects and other invertebrates, thus playing an important role in keeping noxious insects in check. The smallest frogs in the world are in this genus.

TUCK-WHEEP FROG *Eleutherodactylus abbotti*

KEY FEATURES Snout to vent 2.5 cm (1 in.). A small treefrog, variably colored from grayish green to tan above, rarely reddish tan to brown, and flecked with darker, blurred dorsal marks. Some possess a tan mid-dorsal line. The undersides are usually yellow in males and whitish in females. The upper portion of the iris is greenish silver. The call is a series of flat *tuck*s, ending with a higher-pitched *wheep*.
STATUS AND RANGE Endemic to Hispaniola, where it is very common in moist wooded or forested situations, including pine forests from sea level to 1,800 m (6,000 ft.). It also occurs in pastures, gardens, and urban areas. The species often calls during the day, particularly when it is overcast or rainy. Large numbers of males chorus together, and it is the call that gives rise to its name. This frog usually is found beneath ground litter and logs.

PUERTO RICAN RED-EYED FROG *Eleutherodactylus antillensis*

KEY FEATURES Snout to vent 3.3 cm (1.3 in.). A moderate-size treefrog, its upper parts are variably colored, from pale gray and dull grayish-brown to violet red, with faint, dusky markings. It sometimes has a pale mid-dorsal line. The species is easily recognized from other Puerto Rican treefrogs by the upper portion of the iris being red and by the black spotted pattern on the rear of the hind legs. It calls *churee-churee*, with no pause between notes.
STATUS AND RANGE This treefrog is native only to Puerto Rico and the Virgin Islands, where it is very common and widespread in wooded or forested habitat, including dry forest from sea level to the highest mountains. The species is active at night but during the day is found under grass roots, loose bark, rocks, logs, and trash. It calls through the night among leaves of low bushes and branches. Egg clutches are laid on the ground, under leaf litter or a thin layer of soil.

CUBAN GROIN-SPOT FROG *Eleutherodactylus atkinsi*

KEY FEATURES Snout to vent 4.3 cm (1.5 in.). A moderate-size treefrog, its upper parts are reddish brown to tan or gray. Stripes on the back and sides may be present or absent. Its call is a series of birdlike twitters or clicks similar to water dropping from a leaky faucet.

STATUS AND RANGE Endemic to Cuba, where it is very common and widespread in moist habitats, including scrub, woods, forests, coffee plantations, rocky areas, pasture, canals, ditches, gardens, and urban areas from sea level to 1,200 m (4,000 ft.). The species is nocturnal, and males call from the ground. The eggs are laid in a depression in moist soil.

TUCK-WHEEP FROG

PUERTO RICAN RED-EYED FROG

CUBAN GROIN-SPOT FROG

PUERTO RICAN FROG *Eleutherodactylus coqui*

KEY FEATURES Snout to vent 6 cm (2.25 in.). Large for a treefrog, its upper parts
are gray or gray brown and variously marked. The underparts range from whitish
to yellow or orange. The iris is copper, bronze, or gray, never silvery or white.
This frog is easily recognized by its regularly repeated two-note call—*co-quí*, the
second note accented and higher than the first.

STATUS AND RANGE Endemic to Puerto Rico, where it is widely distributed and
abundant in moist broadleaf forest from sea level to the highest mountaintops. It
is found in bromeliads, holes in banks, under trunks, rocks, leaf litter, in palm axils,
curled leaves, and tree holes. Most active at night but also after rains. This is the
most abundant frog in Puerto Rico, with a density estimated at 20,000 per ha (8,000
per acre). As an invasive in Hawaii its density ranges to over 90,000 per ha (36,000
per acre). The diet includes a wide range of invertebrates and small frogs. Coquis,
their common name in Puerto Rico, lay their eggs on leaves and in abandoned bird
nests. The species has been introduced into the Virgin Islands (St. Thomas, St. Croix).

JAMAICAN ROCK FROG *Eleutherodactylus cundalli*

KEY FEATURES Snout to vent 4.5 cm (1.75 in.). A large treefrog, its warty upper
parts are tan, yellowish tan, yellow, reddish, or gray with variable patterning. The
underparts are yellowish, and the upper portion of the iris is golden or greenish
gold. Its call is high pitched, very soft, and fairly erratic.

STATUS AND RANGE Endemic to western Jamaica, where it occurs from sea
level to 640 m (2,100 ft.) in moist wooded areas on shrubs, along limestone cliffs
and rubble, rock piles, caves, and in bromeliads. It is both arboreal and terrestrial.
The species is active at night and retreats to the protection of bromeliads by day.

JAMAICAN FOREST FROG *Eleutherodactylus gossei*

KEY FEATURES Snout to vent 3.4 cm (1.3 in.). A moderate-size treefrog, its upper
parts are rich reddish-brown to tan, with a variable pattern of mottling. There may
be a broad stripe down the back, stripes along the sides, or both. The underparts
are creamy to faintly yellowish with variable markings. The call is a simple repetitive
whistle, a fairly loud *wink*, given rapidly and continuing for a long time without pause.

STATUS AND RANGE Endemic to Jamaica from sea level to over 1,500 m (5,000 ft.),
where it occurs in moist habitats that are sometimes surrounded by dry conditions.
These include shrubs within wooded or forested areas, or in grass. The species is
active by night and retreats under rocks, leaf litter, and rotting logs by day.

YELLOW-STRIPED DWARF FROG *Eleutherodactylus limbatus*

KEY FEATURES Snout to vent 2 cm (0.75 in.). A tiny treefrog, considered the
fourth smallest frog in the world, its upper parts are chocolate brown to purplish
brown, with a white to yellow stripe bordering the back. The underparts are
greenish white to cream and the throat is bright yellow, sometimes with dark
spots. The call is a series of irregular, quiet *peeps*.

STATUS AND RANGE Endemic to Cuba, where it occurs from the lowlands to 550 m (1,800 ft.) in moist and dry forests. Where found it is usually numerous, particularly in pine woods. Active by night, this frog is found under leaf litter or other objects on the ground during the day. The female deposits a single large egg under leaf litter.

PUERTO RICAN FROG

JAMAICAN ROCK FROG

JAMAICAN FOREST FROG

YELLOW-STRIPED DWARF FROG

LESSER ANTILLEAN FROG *Eleutherodactylus johnstonei*

KEY FEATURES Snout to vent 3.5 cm (1.4 in.). A moderate-size treefrog, its upper parts are a dull brown to grayish tan, with variable patterning of at least one chevron in the shoulder area. It often has one or several stripes down its back. The undersides are creamy, often with faint spots on the throat. The two-note call is a weak whistle with a distinct whispery quality and given up to sixty times per minute in a long series.

STATUS AND RANGE Native virtually throughout the Lesser Antilles, it has been introduced into Jamaica and other countries. The species occurs from sea level to 850 m (2,800 ft.) and is very adaptable, occurring in moist, disturbed forests, cut-over fields, gardens, and residential areas. It feeds primarily on ants and is most active at night, retreating by day beneath plant litter, rocks, logs, and in bromeliads. This treefrog probably reached other countries accidentally as a stowaway on boats.

FROGS AND TOADS

SQUIRREL TREEFROG *Hyla squirella*

KEY FEATURES Snout to vent 4.3 cm (1.7 in.). Large for a treefrog, the species is able to change its color to match its background. Most commonly the upper parts are pale green but may be gray or brown. There is a white or yellowish-white line on the upper lip and a light line from below the eye to above the shoulder. The undersides are unmarked and the toes possess moderate disks. The call is a short, nasal, ducklike *quack* uttered in rapid sequence and given in a chorus of many calling males. A second call given before or during rain is a raspy, squirrellike chatter.

STATUS AND RANGE Common on Grand Bahama, where it was introduced and occupies a diversity of habitats, including open woodlands, pastures, gardens, and even residences. It forages in trees and shrubs, usually occurring near pools, in which females lay their eggs. The species is active at night, retreating under logs, bark, leaf litter, and palm thatch during the day. This treefrog is native to eastern North America.

MARINE TOAD OR CANE TOAD *Rhinella marina*

KEY FEATURES Snout to vent 20 cm (8 in.). An enormous toad, covered with warts and possessing large, triangular glands on each side of the head behind its brown eyes. The female is a mottled combination of dusky brown, tan, and chocolate, whereas the male is uniformly brown. Its call is a low-pitched, guttural trill sounding like a boat motor.

STATUS AND RANGE A common and widespread toad introduced throughout much of the Caribbean, including Jamaica, Puerto Rico, U.S. Virgin Islands, Barbados, Grenada, the Grenadines, St. Vincent, St. Lucia, Martinique, Guadeloupe, St. Kitts, Nevis, Montserrat, and Antigua. This toad is found in open and semiopen areas, agricultural lands, suburban gardens, and along roads. It especially frequents moist habitats from sea level to 880 m (2,900 ft.). Terrestrial, it is active from dusk through the night. By day it hides under fallen trees, and debris. Glands behind the eyes and across the back are poisonous to most animals. The tadpoles as well are poisonous. Unlike most toads, it eats both dead and living things, ranging from all sorts of animals to plants and dog food. This toad is native to Central and South America, from whence it was brought to the Caribbean to control sugarcane pests.

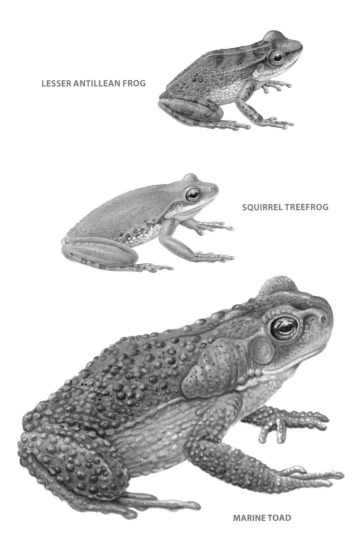

LESSER ANTILLEAN FROG

SQUIRREL TREEFROG

MARINE TOAD

PUERTO RICAN DITCH FROG *Leptodactylus albilabris*

KEY FEATURES Snout to vent 5 cm (2 in.), A moderate-size frog with very variably colored upper parts, from greenish yellow, olive, greenish brown, brownish yellow, to almost black, with darker longitudinal streaks or spots. The underparts range from white to creamy yellow and may be heavily spotted. The upper lip is white, and there are no disks or pads on the toe tips. The distinctive call is a repetitive, loud *pink … pink … pink*.

STATUS AND RANGE A common and widespread frog in Puerto Rico, the Virgin Islands, and northeastern Dominican Republic. It is terrestrial and semiaquatic, occurring in or near streams, ditches, marshes, drains, and gutters in towns, sugarcane fields, and coffee plantations from sea level to 1,030 m (3,400 ft.). This frog is active both day and night. The eggs are laid in a foam nest in a shallow hollow covered by stone, earth, or vegetation. The diet includes a wide range of invertebrates. Male frogs pound their vocal sacs against the ground when calling.

CUBAN TREEFROG *Osteopilus septentrionalis*

KEY FEATURES Snout to vent 14 cm (5.5 in.). The largest treefrog in either the Caribbean or North America, females being larger than males. The upper parts have scattered tubercles and are very variable in color, being whitish to gray, olive colored, or brown, with darker bold blotches. The underparts are creamy white, the iris dull yellow, and the toes, padded at the tips, are about two-thirds webbed. Calls are irregular and consist of a rasping snore.

STATUS AND RANGE Native only to Cuba, the Bahamas, and the Cayman Islands, it has been introduced into Puerto Rico, St. Croix, St. Thomas, and many islands of the Lesser Antilles. This nocturnal frog primarily frequents moist habitats, such as banana plantations, marshes, flooded pastures, roadside ditches, and mangroves, but in the Bahamas it is mostly encountered in dry areas, such as pine forests. Its diet includes frogs, lizards, and virtually any animal it can fit in its mouth. Quite invasive, it is a serious pest where introduced. Toxic mucus is secreted from the skin, which reduces predation.

BULLFROG *Lithobates catesbianus*

KEY FEATURES Snout to vent 15 cm (6 in.). A very large frog with a large, conspicuous eardrum. The upper parts are green or olive green, sometimes mottled with brown. Its underparts are whitish, sometimes mottled with gray or yellow. The call is a monotonous drone.

STATUS AND RANGE Introduced into and now found widely in the lowlands of Cuba, Jamaica, Hispaniola, and Puerto Rico. This is an aquatic frog never found far from water, including ponds, swamps, lakes and irrigation ditches. It eats any animal it can swallow, including rodents, snakes, lizards, turtles, birds, and frogs. In some localities it is highly cannibalistic. The species has been introduced widely around the world as a potential food source, but this is not popular in the Caribbean. It is active both day and night.

PUERTO RICAN DITCH FROG

CUBAN TREEFROG

BULLFROG

MOUNTAIN MULLET *Agonostomus monticola*

KEY FEATURES 15–30 cm (6–12 in.). Usually grayish, it is easily identified by the dusky-yellow dorsal and tail fins and the pale lateral line.

STATUS AND RANGE A fairly common fish of clear streams and rivers throughout the Caribbean. In upper stream reaches these fish tend to be larger, but fewer and more solitary than at lower elevations, where they often form uneven schools. Juveniles are sometimes found in brackish water. It is believed adults migrate to the sea to spawn, primarily during the rainy season. The diet is diverse, including shrimp, insects, and snails. Feeding is primarily near the surface, making this fish a favorite of fly fishers. Its range includes the southern United States, Mexico, and Central America.

RIVER GOBY *Sicydium plumieri*

KEY FEATURES To 13 cm (5 in.). A small, well-camouflaged fish with a flat forehead, large eyes, and large pectoral fins. Generally brownish with horizontal tan stripes, the breeding male is bright blue (or turquoise) and white.

STATUS AND RANGE A common rock-clinging fish of clear, fast-flowing, rocky streams through the Greater and Lesser Antilles. Schools often inhabit rocky pools. The pelvic fins are modified to form a ventral sucking disk, which anchors the body against stream currents and even enables it to climb up waterfalls. Adults spawn in headwaters, the males protecting the eggs. The hatched larvae drift downstream to the river mouths, where they mature to the juvenile stage, at which point they migrate in large numbers back upstream. This goby feeds on algae off rocks. The postlarvae are a delicacy on a number of islands. The species also occurs in Central America. Other common names are Sirajo and Suckstone.

SHRIMP

LONG-NOSED SHRIMP OR YELLOW-NOSED SHRIMP
Xiphocaris elongata

KEY FEATURES To 4 cm (1.5 in.). A small, attractive shrimp with a long, prominent, and brightly colored face, ranging from yellow to orange. The eye stalks and body tend to be translucent.

STATUS AND RANGE Common and widespread in the Greater and Lesser Antilles, this shrimp primarily inhabits the margins of quiet freshwater pools in well-aerated streams. However, it tolerates a wide range of water conditions, including even brackish water and saltwater. When disturbed, it jets quickly away, sometimes leaping out of the water. This shrimp feeds on vegetation.

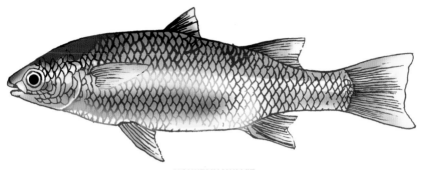

MOUNTAIN MULLET

RIVER GOBY

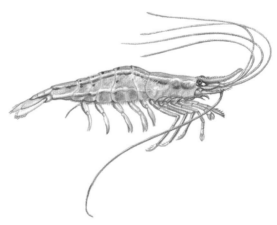

LONG-NOSED SHRIMP

ZEBRA LONGWING OR ZEBRA HELICONIAN *Heliconius charithonia*

KEY FEATURES To 10 cm (4 in.). A large butterfly, its slender black wings are distinctively striped with yellow.

STATUS AND RANGE The species is widespread through most of the Caribbean, occurring on some of the Bahamas, Cuba, Jamaica, Hispaniola, and Puerto Rico south to Montserrat. It frequents an array of habitats, including gardens and road edges. The species is gregarious and at night often roosts communally. Larvae feed on passion flowers, whereas adults feed on pollen rather than nectar. West Indian Lantana is a favored plant of adults. The species stores cyanide in its body and thus is toxic to many potential predators.

GULF FRITILLARY OR SILVER-SPOTTED FLAMBEAU *Agraulis vanillae*

KEY FEATURES To 9.5 cm (3.7 in.). A large butterfly, the upper wing is bright orange with black spots and wing edges. The underwings are light brown, with large, silver teardrop-shaped markings.

STATUS AND RANGE Common and widespread throughout the Caribbean, where it prefers coastal sunlit areas with flowers. These include gardens, scrub, forest edges, and open woodlands. Eggs are placed only on passion flower vines, upon which the larvae depend. Male butterflies have a peculiar habit of courting females by flapping their wings in front of them and trapping their antennae. This is believed to stimulate mating. The species occurs from the southern United States to Argentina.

JULIA OR THE FLAME *Dryas iulia*

KEY FEATURES To 9 cm
(3.5 in.). A beautiful
butterfly with long
narrow forewings. It is
primarily orange, with
black markings varying
among islands. The
underwings are paler
orange. Females are
slightly duller and a bit
blacker.

STATUS AND RANGE
The Julia is fairly
common throughout the Caribbean, where it occurs in open areas such as
clearings, paths, and forest edges. It often frequents wet ground. A fast, active
flyer, the species follows a set route or "trap line" to various nectar sources, a
frequent one being West Indian Lantana. Larvae are confined to passion flower
vines of various species. Adults roost in loose groups low to the ground. Julias
occur from the extreme southern United States south to Brazil. Other names
include Flambeau and Julia
Heliconian.

MALACHITE *Siproeta stelenes*

KEY FEATURES To 8 cm (3 in.). A
large butterfly, black with bright
green markings above and light
brown with pale green markings
below.

STATUS AND RANGE Widespread
and fairly common in the Caribbean
where it occurs in orchards, gardens,
and along forest edges. Generally
solitary, these butterflies sometimes
congregate on rotting fruit, a
primary food. The species also feeds
on nectar, carrion, bird droppings,
and bat dung. It is a slow flyer that
frequently floats, often not high
above the ground. Adults often
roost together under leaves of low
bushes. The Malachite occurs from
the extreme southern United States
south to Brazil. Its name derives from
the similarly colored green mineral.

MONARCH *Danaus plexippus*

KEY FEATURES To 10 cm (4 in.). A large butterfly, it is conspicuously bright orange above with black veins and edging. The underwings are paler.

STATUS AND RANGE The Monarch occurs throughout the Caribbean, where it is generally fairly common in open areas, particularly along beaches but also in gardens, fields, and along roadsides. The species is sedentary in the Caribbean, not moving among the islands. In North America, however, it is famous for its migrations from as far north as Canada to central Mexico. Amazingly, the round-trip migration takes four to five generations to accomplish. The flight south is achieved by the first generation, a single butterfly transiting over 3,200 km (2,000 mi.), at the end of which it hibernates in the mountain forests of central Mexico. Here tens of millions of Monarchs congregate into but a few acres. Several generations are required for the return trip north. Monarch caterpillars occur almost exclusively on milkweeds (Asclepiadaceae), from which they accumulate toxins, which make the larvae and adult inedible by most predators. The orange and black coloration serves as a warning.

BAHAMIAN SWALLOWTAIL *Papilio andraemon*

KEY FEATURES To 10 cm (4 in.). A large butterfly, distinguished by broad yellow bands the length of its wings and by its long tail tips.

STATUS AND RANGE Native to the Bahamas, Cuba, Cayman Islands, and Jamaica, it occurs in open areas and scrubland with flowers, primarily in lowlands. Larvae favor citrus, and in Jamaica they damage orange seedlings. The local name Orange Dog derives from this propensity. Not recorded in Jamaica until the 1940s, the species is believed to have arrived as a result of natural causes such as hurricanes. Four subspecies have been described, suggesting there is very little movement among islands.

COMMON LAND HERMIT CRAB *Coenobita clypeatus*

KEY FEATURES To 8 cm (3 in.). This crab inhabits empty snail shells and is further distinguished by its terrestrial habits and its large purple claw, used to block the shell entrance when disturbed. Most other hermit crabs in the region are primarily aquatic.

STATUS AND RANGE This is the common terrestrial hermit crab of the Caribbean, ranging to elevations of over 600 m (2,000 ft.). It is a scavenger on a wide range of decaying plant and animal matter, even including horse and cow dung. Anglers reputedly catch them for bait using coffee grounds. They migrate annually to the sea at night in such massive numbers that some towns close streets to motorized traffic to protect the crabs. Other hermit crab species occur commonly in the intertidal zone and in tide pools. As they grow, hermit crabs have to find larger shells in which to hide, sometimes a rare commodity. The crab holds onto the shell by grasping it with its specially adapted abdomen. There are numerous species of hermit crabs in many genera.

GREAT LAND CRAB *Cardisoma guanhumi*

KEY FEATURES To 35 cm (14 in.). Note its terrestrial habit, very large size, and brown, gray, or bluish coloration. In males one claw is extremely large.

STATUS AND RANGE This crab occurs widely in coastal lowlands of the Caribbean, where soft soils are available in which to dig a burrow. The large entrance holes, up to 13 cm (5 in.) wide, are a tell-tale sign of the crab's presence. It emerges at night, except when molting. The species may range as far as 8 km (5 mi.) inland.

Omnivorous, the species feeds on leaves, fruits, insects, and carrion. Coastal development, as well as the high popularity of this crab for food, has resulted in its decline in many areas. It also is known as the Blue Land Crab.

FIDDLER CRAB *Uca* spp.

KEY FEATURES To 5 cm (2 in.). There are many similar species, but all are recognized as fiddler crabs by the single huge claw of the male. Fiddler crabs only move sideways.

STATUS AND RANGE Very common in the intertidal zone, where sediments are soft, enabling these crabs to burrow. This includes sand and mudflats, mangroves, and lagoons. The burrow serves many purposes, including protection from predators, safety during molting, and for mating. The mating display occurs outside the burrow, the male rhythmically waving his large claw to attract a female. Should a claw or leg be lost, it is regenerated. Decaying animal and plant material form its primary diet. The name derives from the male, which, while feeding with his small claw, appears to be playing a fiddle, which is his large claw. The large claw only serves for mating displays. Fiddler crabs serve as a food base for many species of birds, including rails and herons.

ATLANTIC GHOST CRAB *Ocypode quadrata*

KEY FEATURES Shell to 8 cm (3 in.). The color of white sand, this crab is well camouflaged. Also note the conspicuous black eyes on lengthy stalks, which enable it to see in every direction.

STATUS AND RANGE The common crab of sandy beaches, where it lives in a burrow up to 1.2 m (4 ft.) in depth. It is active primarily at night, when it feeds on a wide range of plants and animals, including clams, other crabs, decaying matter, and even

hatchling marine turtles. This crab scurries rapidly, up to 16 km (10 mi.) per hour. The name derives from the Ghost Crab's pale coloration and ability to disappear in a flash.

TERMITES *Nasutitermes* spp.

KEY FEATURES Termites are readily located by the large, spherical, dark brown nests they build off the ground, often in the forks of tree branches. Individuals are divided among three castes: workers, soldiers, and reproductives. The first two are readily seen, both being yellowish, the soldiers distinguished by a dark, bulbous head with a pointed snout.

STATUS AND RANGE Termites are common and widespread in the Caribbean, their colonial nests being conspicuous at various heights in trees. From the nests, covered trails are built to feeding sites. These tunnels enable the termites, which are darkness-loving animals, to travel about during the day. Breaking of the tunnels will draw numerous termites to the damaged site. Soldiers can squirt either a sticky or noxious compound. This caste cannot ingest wood and so is fed by the workers. Termites play a major role in breaking down wood, thus recycling nutrients into tropical soils. Winged reproductives leave the nest one night per year to form new colonies.

CUBAN PAINTED TREE SNAILS *Polymita* spp.

Cuba's painted tree snails, the most notable being *Polymita picta*, are among the most handsomely colored land snails on the planet. No other land snail can match them. All white, black, yellow, brown, or orange individuals can be found in the same area, and even the same tree. The majority possess different-colored stripes—narrow or broad, single or multiple. Such an explosion of pigment and design in nontoxic animals is unusual. Most often such coloration serves to warn predators that its bearer is inedible. It is believed that in this

case such diversity eliminates the possibility for predators to "fix" on a definite search image. These snails are in fact very difficult to single out from among yellowing leaves, small red fruits, and blackening seeds, all mottled with sunlight.

Painted tree snails may be found on tree trunks, branches, or the surfaces of leaves. They come to the ground only to lay their eggs. Feeding occurs on the thin layer of blackish fungus and algae that grows on the surface of older leaves. Snails feed only at night or when it is raining. Removal of the fungus serves to clean the leaves and benefits the plant by providing better access to sunlight.

Snail populations have dwindled due to indiscriminate collecting, especially near cities, villages, and in coffee plantations. They can still be found, though, in isolated forests, particularly on the higher mountains.

MARINE LIFE

CONSERVING THE MARINE ENVIRONMENT OF THE CARIBBEAN AND THE WORLD: A GLOBAL IMPERATIVE

BY THE HONORABLE FREUNDEL STUART, Q.C., M.P., PRIME MINISTER OF BARBADOS

The maritime area of Barbados is over 431 times its landmass. Therefore, sustainability as a small island development state cannot be addressed without a special and priority focus on the marine environment or the "blue economy." The survival of the Earth ocean system is crucial.

I share the emerging consensus among the international scientific community that through the combined effect of anthropogenic stressors we are at high risk of causing Earth's next significant extinction event in the oceans.

In spite of this prognosis and the alarming reality of an ever narrowing window of opportunity for corrective action, scientists remain optimistic that these impacts and challenges can be mitigated through concerted and urgent measures, supported by an improved understanding and recognition of the role of oceans and coasts. Now is the moment for action!

Existing oceans-related sustainable development commitments capture well what needs to be done. However, the decline in marine ecosystems continues and this is largely due to States, industries, communities, and livelihoods being structured around unsustainable approaches to the management and use of marine resources. In most instances this is a direct result of issues such as a lack of finance, capacity, and information, as well as a perceived conflict between environmental protection and economic development imperatives.

I champion the perspective that it is essential that any new vision for global sustainability must encompass "the blue economy"—including the conservation and sustainable management of marine and ocean resources. Such a vision would enable developing countries to enjoy a greater share of the benefits derived from those resources.

Within the Caribbean we have recognized that an integrated management approach that involves all relevant stakeholders provides us with the best option for protecting the Caribbean Sea. Barbados has led the regional effort in the Association of Caribbean States to create the Caribbean Sea Commission. The Commission represents an oceans governance framework to promote cooperation towards the effective management of the Caribbean Sea. It is important that we share our experiences and mobilize support for regional initiatives which serve as examples of sustainable development in practice.

Managing oceans on a regional, integrated, long-term and ecosystem scale, as we have attempted to do in the Caribbean, provides all users with a stake in sustainable management of marine resources—from the small scale fisher to the owner of a major hotel. National and regional approaches can only succeed, however, if they are supported by enabling actions and measures at the international level.

First, oceans issues must be placed high on the global agenda. Given the threat posed to life as we know it, leaders from all regions must be more engaged on this issue and we must bring civil society stakeholders, including businesses and non-governmental organizations, into that dialogue.

Second, there are actions that can be taken now that will have a significant positive impact. There is broad international consensus on a range of short-term, high impact actions such as:

- carefully reviewing the capacity of global fishing fleets;
- phasing out harmful fishing subsidies;
- eliminating illegal, unregistered and unreported fishing;
- expanding the global network of marine protected areas to conserve biodiversity.

Third, we must ensure greater predictability in financing for oceans related activities through establishing a new and well-resourced international fund for promoting conservation and management of the marine environment.

We will have little hope of saving our oceans and islands if greenhouse emissions continue to rise.

Time is not on our side. The global nature, complexity, and gravity of the challenges facing the oceans require an immense, comprehensive, and urgent global effort. I end, however, on an optimistic note and affirm that it is well within our capacity to undertake and succeed in this endeavor.

FAIRY BASSLET

BLUEHEAD WRASSE

SHORT-FINNED PILOT WHALE *Globicephala macrorhynchus*

KEY FEATURES To 6 m (20 ft.). A mid-size black whale with a light patch on the belly between the flippers and a bulbous, rounded head. It has a fairly large, broad dorsal fin.

STATUS AND RANGE Occurs throughout the Caribbean in offshore and coastal waters, although not usually very close to shore. It is a sociable whale, usually seen in groups of ten to thirty young animals, usually remaining in the pod of their mother. The Pilot Whale is among the most intelligent and affable of whales. It feeds primarily on squid, which it will chase at great speeds. Feeding dives may last over ten minutes. In some parts of the world it continues to be hunted for food. This whale is well known for large groups periodically becoming stranded on beaches. The cause of this remains a mystery.

HUMPBACK WHALE *Megaptera novaeangliae*

KEY FEATURES To 16 m (52 ft.). A huge whale with very long whitish flippers and varying amounts of white on the underside of the tail.

STATUS AND RANGE Of regular occurrence in coastal and offshore waters throughout most of the Caribbean from December to March. During this period females do not feed, living off fat reserves. At this time they give birth to a single calf. Reproduction takes place every two to three years. In March they migrate north to the coasts of New England and eastern Canada. Humpbacks are often seen in small, loose groups of two to eight whales. They sometimes breach (jump entirely out of the water) or spy hop (push their head out of the water). Lacking teeth, the humpback's mouth is lined with baleen plates, which serve as a sieve to strain small fish and krill from the water. Formerly endangered due to overhunting, this whale has recovered dramatically and is now a favorite of whale-watching tours.

SHORT-FINNED PILOT WHALE

HUMPBACK WHALE

BOTTLENOSE DOLPHIN *Tursiops truncatus*

KEY FEATURES 2–3.5 m (6.5–11.5 ft.). A large marine mammal with a moderate-size dorsal fin. The coloration is gray or slate blue, slightly darker above than below, with darker flippers and flukes. Its snout is short and the curved line of the mouth resembles a smile. The lower jaw is slightly longer than the upper.

STATUS AND RANGE Fairly common throughout the Caribbean, in coastal bays and lagoons as well as offshore areas. It is not uncommon to see these dolphins ride the bow waves of vessels or leap out of the water. Typically they occur in pods of ten to thirty individuals. Fish are their primary food, and they often work as a team to capture prey. Dolphins are highly intelligent, and there are many stories of their interactions with and assistance of humans.

WEST INDIAN MANATEE *Trichechus manatus*

KEY FEATURES To 4.5 m (15 ft.). A very large, nearly hairless, gray aquatic mammal with a rounded body and paddlelike front limbs and tail. It has a small head, squared snout, and tiny eyes.

STATUS AND RANGE Formerly throughout Caribbean waters, it is now rare or absent from most of the region. The manatee inhabits shallow coastal waters, including lagoons, estuaries, mangrove channels, and river mouths. Its movements are sluggish, the head popping above the water surface from time to time. Considered endangered, the manatee was formerly hunted extensively for food, a major reason for its decline. Presently habitat degradation and destruction, along with injuries from boat propellers, are serious threats.

BOTTLENOSE DOLPHIN

WEST INDIAN MANATEE

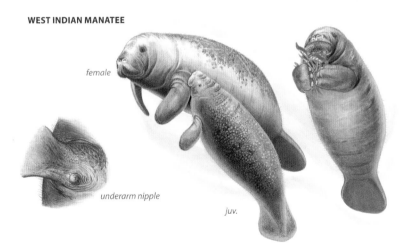

female

underarm nipple

juv.

The Caribbean's marine turtles, particularly the Green and Hawksbill, are widespread and well known to local coastal residents throughout the region. Formerly their eggs were an important food resource, as was their meat. In the case of the Hawksbill, its shell too was prized, for crafting into combs, necklaces, and other ornaments. Overharvesting, the development and destruction of beaches, reefs, and marine sea grass beds, as well as folklore suggesting marine turtle eggs are an aphrodisiac, have greatly diminished marine turtle numbers to the point where all the species of the region are either threatened or endangered. Marine turtles play an important role in reef and sea grass ecology, as indicators of marine ecosystem health, and as an important attraction for tourists. Their sustained management should be an important priority of every Caribbean nation.

HAWKSBILL TURTLE *Eretmochelys imbricata*

KEY FEATURES Shell to 90 cm (35 in.). Medium size for a marine turtle, it has a shield-shaped upper shell with a keel down the center. Note the hooked "beak," which gives the species its name.

STATUS AND RANGE Throughout the Caribbean it occurs in clear, shallow coastal waters near rocks and coral reefs, and also in shallow bays, estuaries, and lagoons. As with all marine turtles, mating takes place at sea, but females dig holes on the beach in which they deposit their eggs. The species is endangered.

GREEN TURTLE *Chelonia mydas*

KEY FEATURES Shell to 1.5 m (5 ft.). A large marine turtle whose upper shell is heart shaped, black, gray, greenish, or brown, often with bold spots or streaks. The undershell is yellowish white.

STATUS AND RANGE Throughout the Caribbean it occurs in coastal waters, where it feeds on Turtle Grass. The common name refers to its greenish body fat. Adulthood may not be reached until the age of thirty. This turtle is considered endangered due to overharvesting of adults and eggs for food. The species migrates immense distances, sometimes over thousands of kilometers, but most return to nest on the beach where they were hatched.

LEATHERBACK TURTLE *Dermochelys coriacea*

KEY FEATURES Shell to 2.4 m (8 ft.); to a weight of 550+ kg (1,200+ lb.). Largest of the world's marine turtles, its back is black or brown, often white-splattered, and covered with smooth, leathery skin (unlike hardened plates of other marine turtles). Seven ridges along the back run from front to rear.

STATUS AND RANGE An open-ocean turtle that occurs throughout the Caribbean but occasionally feeds in shallow waters of bays and estuaries. Major breeding sites include Hispaniola, Puerto Rico, and St. Croix (Virgin Islands). Like all other marine turtles, females only come to shore to lay eggs. Males never come ashore. The turtles' throats are coated with spines to grasp their primarily prey— jellyfish. The species is endangered primarily due to overharvesting of its eggs.

HAWKSBILL TURTLE

GREEN TURTLE

LEATHERBACK TURTLE

REEF BUTTERFLYFISH *Chaetodon sedentarius*

KEY FEATURES To 10 cm (4 in.). Note pale yellow on the upper body and tail, plus the vertical black bar through the eye and a second along the rear of the body.

STATUS AND RANGE Generally common on reefs throughout the Caribbean, where it swims about openly among the corals. It is not wary unless approached. Generally solitary or in pairs, the species appears to mate for life. The slender snout serves to probe for coral polyps, marine worms, and other invertebrates. The name *butterflyfish* derives from the bright coloration of this group and their habit of flitting about on the reef.

SPOTFIN BUTTERFLYFISH *Chaetodon ocellatus*

KEY FEATURES To 15 cm (6 in.). Note the circular silver body fringed with yellow and the single vertical black bar through the eye. Often there is a black spot on the rear of the dorsal fin.

STATUS AND RANGE Common on shallow reefs throughout the Caribbean. The species swims openly among corals, where it is conspicuous. It is not wary unless approached and generally is solitary or in pairs. The eye bar on most butterflyfish serves as camouflage to confuse predators as to which end is the front. This species feeds on anemones, tube worms, and other invertebrates. The slender snout and protractible mouth are ideal for probing in crevices for prey. It is a popular aquarium fish.

BANDED BUTTERFLYFISH *Chaetodon striatus*

KEY FEATURES To 12.5 cm (5 in.). The silver coloration with broad, vertical black bars, accompanied by the pointed snout, is diagnostic. Juvenile is similar, but with a large "eye spot" at the rear of the dorsal fin.

STATUS AND RANGE Common on shallow reefs throughout the Caribbean, where it swims openly among the corals. It is not wary unless approached and generally is solitary or in pairs. Butterflyfish tend to have small home ranges. At night they hide in crevices and become inactive. In some species their nocturnal coloration turns paler. It is a popular aquarium fish.

QUEEN ANGELFISH *Holacanthus ciliaris*

KEY FEATURES To 35 cm (14 in.). One
of the most majestic reef fish; note
the distinctive body shape, plus
the blue and yellow patterning
and entirely yellow tail. It has a
dark-blue crown spot circled
with paler blue. Juvenile
is identified by a series of
curved, vertical blue bars along
the length of the body.

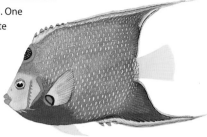

STATUS AND RANGE Fairly common on reefs
throughout the Caribbean, where it swims about deliberately. It is generally
solitary and is rather wary and not easily approached. The species feeds almost
exclusively on sponges. Dominant males have female harems. If the male is lost, a
female changes sex and becomes a dominant male.

FRENCH ANGELFISH *Pomacanthus paru*

KEY FEATURES To 35 cm (14 in.). Distinguished by its form,
black coloration, and yellow-edged body scales.
Juvenile is black with vertical yellow bars, and its
tail has a broad, black patch edged with yellow.
The species swims with a fluttering motion.

STATUS AND RANGE Common on reefs
and among sea fans throughout the
Caribbean. It generally is solitary or in
pairs and is not wary. This fish feeds almost
exclusively on sponges. It is believed to form
permanent pair bonds.

GRAY ANGELFISH *Pomacanthus arcuatus*

KEY FEATURES To 45 cm (18 in.). Note the body shape and overall gray
coloration. Juvenile is black with vertical yellow bars, and its tail has a narrow,
black bar.

STATUS AND RANGE Common on reefs in the
Bahamas and Greater Antilles, less common
farther south. It generally is solitary or in pairs
and is not wary. The conspicuous black-
and-yellow coloration of the juvenile of
this and the French Angelfish advertise
them as cleaners that glean parasites
from other fish. It feeds primarily on
sponges but also soft corals and to a
lesser extent other invertebrates.

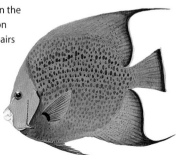

239

ROCK BEAUTY *Holacanthus tricolor*

KEY FEATURES To 20 cm (8 in.). Identified by its distinctively yellow-black-yellow body pattern. Juvenile is almost entirely yellow, with a dark, circular "eye spot," ringed with blue, beneath the dorsal fin.

STATUS AND RANGE Fairly common on reefs throughout the Caribbean, where it swims in the open but is somewhat wary. This fish is generally solitary. Large males have harems of two to four smaller females. It appears that females upon reaching a certain size undergo a sexual transformation and become males.

GREAT BARRACUDA *Sphyraena barracuda*

KEY FEATURES To 1.5 m (5 ft.). Note its large size, slender body, and protruding lower jaw with conspicuous teeth.

STATUS AND RANGE Fairly common near reefs and most shallow water habitats throughout the Caribbean. Typically it is solitary or in small groups. Inquisitive, it is thus disconcerting to divers. Barracuda are a popular game fish. Small ones serve as a food fish.

CAUTION Divers should be careful not to wear items that might sparkle in the presence of barracudas, as these could appear as prey and thus prompt an attack. Full-grown Great Barracuda are considered by many to be potentially poisonous when eaten.

BERMUDA SEA CHUB *Kyphosus saltatrix*

KEY FEATURES To 0.6 m (2 ft.). Note its shape and the pale yellow stripes running the length of its body.

STATUS AND RANGE Fairly common over reefs and rocky areas throughout the Caribbean, primarily in shallow waters but sometimes to depths. It also occurs on sandy flats. The species usually schools and feeds primarily on vegetation. It is a popular food fish in some locales.

OCEAN SURGEONFISH *Acanthurus bahianus*

KEY FEATURES To 30 cm (12 in.). Note its shape and nearly uniform coloration, which it can change from gray to blue or brown. The tail is often pale at the base, and the tail tips taper to points. It has a spine at the tail base.

STATUS AND RANGE Common and conspicuous on shallow reefs throughout the Caribbean. It is not wary and often forms schools. The diet is primarily plant matter, which is grazed on sandy bottoms and includes sea grass beds. Sometimes large spawning aggregations are formed. The name of this and the Doctorfish derive from the presence of the spine at the tail base, reminiscent of a scalpel.

DOCTORFISH *Acanthurus chirurgus*

KEY FEATURES 30 cm (12 in.). Nearly uniform in color, it can change coloration from gray to blue or brown. It is distinguished from the Ocean Surgeonfish by vertical bars the length of its body and its less finely tipped tail. The tail has a spine at its base.

STATUS AND RANGE Common and conspicuous on shallow reefs and sea grass beds throughout the Caribbean. It is solitary, in pairs, or in small schools and is not wary. The species feeds primarily on plant matter, filamentous algae, and other organisms it scrapes from hard surfaces or extracts from bottom sediments. The young sometimes form cleaning stations with other fish.

BLUE TANG *Acanthurus coeruleus*

KEY FEATURES To 25 cm (10 in.). The form and entirely blue coloration distinguish it. This fish can change shades. Subadult is blue with a yellow tail; juvenile, entirely yellow. There is a spine at the base of the tail.

STATUS AND RANGE One of the most common and conspicuous fish of shallow reefs in the Caribbean. It often occurs in schools and is not wary. This tang feeds exclusively on algae. Schools of tang will often overwhelm the territories of damselfish to feed on their algae gardens. Blue Tang sometimes form large spawning aggregations.

intermediate juv.

juv.

BAR JACK *Caranx ruber*

KEY FEATURES To 35 cm (14 in.). Note the blue and black stripes running from beneath the dorsal fin to the tip of the lower tail fin. Body color can vary. Juvenile has vertical black bars.

STATUS AND RANGE Common in open water near reefs and over sand flats throughout the Caribbean. It swims rapidly, typically in schools, and is not wary. Taken commercially for food, it is also a sport fish. The species feeds primarily on small fish taken in open water or off the bottom. Sometimes it follows sting rays, which scare up prey.

HORSE-EYE JACK *Caranx latus*

KEY FEATURES To 0.6 m (2 ft.). Note its shape and silver body, with yellow tail and black-tipped dorsal fin.

STATUS AND RANGE Generally common in the Caribbean, passing over reefs and occurring widely in other habitats including, at times, freshwater. It occurs in schools and is moderately wary. This jack feeds primarily on small fish. It is sought as a game fish.

PORKFISH *Anisotremus virginicus*

KEY FEATURES To 25 cm (10 in.). Distinguished by two broad, black facial bars, which converge toward the top of the head. Juvenile is primarily yellow, with two horizontal body stripes and a black tail spot.

STATUS AND RANGE Fairly common in the Caribbean, but rather rare in the Bahamas. Generally it is seen drifting inactively in schools over reefs, sea grass, or rocky bottoms. The species is active at night, at which time it feeds on a diversity of bottom-dwelling invertebrates. Juveniles pick parasites off other fish.

juv.

FRENCH GRUNT *Haemulon flavolineatum*

KEY FEATURES To 25 cm (10 in.). Observe the stripes on the flanks, which run obliquely across the body. The yellow stripes are paired with blue, silver, or white stripes.

STATUS AND RANGE The most abundant grunt in the Caribbean, it is typical of shallow reefs. Generally inactive during the day, this grunt occurs in schools of varying size. It is moderately wary, a popular food fish, and feeds on a wide range of invertebrates.

WHITE GRUNT *Haemulon plumierii*

KEY FEATURES To 35 cm (14 in.). The
horizontal stripes, confined to the head, are
generally yellow and blue in color.
STATUS AND RANGE Common on shallow reefs
in inactive schools during the day throughout the Caribbean. Active at night,
schools move away from the reef to sand flats or grass beds to feed on bottom-
dwelling organisms, including fish and a variety of invertebrates. The species is
moderately wary. Juveniles frequently seek protection among the spines of sea
urchins. This is a popular food fish.

BLUE-STRIPED GRUNT *Haemulon sciurus*

KEY FEATURES To 35 cm (14 in.). Note the blue stripes the length of the body
over a yellow background. The tail and dorsal fin are dark.
STATUS AND RANGE Common on shallow reefs throughout the Caribbean,
often near drop-offs, occurring in inactive schools
during the day. It also occurs in sea grass beds
and mangroves, where it feeds primarily on
invertebrates. The name *grunt* derives
from the sound this group of fish makes
when caught, a sound they make rubbing
their teeth— located in their throats—together.

MARGATE *Haemulon album*

KEY FEATURES To 0.6 m (2 ft.). Note the shape and gray
coloration, with the dark tail and dorsal fin. This is the
largest of the grunts.
STATUS AND RANGE Fairly common and
widespread in the Caribbean over sand
flats and sea grass beds, but also coral
rubble, rocky areas, and among sea fans.
It usually is solitary or in small groups and feeds on fish
and crustaceans. A popular food fish, the name derives from an English seaport.

SPANISH GRUNT *Haemulon macrostomum*

KEY FEATURES To 38 cm (15 in.). Note the yellow stripe below the dorsal fin,
yellow "saddle" before the tail, and black stripes on the
upper body.
STATUS AND RANGE Fairly common
throughout the Caribbean, where it often
drifts in open areas over reefs. A wary
species, it occurs alone, in small groups,
or in dense schools. The diet is primarily sea
urchins and crustaceans. Like other grunts, it is a popular
food fish. Young occur in sea grass beds and feed on zooplankton.

ATLANTIC SPADEFISH *Chaetodipterus faber*

KEY FEATURES 0.75 m (2.5 ft.). Observe the distinctive shape and black vertical bars.
STATUS AND RANGE Generally common, especially in the western Caribbean. It frequents shallow, open water, both marine and brackish. Inquisitive, the species generally occurs in small schools, though sometimes in large ones. It feeds primarily on a wide range of bottom-dwelling invertebrates, particularly sponges. The name derives from its shape, similar to the spade on a playing card. A female may release up to a million eggs per season.

MUTTON SNAPPER *Lutjanus analis*

KEY FEATURES To 0.6 m (2 ft.). The coloration and barring are variable. Note the black spot on the upper back and the pointed anal fin.
STATUS AND RANGE Fairly common throughout the Caribbean over sandy bottoms and around reefs, mangrove lagoons, rock rubble, and sea grass flats. This snapper is generally solitary and inquisitive. The diet includes various invertebrates and other fish. It is popular both as a game fish and for food.

var.

YELLOWTAIL SNAPPER *Ocyurus chrysurus*

KEY FEATURES To 0.6 m (2 ft.). Note the pronounced yellow stripe down the middle of the body and the yellow tail. Yellow spots on the upper body are often faint.
STATUS AND RANGE Common and widespread in the Caribbean about reefs, whereas young frequent sea grass beds. The species usually occurs in schools and is often inquisitive. It is a popular sport fish and is commercially harvested as a food fish. Primarily a nocturnal feeder, it eats crabs, shrimp, and small fish, which it takes from the bottom and the water column. Spawning is in schools, and females average well over one million eggs per season.

SCHOOLMASTER *Lutjanus apodus*

KEY FEATURES To 0.6 m (2 ft.). This snapper is distinguished by its entirely yellow fins.

STATUS AND RANGE Common throughout the Caribbean in schools generally over reefs near the shelter of corals or gorgonians. Juveniles range primarily over sea grass beds but also sandy bottoms around reefs, in mangrove channels, lagoons, and even brackish water. Individuals disperse at night to feed on invertebrates and small fish. This is a popular game and food fish. The species is wary.

DUSKY DAMSELFISH *Stegastes adustus*

KEY FEATURES To 13 cm (5 in.). Olive brown overall, with body scales edged with dark vertical lines. Juvenile is orange from the forehead to the dorsal fin, with a large black spot near the rear of that fin.
STATUS AND RANGE Common throughout the Caribbean in both rocky and sandy areas, including tide pools. It occurs primarily in shallow waters, but also to substantial depths. The species is generally solitary. It aggressively defends a territory containing an "algae garden," which it nurtures and where it forages. Damselfish with such gardens will defend them against much larger fish.

juv.

THREESPOT DAMSELFISH *Stegastes planifrons*

KEY FEATURES To 10 cm (4 in.). The coloration is variable, becoming darker with age. Note the black spots at the base of the tail and pectoral fins. It has a yellow mark above the eye. Juvenile is yellow, with black spots on the dorsal fin and base of the tail.
STATUS AND RANGE Very common throughout the Caribbean, from reef shallows to substantial depths, particularly among the branches of Staghorn Coral. Generally solitary, each individual aggressively defends a territory that includes an "algae garden," algae being its primary food. Territories of this and other algae-feeding damselfish include a central cavity that serves for shelter during the night and as a nest site.

juv.

COCOA DAMSELFISH *Stegastes variabilis*

KEY FEATURES To 10 cm (4 in.). Dull, dark brown overall, with a dark spot at the base of the dorsal fin. Juvenile is yellow with extensive blue upper parts; it has a black spot on the dorsal fin and at the tail base.
STATUS AND RANGE Fairly common throughout the Caribbean in reef shallows. Generally solitary, it is not wary. It defends a large territory but weakly, and it feeds primarily on algae but also on sponges, sea squirts and anemones. The male makes the nest and broods the eggs.

juv.

BEAUGREGORY *Stegastes leucostictus*

KEY FEATURES To 9 cm (3.5 in.). Dull, dark brown with yellowish highlights in the tail and on the upper back. Juvenile is yellow with extensive blue upper parts; it has a black spot on the dorsal fin but none at the tail base.

STATUS AND RANGE Very common throughout the Caribbean in shallow waters of reefs, coral rubble, underwater grass beds, mangrove channels, and tide pools. One of the first fish seen upon donning a mask and snorkel, it is not wary. The diet includes a wide array of invertebrates, eggs, small fish, and algae. Some males weakly defend large territories, which include various cavities in which to hide. The male makes the nest and tends the eggs, which can number from 4,000 to 25,000 per brood.

juv.

BICOLOR DAMSELFISH *Stegastes partitus*

KEY FEATURES To 9 cm (3.5 in.). Note the two-tone appearance, the front half of the body dark and rear half primarily white. Coloration is quite variable.

STATUS AND RANGE Common and widespread in the Caribbean among the shallows of reefs and beds of sea grass. Not wary, it is highly solitary and defends its territory aggressively, but it never strays far from cover. The species feeds primarily on plankton, including larvae, copepods and sea squirts.

YELLOWTAIL DAMSELFISH *Microspathodon chrysurus*

KEY FEATURES To 18 cm (7 in.). Note the dark body and yellow tail. Juvenile: Dramatic sky blue spots speckle the body, and the tail is white.

STATUS AND RANGE Common and widespread in the Caribbean among shallow reefs where large females are often associated with Elkhorn Coral and males with rubble of the same coral in deeper waters. It is generally solitary and not wary. Juveniles sometimes clean parasites off other fish. The primary food is algae, but it also grazes on coral polyps. The male prepares the nest and later guards the eggs. This is a popular aquarium fish.

juv.

SERGEANT MAJOR *Abudefduf saxatilis*

KEY FEATURES To 15 cm (6 in.). Distinguished by black vertical bars and a yellow wash on the upper body.
STATUS AND RANGE Very common throughout the Caribbean in all shallow water habitats, including reefs, rocky areas, sea grass flats, tide pools, and around docks. Generally in loose schools, it is quite tame. The diet includes a wide array of items including small fish, invertebrates, zooplankton, and plants. The name derives from the fish's similarity to the military insignia. When nesting, males turn grayish blue and very territorial. As many as four females may contribute up to 20,000 eggs to a single nest, which the male then broods.

BLUE CHROMIS *Chromis cyanea*

KEY FEATURES To 10 cm (4 in.). Blue overall, with a black stripe along the back and outer edges of the tail. The tail is deeply forked.
STATUS AND RANGE Common and widespread in the Caribbean above reefs and along outer slopes, but never far from protective cover. Not wary, it often occurs in loose schools of varying size. The diet consists of plankton floating over the reef. From the plankton, algae are its principal food, but eggs, larval fish, and invertebrates are also taken. The male makes a scant nest and tends the eggs.

BROWN CHROMIS *Chromis multilineata*

KEY FEATURES To 15 cm (6 in.). Note the yellow tips on the dorsal and tail fins, as well as the black spot at the base of the pectoral fin.
STATUS AND RANGE Common and widespread in the Caribbean above reefs and along outer slopes. Often in loose schools, it will form aggregations in the hundreds where currents are rich in food. Like the Blue Chromis, it is not wary and feeds on plankton, but it strays farther from the protection of the reef to do so. The species sometimes forms very large spawning aggregations.

TOBACCOFISH *Serranus tabacarius*

KEY FEATURES To 15 cm (6 in.). Variable in coloration but typically distinguished by a broad, orangish band the length of the body, as well as by white upper parts with large black markings.
STATUS AND RANGE Generally common and widespread in the Caribbean on reefs, rocky areas, and coral rubble, where it occurs from shallow waters down to over 70 m (200 ft.).
This fish is typically seen resting on the bottom or swimming just above it. The species is solitary or in occurs in small aggregations, is fairly curious, and feeds on fish and crustaceans.

BARRED HAMLET *Hypoplectrus puella*

KEY FEATURES To 11 cm (4.5 in.). The large dark patch on the center of body, edged with white, is distinctive.
STATUS AND RANGE Common and widespread in the Caribbean on shallow reefs, where found near the bottom close to cover. The species is generally inactive, solitary, and not wary. It feeds primarily on crabs and shrimp, though infrequently on fish.

Adults possess both male and female organs. Hamlet taxonomy is confused, and it may be that all hamlets actually belong to a single species. Their genetic material thus far appears identical.

BLACK HAMLET *Hypoplectrus nigricans*

KEY FEATURES To 13 cm (5 in.). Entirely dark; note the long pelvic fins.
STATUS AND RANGE Fairly common and widespread in the Caribbean on shallow reefs. The species is relatively inactive, solitary, and not wary. It feeds on crustaceans and fish. Adults possess both male and female organs and undergo role reversals during the course of mating. This hamlet mimics the Dusky Damselfish in shape and coloration. Mimicry of this common damselfish, which feeds on algae and thus is not a threat to other fish, enables the Black Hamlet to approach its prey more readily.

NASSAU GROUPER *Epinephelus striatus*

KEY FEATURES To 1 m (3 ft.). Note the banding pattern and black saddle at the tail base. It can change colors dramatically.
STATUS AND RANGE Common throughout the Caribbean on reefs, where it is typically found inactive near the bottom and close to cover. Generally it is solitary and moderately territorial. Not wary, it is easily tamed to eat from one's hand. The diet includes fish and crustaceans. Nassau Groupers undertake migrations of sometimes well over 160 km (100 mi) to spawning sites where impressive numbers, formerly of as many as one hundred thousand individuals, aggregate. Being a very popular food fish, the species has been overharvested to the point where numbers have dramatically declined and some former areas of commercial fishing no longer exist. Harvesting of breeding aggregations is the most likely reason for this decline. The species is a frequent visitor to cleaning stations.

TIGER GROUPER *Mycteroperca tigris*

KEY FEATURES To 1 m (3 ft.). It has a
distinctive barred pattern.
The coloration is widely
variable, but it frequently
displays red tones at
cleaning stations. Juvenile
is yellow, with a central band down
the body.

STATUS AND RANGE Common and widespread in the Caribbean on reefs and
rocky areas. It frequents the bottom, is generally solitary and moderately wary.
The species feeds exclusively on fish. It sometimes forms spawning aggregations
of hundreds, a period during which it is frequently fished commercially for food.

BLACK GROUPER *Mycteroperca bonaci*

KEY FEATURES To 1.2 m (4 ft.). A large
fish known to grow to over 100 kg
(220 lbs), it is extremely
variable in color. Best
distinguished by the
broad, dark band on
the end of the tail and the
large, dark body markings that are
aligned in rows.

STATUS AND RANGE Fairly common and widespread in the Caribbean on reefs
and rocky areas at medium and deep depths, where it usually hovers close to
the bottom but sometimes swims well above the reef. It is solitary and wary. The
diet is small fish, squid, and crabs. A popular recreational and food fish, it is of
important commercial value. Some individuals change sex from female to male.
Breeding occurs in spawning aggregations.

GRAYSBY *Cephalopholis cruentata*

KEY FEATURES To 25 cm (10 in.). Note the pale or dark spots, three to five
in number, at the base of the dorsal fin. The species can change coloration
dramatically. The tail is more rounded than similar-
appearing species.

STATUS AND RANGE Common and
widespread on reefs in the Caribbean.
It is typically found resting on the
bottom, under ledges or near crevices
in which to hide. Generally solitary, it is not wary and is
easy to tame. Territories are shared by a male and his harem of several females. A
nocturnal predator on small fish, it feeds heavily on Brown Chromis. The Graysby
is a popular food fish. Juveniles are all females and transform to males when
about 20 cm (8 in.) in length.

RED HIND *Epinephelus guttatus*

KEY FEATURES To 0.6 m (2 ft.). The body is spotted with red, and the rear body fins are edged with dark bands.

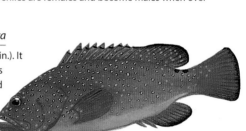

STATUS AND RANGE Generally fairly common and widespread in the Caribbean on reefs from shallows to substantial depths. It also occurs in rocky areas. The species typically perches or drifts motionless on the bottom, waiting for unwary prey to swim by, at which point it lunges. Not wary, it feeds on fish and crustaceans. This is a popular food fish of commercial importance. Overfishing of spawning aggregations has reduced its numbers in some areas. All juveniles are females and become males when over 25 cm (10 in.) in length.

CONEY *Cephalopholis fulva*

KEY FEATURES To 40 cm (16 in.). It possesses various color phases varying from red to yellow and is sometimes two-toned, but all display blue spots on the head, two black dots on the upper base of the tail, and black dots on the lower lip.

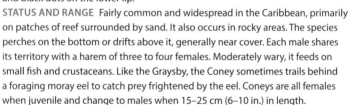

STATUS AND RANGE Fairly common and widespread in the Caribbean, primarily on patches of reef surrounded by sand. It also occurs in rocky areas. The species perches on the bottom or drifts above it, generally near cover. Each male shares its territory with a harem of three to four females. Moderately wary, it feeds on small fish and crustaceans. Like the Graysby, the Coney sometimes trails behind a foraging moray eel to catch prey frightened by the eel. Coneys are all females when juvenile and change to males when 15–25 cm (6–10 in.) in length.

FAIRY BASSLET *Gramma loreto*

KEY FEATURES To 8 cm (3 in.). The front of the body is purple and the rear is yellow.

STATUS AND RANGE A fairly common and widespread fish in the Caribbean over corals, which have nooks and crannies in which to hide, especially where there are tall corals or reef walls. It occurs at depths from 1–55 m (3–180 ft.). Also known as the Royal Gramma, it is territorial and feeds on floating plankton. The species is wary and retires into a crevice when approached. It is highly sought after for the aquarium trade.

GREATER SOAPFISH *Rypticus saponaceus*

KEY FEATURES To 30 cm (1 ft.).
Note its distinctive body shape,
gradually sloping forehead, mottled
coloration, and protruding lower jaw.
STATUS AND RANGE Moderately common
and widespread in the Caribbean, it hangs out inactively on
reef bottoms from shallow water to depths of 55 m (180 ft.). It is more active at
night, when it feeds on other fish. When disturbed, soapfish produce toxic mucus
that appears like soapsuds, a repellent against predators. The species is solitary
and not wary.

CLEANING GOBY *Elacatinus genie*

KEY FEATURES 4 cm (1.5 in.). Note the
body form and bright yellow V on the
forehead, which extends as a yellow
and/or white stripe the length of the
body.
STATUS AND RANGE Common and widespread in the Caribbean on shallow
reefs, where it rests on suckerlike pelvic fins on coral or rock surfaces. These
gobies often congregate to form "cleaning stations," where they pick parasites
off larger fish, even entering their mouths and gill covers to do so. Other fish
sometimes wait in line to be serviced. This species is not wary.

QUEEN PARROTFISH *Scarus vetula*

KEY FEATURES To 0.6 m (2 ft.). The much more abundant initial female phase is
gray with a broad white band the length of the body. The terminal male phase is
blue green, with yellow markings around the mouth.
STATUS AND RANGE Common and
widespread in the Caribbean on reefs
from shallows to depths of
24 m (80 ft.), where it
tends to move actively
close to the bottom.
Like most parrotfish this
species begins life as a female,
and some subsequently change their
sex and become a male. The latter possess
the terminal coloration. Males have
harems generally of three or four
females. The species gnaws
algae from rocks and
corals during the day. At
night it sleeps in a mucus
cocoon.

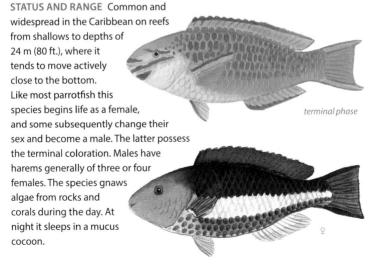

terminal phase

♀

STRIPED PARROTFISH *Scarus croicensis*

KEY FEATURES To 28 cm (11 in.). The abundant initial phase, all believed to be females, is white with three black stripes the length of the body. Often the tip of the snout is yellowish. The terminal phase, all males, has a yellowish spot above and behind the pectoral fin, and the dark tail has pink horizontal stripes.

terminal phase

STATUS AND RANGE Common on reefs and rocky areas throughout the Caribbean. The initial phase forms schools of three to ten individuals, but sometimes forms much larger ones. Like other parrotfish, they regularly scrape algae and corals from the

initial phase

reef with their chisellike teeth. Parrotfish excrement, consisting primarily of fine stony material gnawed from the reef, is important in the deposition of sand. This species occurs at depths of 3–24 m (10–80 ft.).

STOPLIGHT PARROTFISH *Sparisoma viride*

KEY FEATURES To 46 cm (1.5 ft.). Terminal phase: Note the yellow mark at the tail base, yellow or pinkish crescent on the tail, and small yellow spot well behind the eye. Initial phase has red underparts with a checkered scale pattern.

initial phase

STATUS AND RANGE Common over all parts of reefs throughout the Caribbean. Not wary, it feeds on algae off stones and corals. Stoplights in the intermediate-phase, fish which are changing from one phase to another, are most common and may be either male or female. Terminal-phase Stoplight Parrotfish are all males. The excrement of parrotfish,

terminal phase

derived from the coral skeletons they eat and pulverize in their throats, has been estimated to produce as much as one ton of sand per acre of reef each year.

REDSPOTTED HAWKFISH *Amblycirrhitus pinos*

KEY FEATURES To 10 cm (4 in.). Distinguished by red dots over its upper parts, vertical stripes, black bar at the base of the tail, and its habit of perching motionless.

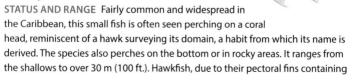

STATUS AND RANGE Fairly common and widespread in the Caribbean, this small fish is often seen perching on a coral head, reminiscent of a hawk surveying its domain, a habit from which its name is derived. The species also perches on the bottom or in rocky areas. It ranges from the shallows to over 30 m (100 ft.). Hawkfish, due to their pectoral fins containing extended rays, are able to perch on stinging corals, which serve as protection. They dart out to catch crustaceans and other unwary prey. Born as females, some change to males later in life. The species is solitary and wary.

SPANISH HOGFISH *Bodianus rufus*

KEY FEATURES To 40 cm (16 in.). Note the irregular patch over much of the upper body, which varies from red to purple.

STATUS AND RANGE Widespread in the Caribbean, it is generally common on reefs and in rocky areas at many depths. An active swimmer, it is not wary. The species is a popular food fish. Juveniles pick parasites from larger fish. Adults feed on a wide range of invertebrates, including mollusks, crabs, and sea urchins. They have a separate set of teeth in their throats for crushing hard shells. Young fish are all females and transform to males later in life.

HOGFISH *Lachnolaimus maximus*

KEY FEATURES To 1 m (3 ft.). Distinguished by the broad facial band and form of the head. It can alter coloration substantially.

STATUS AND RANGE Fairly common in the Caribbean on reefs, particularly among soft corals. Not wary, it is generally solitary but regularly occurs in small groups. The species feeds on bottom-dwelling crustaceans, primarily shellfish, but also on crabs and sea urchins. It is a popular food fish. Young are all females and transform to males upon reaching about 35 cm (14 in.) in length. The name derives from its hoglike snout and its habit of rooting around on the seafloor for prey.

SLIPPERY DICK *Halichoeres bivittatus*

KEY FEATURES To 20 cm (8 in.). Very variable in coloration, which it changes with surroundings. Distinguished by its dark tail tips and stripe, often two, the length of the body. Juvenile is pale, with a broad, dark stripe down the body. Wrasses, of which this is one, swim primarily using their pectoral fins, giving the appearance of dragging their tails.

STATUS AND RANGE Very common and widespread in the Caribbean, swimming about reefs, sea grass flats, rocky areas, and most other shallow-water habitats. Not wary, it is often in loose schools. The species feeds on fish and

juv.

invertebrates. This and many other wrasses bury in the sand at night to sleep.

YELLOWHEAD WRASSE *Halichoeres garnoti*

KEY FEATURES To 18 cm (7 in.). The head is primarily yellow, edged with a black vertical bar. Juvenile is yellow, with a blue stripe the length of the body. Other intermediary colorations occur.

STATUS AND RANGE Common and widespread in the Caribbean on reefs at various depths but primarily deeper waters. Not wary, it swims actively, frequently probing in cavities for food. A male and several females occupy a territory, which is weakly defended. The species feeds on invertebrates. At night it dives out of sight under soft sand.

juv.

BLUEHEAD WRASSE *Thalassoma bifasciatum*

KEY FEATURES To 15 cm (6 in.). Note the blue head, as well as the black and white collar. Juvenile is yellow, with a black spot on front of the dorsal fin. Many other colorations are difficult to identify. Mature males with blue heads represent a very small fraction of the population (4 percent in the Bahamas).

STATUS AND RANGE A very common wrasse of shallow reefs and sea grass flats throughout the Caribbean. Very tame, it is solitary or occurs in schools, which roam widely over the reef. Young feed on fish eggs and plankton and sometimes pick parasites off larger fish. Adults feed on bottom-dwelling invertebrates.

juv.

CREOLE WRASSE *Clepticus parrae*

KEY FEATURES To 25 cm (10 in.). Often purplish overall with a black saddle on the forehead. There are other very variable colorations including blue and lavender. With age, the posterior portion of the body turns increasingly yellow or reddish. Note the heavy use of the pectoral fins for swimming. The coloration is quite similar to the Blue Chromis, with which it associates.

STATUS AND RANGE Common and widespread in the Caribbean in open water over outer reef drop-offs and along vertical faces. Very tame, it swims actively, usually in large schools and often as a lengthy stream of fish. It feeds on plankton and is a frequent user of cleaning stations. Juveniles are all females and change to males at approximately 18 cm (7 in.) in length.

YELLOW GOATFISH *Mulloidichthys martinicus*

KEY FEATURES To 38 cm (15 in.). The two long
barbels beneath the mouth, coupled with
the yellow tail and mid-body stripe, are
characteristic. Coloration is variable.
STATUS AND RANGE Common and
widespread in the Caribbean on shallow sandy flats and sandy areas of reefs.
This goatfish is usually seen swimming lethargically in small groups and
sometimes in large schools. It feeds at night, primarily on a variety of
invertebrates, which it locates by probing the sand with its barbels. It is not wary
and is a popular food fish.

SPOTTED GOATFISH *Pseudupeneus maculatus*

KEY FEATURES To 25 cm (10 in.). Note the three
large spots along the sides and the two long
barbels beneath the mouth. Coloration is very
variable.
STATUS AND RANGE Fairly common and
widespread in the Caribbean on shallow sandy flats, open
areas of reefs, and in sea grass beds. It rests and feeds on the bottom, often a few
individuals together. The species probes around in sand for small invertebrates
and is sometimes followed by small wrasses, which catch prey scared up by the
goatfish. The name derives from its scavenging for all sorts of prey, as do goats. It
is not wary and is a popular food fish.

SQUIRRELFISH *Holocentrus adscensionis*

KEY FEATURES To 30 cm (1 ft.). Note the red and
white stripes and the large black eye.
STATUS AND RANGE Very common
throughout the Caribbean, swimming
slowly about reefs and rocky areas, usually
near the bottom and not far from protective
crevices. It occurs from shallows to depths of over 15 m (50 ft.). Most active at
night, it is not wary and is generally solitary. The species feeds on invertebrates.
Its name derives from its large, squirrellike eyes.

BLACKBAR SOLDIERFISH *Myripristis jacobus*

KEY FEATURES To 20 cm (8 in.). Entirely red; note
the broad, black bar behind the eye.
STATUS AND RANGE Fairly common and
widespread in the Caribbean on reefs, usually
drifting under ledges or hiding in crevices. Active
at night, it sometimes swims upside down. Not wary, the species occurs singly
and in small schools. It feeds on invertebrates and zooplankton. This is a popular
aquarium fish. The name derives from the black bar similar to a soldier's stripe.

255

GLASSEYE SNAPPER *Heteropriacanthus cruentatus*

KEY FEATURES To 30 cm (1 ft.). Note the large eye, continuous dorsal fin lobed at the rear, and the silver stripes, sometimes faint, on the back.
STATUS AND RANGE Fairly common in lagoons and on shallow reefs, but it occurs to depths of 15 m (50 ft.). Widespread in the Caribbean, it is inactive during the day, when generally found under ledges or in crevices, occurring singly or in small groups. It becomes active at dusk, at which time it may gather in large schools. The Glasseye is not wary and feeds on octopus, shrimp, crabs, fish, and marine worms.

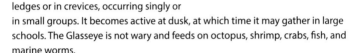

FLAMEFISH *Apogon maculatus*

KEY FEATURES To 10 cm (4 in.). The red coloration, two white lines through the large eye, and the black spot behind it distinguish this species. It may also have a dark spot at the base of the rear dorsal fin and a black saddle at the base of the tail.
STATUS AND RANGE Common and widespread in the Caribbean in shallow waters in various habitats from piers to reefs, but it is seen only infrequently, due to its shyness and nocturnal habits. During daylight it hides in caves and crevices, sometimes in large numbers. The Flamefish feeds in the open at night on tiny fish, crustaceans, and plankton. The male broods the eggs of its mate in its mouth until ready to hatch. This species is also known as the Flame Cardinal.

REDLIP BLENNY *Ophioblennius atlanticus*

KEY FEATURES To 11 cm (4.5 in.). It has a distinctive body shape and dark coloration with red highlights. The coloration is variable.
STATUS AND RANGE Generally common and widespread in the Caribbean on shallow reefs and especially rocky areas, where it sits motionless on the hard surface, to which it clings with its pectoral fins. When disturbed it retreats to a nearby cavity, but it is not especially wary. It is an algae feeder and very territorial in nature. Other names include Lipstick Blenny and Devilfish, the latter because of its typically red-and-black coloration.

TRUMPETFISH *Aulostomus maculatus*

KEY FEATURES To 1 m
(3 ft.). Note the elongated
body and distinctive snout. It has variable coloration.
STATUS AND RANGE Common throughout the Caribbean on shallow reefs,
where detecting it is sometimes difficult, due to its camouflaged appearance and
habit of drifting vertically to imitate sea grasses. It is not wary and feeds primarily
on small fish, which it sucks into its mouth. The male carries the eggs in a pouch
until they hatch. Its name derives from its somewhat trumpetlike shape.

SAND TILEFISH *Malacanthus plumieri*

KEY FEATURES To 0.6 m (2 ft.). It has an
elongated body, with lengthy dorsal and
anal fins and a crescent-shaped tail with a distinctive
dark mark on the upper lobe.
STATUS AND RANGE Common and widespread in the Caribbean in turtle grass
beds, where it excavates a burrow in the sand around which it hovers. It also
occurs on sand flats. Young are pelagic and are so dramatically different from the
adult they were long considered an entirely unrelated species.

YELLOWHEAD JAWFISH *Opistognathus aurifrons*

KEY FEATURES To 10 cm (4 in.). Note its yellow head
and unusual body form.
STATUS AND RANGE Common and
widespread in the Caribbean in sand beds
and coral rubble where, with its mouth, it
excavates a burrow into which it retreats when
disturbed. Usually seen hovering vertically over its burrow, it
generally occurs in small colonies. The male incubates the eggs in its
mouth, leaving them in the burrow while feeding. Not wary, it is a popular
aquarium fish. Zooplankton is its primary food.

SAND DIVER *Synodus intermedius*

KEY FEATURES To 45 cm (1.5 ft.).
It has the habit of perching on the
bottom with its foreparts propped
up on its large ventral fins. Note the large
mouth, banded pattern, and distinctive body shape.
STATUS AND RANGE The most common of the lizardfish in the Caribbean, this
name derives from its head appearing like that of a lizard. This bottom dweller
typically sits motionless on sand, sometimes buried with only the head showing.
It is most abundant in shallow waters, though it occurs to depths of over 30 m
(100 ft.). Another name is Grinner, due to its large mouth and seeming smile. The
mouth is full of sharp teeth, even on the tongue. Lizardfish dart out to feed on
fish, shrimp, and other prey. The species is not wary.

CARIBBEAN SHARPNOSE PUFFER *Canthigaster rostrata*

KEY FEATURES To 10 cm (4 in.). Note the distinctive body shape, with pointed snout and large eyes. The back is brown, and the upper and lower tail borders are black. Juvenile's back is orange. **STATUS AND RANGE** Fairly common and widespread in the Caribbean, occurring in a variety of habitats, including reefs, sand flats, grass beds, and even tide pools. It is perhaps most common among sea fans. This species swims lethargically about, generally is solitary, and is not wary. It can inflate itself like a balloon for protection. The diet is primarily invertebrates.

BALLOONFISH OR LONGSPINED PORCUPINEFISH
Diodon holocanthus

KEY FEATURES To 0.5 m (1.7 ft.). Note the spines, distinctive body shape, large bulging eyes, and body spots of varying size. **STATUS AND RANGE** Probably the most common of the porcupinefish in the Caribbean, occurring in a wide range of shallow water habitats, including reefs, grass and sand flats, bays, harbors, and mangrove channels. Slow swimmers, some porcupinefish propel themselves by squeezing jets of water out their gill slits. Generally wary and solitary, the species sometimes occurs in small schools. It inflates its body when alarmed, making its spines stand upright. It feeds primarily on snails, which it crushes with its beak. Balloonfish, in their inflated form, are frequently lacquered and sold as curios.

SMOOTH TRUNKFISH *Rhinesomus triqueter*

KEY FEATURES To 30 cm (1 ft.). Told by the distinctive body form, dark body coloration covered with white spots, and the yellowish sides. Juvenile is black with yellow-white spots. **STATUS AND RANGE** Generally common and widespread in the Caribbean, swimming casually over reefs. Not wary, it typically is solitary. The species feeds on invertebrates in bottom sediments. A member of the boxfish family, it has a bony body-armor. Fish in this group possessing a spine over the eye are called *cowfish*. A popular aquarium fish, some boxfish exude a toxin when alarmed. It is also popular as a food fish, whereas some are lacquered and sold as curios.

QUEEN TRIGGERFISH *Balistes vetula*

KEY FEATURES To 0.6 m (2 ft.). The distinctive shape and patterning are characteristic. Coloration varies.
STATUS AND RANGE Fairly common and widespread in the Caribbean over reefs, rocky areas, sand flats, and grass beds. It swims slowly, generally alone, and is moderately wary. The species feeds primarily on sea urchins, which it picks up by a spine and drops until the urchin lands upside down and is defenseless. The eyes of the triggerfish are placed high on the head, an adaptation to protect them from urchin spines. Each eye can move independently. The name derives from the first dorsal spine being able to be locked in place, allowing the fish to be lodged in a crevice for protection. It is a food fish in some areas.

BLACK DURGON *Melichthys niger*

KEY FEATURES To 0.6 m (2 ft.). It appears entirely black, with white borders to the dorsal and anal fins.
STATUS AND RANGE Generally fairly common and widespread in the Caribbean, swimming over outer reefs. It is wary and usually occurs in loose schools. The species hides in crevices, where it uses its dorsal "trigger" to lock itself in place. The diet consists of algae attached to coral and rocks, as well as zooplankton. It makes vocalizations by grinding muscles against its swim bladder.

SCRAWLED FILEFISH *Aluterus scriptus*

KEY FEATURES To 1 m (3 ft.). Note the distinctive body shape, including the long tail. The body is covered with pale blue spots and squiggles and a spattering of black spots. Coloration is highly variable.
STATUS AND RANGE Fairly common and widespread in the Caribbean in open waters of reefs and sometimes in lagoons. It is wary, solitary, and swims about lethargically. The dorsal "file" along with a spine on the belly serve to wedge it into crevices for protection. The species often drifts vertically, blending effectively with soft corals and making it easy to overlook. It feeds on poisonous blue-green algae growing on dead coral, as well as sea grasses, anemones, and other organisms. The scales have spines, making them extremely rough, the skin formerly being used to light matches.

GLASSY SWEEPER *Pempheris schomburgkii*

KEY FEATURES To 15 cm (6 in.). Distinguished by the laterally compressed deep body, large eyes, and black band edging the belly.

STATUS AND RANGE Generally common and widespread in the Caribbean in caves and holes in reefs during the day, and sometimes under wharves. The species is active at night, when it feeds primarily on zooplankton. It typically occurs in schools of varying sizes. The first name of the species likely derives from the juvenile form, which is transparent to the point that you can see its backbone. Another name, Hatchetfish, derives from its shape. Other species of sweepers have bioluminescent organs. This species is not wary.

SPOTTED DRUM *Equetus punctatus*

KEY FEATURES To 28 cm (11 in.). A distinctive black-and-white fish with the front dorsal fin extending up like a plume. This is especially the case in the juvenile, in which this plume is greater than the length of the body. Adults have a spotted rear dorsal fin and tail.

STATUS AND RANGE A spectacular but uncommon reef fish, which is secretive during the day, taking shelter under ledges and in cavities, where it swims about in a fixed pattern. It is more active at night, when it emerges to feed on small fish, crabs, shrimp, and worms. This drum ranges from shallows to depths of approximately 30 m (100 ft.). It is solitary and not wary. The name of this group derives from a drumming sound made by resonations of the swim bladder.

SPOTTED MORAY *Gymnothorax moringa*

KEY FEATURES To 1.2 m (4 ft.). This eel is distinguished by dark splotches and squiggles on a pale background.

STATUS AND RANGE A common eel of reefs, rocky areas, and Turtle Grass beds, but very retiring and difficult to see during the day, when sometimes its head is seen protruding from a crevice. At night it emerges to feed on fish. Prey is located by smell. This eel, widespread in the Caribbean, is found primarily in shallow water but occurs to depths of 15 m (50 ft.). Many other morays occur in the Caribbean, but all are difficult to see during daylight hours. It is solitary and not wary.

CAUTION Molesting morays can lead to a serious bite.

SOUTHERN STINGRAY *Dasyatis americana*

KEY FEATURES To 1.5 m (5 ft.). The shape of this gray-brown ray is enough to distinguish it.

STATUS AND RANGE Fairly common and widespread in the Caribbean on sandy bottoms of reefs, sea grass beds, and lagoons, it frequents shallow waters but occurs to 55 m (180 ft.) depths. Generally solitary or in pairs, often nearly buried in the sand, it sometimes occurs in large groups, particularly during migration. Primarily nocturnal, it feeds by flapping its "wings" to expose mollusks, crustaceans, and other prey, which it sucks into its mouth. Stingray cities, where these fish congregate to be fed by divers, are popular tourist destinations in the Caribbean.

CAUTION If a stingray is molested, the whiplike tail has two venomous spines, which can inflict a serious wound.

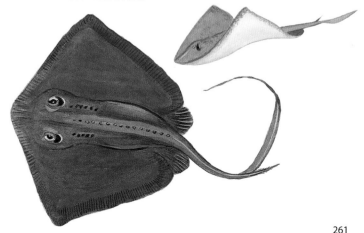

NURSE SHARK *Ginglymostoma cirratum*

KEY FEATURES To 4 m (13 ft.). Distinguished by its habit of sitting motionless on the bottom, its dull rusty-brown coloration, and broad head with flat snout.
STATUS AND RANGE Fairly common throughout the Caribbean on reefs, sand flats, and in mangrove channels. It is usually found resting under ledges or coral formations, primarily in shallow waters but found to depths of over 30 m (100 ft.). Individuals often return to the same spot to rest each day. Sometimes the species rests in large groups, but at night it hunts alone. It probes in bottom sediments for food, feeding primarily on an array of invertebrates, with stingrays also a regular prey item. Smaller prey items are sucked into its mouth. The skin is popular as leather, and the liver is taken for its oil.

CARIBBEAN REEF SHARK *Carcharhinus perezii*

KEY FEATURES To 3 m (10 ft.). Gray above and white below, the undersides of its fins are dusky. Several similar species of sharks occur in the region but are less common.
STATUS AND RANGE Probably the second most common species of shark in the Caribbean after the Nurse Shark. It cruises singly, sometimes in groups, around reefs and other shallows, though found to depths of over 60 m (200 ft.). The species feeds primarily at night on fish and squid. Moderately wary, it is not aggressive. The species is taken for its leather, liver oil, its fins, and to make fishmeal. It is the principal species around which the "shark feeding" ecotourism industry has developed in the region. This species is commonly caught via long-line fishing.
CAUTION This shark is potentially dangerous if disturbed or around speared fish.

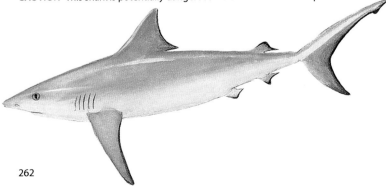

MOLLY MILLER *Scartella cristata*

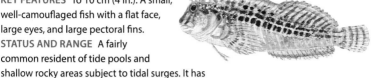

KEY FEATURES To 10 cm (4 in.). A small, well-camouflaged fish with a flat face, large eyes, and large pectoral fins.
STATUS AND RANGE A fairly common resident of tide pools and shallow rocky areas subject to tidal surges. It has the distinctive habit of perching motionless, resting on its pectoral fins, only to race off to a crevice when disturbed. The females lay their eggs in cavities, including abandoned shells, which are then brooded by the males. Also called the Combtooth Blenny, the name derives from its tooth structure for feeding on algae. There are many species of blenny. The Saber-toothed Blenny has fangs with venom glands for immobilizing prey. Other species mimic cleaner wrasses in color and behavior so they can approach unwary prey and take a nip out of them. The Molly Miller is not wary unless closely approached.

REDFIN NEEDLEFISH *Strongylura notata*

KEY FEATURES To 0.6 m (2 ft.). Very slender with a greatly extended jaw. Note the red-tipped dorsal and upper tail fins.
STATUS AND RANGE Common and widespread in the Caribbean in shallow waters of bays, harbors, around piers, and sometimes in freshwater. Often seen motionless just beneath the surface. It generally schools and feeds on small fish. Other species of needlefish and halfbeaks, which look alike from afar, occur in the region.

WHITE MULLET *Mugil curema*

KEY FEATURES To 35 cm (14 in.). Note the dark tips of the dorsal fin, tail, and base of the pectoral fin.
STATUS AND RANGE Common and widespread in the Caribbean over soft bottoms, including sea grass flats, lagoons, and estuaries, and it even enters freshwater. Often in large schools, it is moderately wary. The species feeds primarily on vegetable material by gulping bottom sediment and spitting out larger particles. It is a favored food fish.

263

BONEFISH *Albula vulpes*

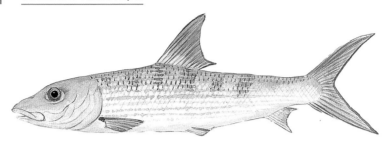

KEY FEATURES To 1 m (3 ft.). The snout extends beyond the lower jaw, and the tail is forked.

STATUS AND RANGE Common and widespread in the Caribbean on shallow flats of mud or sand and on coral rubble. It frequently feeds on flats following a rising tide. Primary prey includes crabs and shrimp. At times it follows rays, which probe around in the sand, to catch fleeing organisms. It is a popular game fish for fly fishers due to its fighting ability, though it is not typically eaten. Other names include Phantom and Gray Ghost.

COMMON SNOOK *Centropomus undecimalis*

KEY FEATURES To 1.2 m (4 ft.). Distinguished by the black lateral line, protruding lower jaw, and depressed forehead.

STATUS AND RANGE Common and widespread in the Caribbean in estuaries, lagoons, and mangroves, where it frequents muddy flats. It sometime occurs in deeper waters. Primary prey includes small fish and crustaceans. A popular food fish, it is caught commercially and sometimes raised through aquaculture. Snook are also a very popular game fish. Other names are Sergeant Fish and Robalo.

TARPON *Megalops atlanticus*

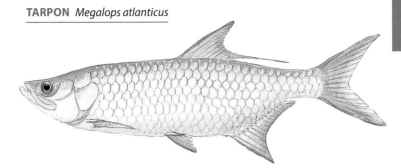

KEY FEATURES To 2.4 m (8 ft.). Very large, with a silvery body and upturned mouth.

STATUS AND RANGE Fairly common and widespread in the Caribbean in bays, lagoons, mangroves, and estuaries, including brackish waters. A popular game fish, it often occurs in schools. In water with low oxygen levels it can breathe air using its swim bladder, which is adapted to serve as a primitive lung. Juvenile tarpon are obligate air-breathers, and adults are believed to require oxygen from the air for their survival. The species feeds primarily on small fish, shrimp, and crabs.

OPEN-WATER GAME FISH

DORADO *Coryphaena hippurus*

KEY FEATURES To 1.8 m (6 ft.). Distinguished by its beautiful blue, green, and gold coloration and distinctive body shape. The male has a more pronounced forehead than the female. The coloration fades out of water and even more so in death.

STATUS AND RANGE An offshore surface fish often occurring around flotsam, particularly Sargasso. Frequently in schools, it is highly migratory. The Dorado is prized as a game fish for its strength, beauty, and edibility. The latter factor has made it important commercially. The Dorado feeds on Flying Fish, among other fish, and crabs. It is one of the fastest growing and fastest swimming fish reaching speeds of nearly 100 km (60 mi.) per hour. Other names include Mahi-mahi (meaning "strong-strong" in Hawaiian) and Dolphin (unrelated to the mammal of the same name). It sometimes carries the toxin ciguatera.

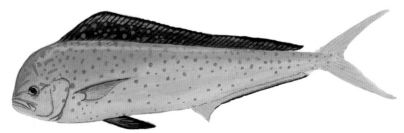

ATLANTIC WHITE MARLIN *Kajikia albida*

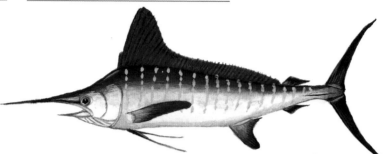

KEY FEATURES To 2.7 m (9 ft.). This large, long-billed fish is generally dark blue above and silvery below. It is best distinguished from similar species by its first dorsal fin, which is spotted and has a round lobe at its front. Females are larger than males. Coloration changes as the fish becomes excited.

STATUS AND RANGE An open ocean fish, occurring primarily alone or in pairs, but sometimes aggregating when feeding. It is migratory and frequents upwellings, and the margins of currents. A popular recreational charter fish and a desirable food fish, it is also taken commercially via long lines. Overfishing has caused serious population declines. It feeds primarily on squid and fish, the Dorado and Flying Fish being among the most common prey.

BLUE MARLIN *Makaira nigricans*

KEY FEATURES To 4.3 m (14 ft.). A very large, long-billed fish, dark blue above and silvery below. Distinguished from the similar Atlantic White Marlin by the lobe on its first dorsal fin being pointed and lacking spots, or, rarely, possessing a few. Females are much larger than males.

STATUS AND RANGE Occurs in the open ocean, where it is highly migratory, at times crossing the Atlantic Ocean. It is a popular recreational charter fish and a desirable food fish. It is also caught commercially via long-line fishing, from which it is under intensive pressure in the Caribbean. It uses its bill to slash prey such as squid and fish, on which it feeds. One of the fastest of fish, it is reputed to have exceeded 100 km (60 mi.) per hour.

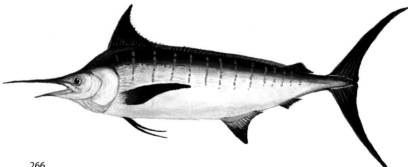

CERO *Scomberomorus regalis*

KEY FEATURES To 1 m (3 ft.). Note the horizontal side stripes, finlets on rear of the body, and deeply forked tail.

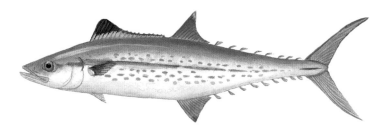

STATUS AND RANGE Common and widespread in the Caribbean in open water, sometimes over reefs. Generally solitary, it feeds primarily on small schooling fish but also on squid and shrimp. Individual females are reputed to release as many as 2.2 million eggs. It is a popular sport fish.

SWORDFISH *Xiphias gladius*

KEY FEATURES To nearly 5.5 m (18 ft.). Its long sword-like bill and crescent-shaped dorsal fin are distinctive.

STATUS AND RANGE An ocean-going fish highly sought by recreational charter anglers. It is often fished by trolling. A desirable food fish, it is commercially taken, frequently by long line. Overfishing has caused serious population declines. The Swordfish typically is solitary but may travel in loose schools. It is sometimes seen basking at the surface or leaping high into the air. Highly migratory, it is extremely fast, recorded at speeds to 80 km (50 mi.) per hour. The bill serves to slash and injure prey, which include other fish and squid. Its few predators include large sharks, the Sperm Whale, and Orca. The Swordfish has an unusual organ that heats the eyes and brain, enabling it to see prey better and to be more active.

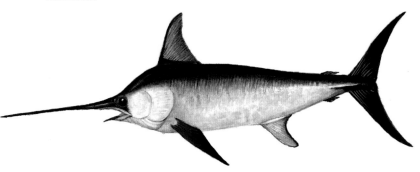

MARINE PLANTS AND INVERTEBRATES

MARINE PLANTS

TURTLE GRASS *Thalassia testudinum*

KEY FEATURES To 30 cm (1 ft). Clusters of green, slender leaves appear like broad blades of grass rising from the sea floor. It typically occurs in large patches or extensive beds.

STATUS AND RANGE The most abundant flowering plant beyond the low tide zone. It occurs primarily on sandy bottoms. Turtle Grass provides shelter and food for many species including the Green Turtle for which it is named. Diverse algae use Turtle Grass on which to grow and, in turn, provide a major food source for many grass bed inhabitants. Turtle Grass can grow up to 2.5 cm (1 in) per week.

MARINE INVERTEBRATES

Marine invertebrates make up a vast assemblage of unrelated organisms. This includes well-known forms such as the crabs, corals, and jellyfish. But it also encompasses common groups scarcely known to the general public. The sea squirts and bryozoans are among these.

STONY CORALS

This large group forms the basis of the coral reef community. Each stony coral is actually a colony of numerous, tiny polyps. A polyp is an individual animal resembling a diminutive sea anemone with a ring of tentacles surrounding a central mouth opening. Each polyp exudes a hard, external skeleton (exoskeleton) for protection. Each exoskeleton is attached to several others forming an immobile, connected colony. Over fifty species of stony corals occur in the Caribbean. Tentacles of coral polyps are armed with venomous stinging cells which immobilize small fish and other tiny organisms. The tentacles draw these animals, and trapped plankton, into the mouth. Many polyps contain minute photosynthetic algae called zooxanthellae which convert sunlight into energy for the corals. These zooxanthellae are essential to the survival of many coral species, which account for the importance of coral reefs being in clear water and near the ocean surface to better access the sun's rays. Stony corals serve as food, protection, and substrate for fish, sponges, mollusks, crustaceans, marine worms, and sea urchins, among many others.

FINGER CORAL *Porites* spp.

KEY FEATURES To 1.2 m (4 ft). There are various forms of Finger Corals. They vary in thickness, fragility, and shape, but are of the same general form – like gnarly fingers.

STATUS AND RANGE Several forms of Finger Coral are common in the shallow, in-shore portions of reefs, sometimes growing in expansive stands. Other forms occur in deeper waters of the outer reef.

Turtle Grass

Finger Coral

STAGHORN CORAL *Acropora cervicornis*

KEY FEATURES To 2.5 m (8 ft.). A branching coral reminding one of deer antlers, thus the name.

STATUS AND RANGE A common coral of the reef community, growing from just beneath the surface to depths of over 18 m (60 ft.). It prefers clear, calm waters. Dense stands provide both food and shelter for numerous marine organisms. Sometimes it grows in solitary colonies.

ELKHORN CORAL *Acropora palmata*

KEY FEATURES To 3.7 m (12 ft.). A magnificent coral similar to Staghorn but with flattened branches, more like the antlers of a caribou or moose than an elk.

STATUS AND RANGE A common reef coral occurring from just beneath the surface to depths of over 9 m (30 ft.). It prefers clear, moving waters. An excellent provider of food and shelter for numerous marine organisms.

BLADE FIRE CORAL *Millepora complanata*

KEY FEATURES To 50 cm (1.6 ft.). Note the tan-colored vertical plates of distinctive form.

STATUS AND RANGE A common reef coral occurring from the surface to substantial depths. It prefers clear, moving waters.

CAUTION Touching Fire Coral produces a burning sensation that can last for days if one is sensitive. Normally the pain is short lived.

COMMON BRAIN CORAL *Diploria strigosa*

KEY FEATURES To 1.8 m (6 ft.). Colonies form as distinctive, round heads or encrust over rock surfaces.

STATUS AND RANGE There are various species of brain coral, Common Brain Coral being most prevalent. This species occurs widely on most reefs and ranges from just beneath the surface to over 30 m (100 ft.) in depth. The largest specimens are up to nine hundred years old. Numerous species of related corals are in various genera.

Staghorn Coral

Elkhorn Coral

Blade Fire Coral

Common Brain Coral

Like the stony corals, soft corals are colonial in nature and are made up of individual polyps. However, soft corals, also referred to as *gorgonians*, are flexible in structure, their external skeletons being composed of protein compounds rather than calcium carbonate. Such flexibility enables them to wave in the water currents. This feature, coupled with the branching and plumelike nature of many species, gives one the impression of being in an underwater garden. Primarily filter feeders on plankton, soft corals tend to inhabit areas with active currents. In such environments they sometimes grow to very large sizes. Soft corals are less diverse than stony corals in the Caribbean, there being somewhat over twenty species present.

COMMON SEA FAN *Gorgonia ventalina*

KEY FEATURES To 1.8 m (6 ft.). A distinctively fan-shaped gorgonian, commonly referred to as a *soft coral*, with a delicate lattice design. Usually purple, but sometimes yellow or brown. A sea fan is actually a colony in individual coral polyps united by their external skeletons. There are many species in different genera.
STATUS AND RANGE Common on the outer rim of reefs, where it can benefit from active water flow. Fans are oriented to face water currents, which carry the zooplankton on which they feed. This food is complemented by the presence of zooxanthellae, which are minute organisms living commensally inside the coral and which photosynthesize additional nutrients. Dried sea fans are commonly sold as souvenirs and for aquaria.

SEA RODS Family: Plexauridae

KEY FEATURES To 2 m (7 ft.). The Caribbean supports many species of sea rods. They are distinguished by a bushlike structure made up of club-like branches that do not taper at their tips. A soft coral, they wave in the current.
STATUS AND RANGE Common in the reef community, usually in clear water where bathed by active water movement. Where gorgonians occur in concentrations they are referred to as *gardens*, due to their convergence in appearance to their terrestrial plant counterparts. As with all soft corals, the numerous polyps that compose the sea rod each has eight tentacles for filtering plankton from the passing currents.

Common Sea Fan
Sea Rods

SEA PLUMES *Pseudopterogorgia* spp.

KEY FEATURES To 2 m (7 ft.). Note the distinctive, featherlike plumes, which wave gracefully in the current. Distinguishing them to species is a job for specialists.
STATUS AND RANGE Sea plumes are common in many reef areas but primarily in waters that are clear and moving. They look like plants but are gorgonians: colonial animals. Sea plumes and other gorgonians should be inspected closely for fish, snails, and other organisms that use them for cover or on which they feed. There are various species.

SPONGES Phylum Porifera

KEY FEATURES 1 cm to 2 m (0.4 in to 7 ft.) Sponges occur in many sizes, shapes, and colors. They are permanently attached to a rock, coral, or other firm substrate. Their form varies from being shaped like a cup, barrel, tube, or soft coral, or from encrusting over a surface. Most have a conspicuous opening. The shape and color of a single species may vary due to age, location, or other factors.
STATUS AND RANGE Sponges are common on all Caribbean reefs, where they feed by filtering plankton and other microscopic material from the water through small pores on their bodies. They also serve as food for a number of fish and marine invertebrates. Over five thousand species are known worldwide; three examples found in the Caribbean are illustrated here. One of the most primitive of animals, sponges have no organs.

MAGNIFICENT FEATHER DUSTER *Sabellastarte magnifica*

KEY FEATURES Gill length: 10 cm (4 in.). The body of this marine worm is concealed in a tube, but it typically exposes a pair of feathery gills of various coloration but primarily barred brown and white. The gills are composed of fine tentacles, which remind one of a feather duster.
STATUS AND RANGE Common on coral reefs, where it forms a burrow in coral, sand, or rubble. The gills filter plankton from the water and also serve for respiration. When disturbed this worm quickly withdraws into its soft tube. After several minutes undisturbed it will slowly emerge.

CHRISTMAS TREE WORM *Spirobranchus giganteus*

KEY FEATURES Gill diameter: 3.8 cm (1.5 in.). The two distinctive Christmas tree-shaped organs, actually modified mouth parts, easily identify this worm. Coloration varies widely. Most of the worm is hidden in its burrow.
STATUS AND RANGE A common tube worm of the coral reef, where the young burrow into corals and limestone and then surround themselves with a calcium-carbonate tube. The spiral organs, commonly referred to as *gills*, serve both to capture food and for respiration. The gills consist of slender tentacles, each with rows of fine hairs called *cilia*, which transport food, primarily plankton, to the digestive tract. The Christmas Tree Worm is a filter-feeder. When disturbed, the worms quickly withdraw into their burrows, which they can cover for safety.

Sea Plumes

Barrel sponge

Tube sponge

Encrusting Sponge

Magnificent Feather Duster

Christmas Tree Worm

CARIBBEAN REEF SQUID *Sepioteuthis sepioidea*

KEY FEATURES 20 cm (8 in.). Note the distinctive torpedo-shaped body form, large eyes, eight arms, and two longer tentacles. Also distinctive is its habit of swimming backward. Typically mottled brown, squid can change coloration quickly and dramatically.

STATUS AND RANGE Common in small schools around shallow reefs, where they move effortlessly backward or forward or hover in place. Movement is generated by jet propulsion. Communication is via changes in body color. When threatened, squid squirt a cloud of dark ink. Voracious feeders on small fish and invertebrates, squid can eat up to 60 percent of their weight per day. Adults die after reproduction. The species is not wary. Giant Squid, from the ocean depths, have the largest eyes in the animal kingdom. Squid are mollusks that lack an external shell but possess an internal equivalent. They are a popular dish in restaurants.

OCTOPUS *Octopus* spp.

KEY FEATURES 5 cm–1 m (2 in.–3 ft.). The octopus, with its eight long arms covered with tentacles, bulbous body, and large eyes, is well known to everyone.

STATUS AND RANGE Several species of octopus occur among the reefs, sea grass beds, and rocky areas of the Caribbean, where they are primarily nocturnal, hiding by day in crevices, large sponges, or other cavities. They can quickly change color to blend with their environment. To escape predators they squirt jets of water to propel themselves or spray a cloud of dark ink. Octopuses are highly intelligent and can learn from one another. They feed on crabs, shrimp, and other invertebrates. Highly prized for food, they are widely harvested.

CARIBBEAN SPINY LOBSTER *Panulirus argus*

KEY FEATURES To 60 cm (2 ft.), excluding antennae. This large, spiny crustacean is quite distinctive, possessing two extremely long antennae of greater length than the body. Coloration varies with age.

STATUS AND RANGE Common and widespread on reefs throughout the Caribbean, but not readily seen due to its nocturnal habits. During the day, this shy lobster retreats to crevices and is not easily seen. Sea grass beds and mangroves serve as nurseries for young lobsters. Very popular for food, the species is heavily harvested commercially and is the number one food export of the Bahamas. Overharvesting in many areas has caused population declines. Lobsters swim backwards by flipping their tails. They feed on snails, clams, carrion, and detritus. Seasonally they form a single line and migrate for reasons that are still unclear.

Caribbean Reef Squid

Octopus

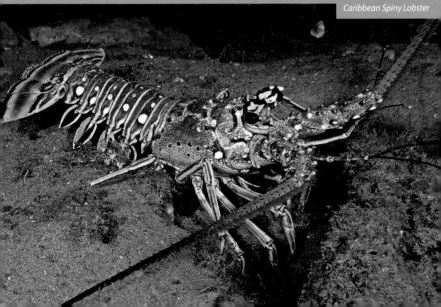

Caribbean Spiny Lobster

LONG-SPINED SEA URCHIN *Diadema antillarum*

KEY FEATURES Diameter to nearly 0.6 m (2 ft.). This urchin has the appearance of a large, black pincushion.

STATUS AND RANGE A bottom-dweller at shallow depths of coral reefs, sea grass beds, and sand flats. It typically inhabits crevices, from which it wanders small distances at night, using its unique tube feet similar to those of the starfish. Once abundant, a massive die-off in 1983–84 wiped out nearly the entire Caribbean population, leaving only one animal for every fifty that had been there before. Previously the most important grazer of algae in the reef community, the demise of this urchin resulted in algal blooms that suffocated many reefs, dramatically reducing their species diversity. In recent years this urchin is recovering in numbers. It is fed upon by various fish, gastropods, starfish, and crabs. Also know by the name of Black Sea Urchin.

CAUTION Urchins are a potential threat to careless waders or to divers who accidentally bump into them. The spines break off easily and are soft, thus are difficult to remove and cause much pain.

DONKEY DUNG SEA CUCUMBER *Holothuria mexicana*

KEY FEATURES To 0.5 m (20 in.). A wrinkled, dark blob reminiscent of its name, motionless on the seafloor. Coloration may vary but typically is dark brown, gray, or black, with a warty surface. Several related species occur in the region.

STATUS AND RANGE Common singly in calm shallow waters, particularly on sandy bottoms and among sea grass beds. Also on reefs and in mangroves. The sea cucumber has unique tube feet, making it a relative of the sea star and sea urchin, but it moves extremely slowing, scarcely covering 1 m (3 ft.) in a day. Sea cucumbers ingest sediments, from which they digest the algae and other minute organisms associated with it. When threatened, sea cucumbers may expel fine, sticky threads or even their internal organs as a defense mechanism. They are commercially harvested in some areas, primarily for export to China.

CUSHION SEA STAR *Oreaster reticulatus*

KEY FEATURES To 45 cm (1.5 ft.). Easily distinguished by its distinctive heavy body and short arms, usually five, arrayed with stubby spines. It is typically red, orange, yellow, or brown. The young are greenish and mottled.

STATUS AND RANGE Fairly common on sand flats and sea grass beds, but it also occurs in mangroves and on reefs. It moves about on tube feet, which also serve for respiration and to rake together algae, invertebrates, and detritus on the ocean floor into a small mound. It then everts its stomach and digests the food external to its body. Sponges are a primary food source. Sometimes dense aggregations form to feed or migrate. The largest sea star in the Caribbean, it has been overcollected for souvenirs and the aquarium trade. A lost arm can be regenerated. Formerly referred to as *starfish*, this term is in disuse because sea stars are unrelated to fish. Their closest relatives are sea urchins and sea cucumbers.

Long-spined Sea Urchin

Donkey Dung Sea Cucumber

Cushion Sea Star

279

SEASHELLS (MOLLUSKS)

Seashells that wash up on beaches are the hard, external skeletons of formerly living creatures known as *mollusks*. Mollusks form an immense and diverse group of organisms. One subgroup is the cephalopods, represented by the squid and octopus discussed earlier, but one of which, the Common Spirula, is included in this section because it is best known as a "seashell" after death, when its hard body part washes ashore. The most diverse and abundant of the seashells are the gastropods, commonly known as *snails*. Snails possess a single shell. Some mollusks have two opposing shells and are called bivalves. Oysters, clams, and scallops are examples. Not all mollusks are marine. Some occur well away from the sea or even freshwater. The Cuban land snails, discussed in the Terrestrial Invertebrate section, are examples of these.

SINGLE-SHELLED SNAILS (GASTROPODS)

BARBADOS KEYHOLE LIMPET *Fissurella barbadensis*

KEY FEATURES To 4 cm (1.5 in.). Like a small volcano with a nearly circular hole on top. More irregular in form and more delicate than many other limpets. The shell interior bordering the hole has a green ring.
STATUS AND RANGE Extremely common and widespread in the Caribbean. It adheres to rocks in the intertidal zone, where it grazes algae from rocks using a rasplike structure called a *radula*. There are many limpet species of similar appearance in the region, but some are quite unrelated. Their similarity of appearance derives from them evolving to occupy the harsh environment of the intertidal zone.

KNOBBY KEYHOLE LIMPET *Fissurella nodosa*

KEY FEATURES To 4 cm (1.5 in.). Volcano-shaped with a figure-eight hole on top and thick, elevated ridges down the sides with knobs protruding from them. The interior is white.
STATUS AND RANGE Common and widespread in the Caribbean, where it adheres to rocks just below the low tide zone and grazes algae from them. The name derives from a meaning of the word limpet: "one that clings persistently."

WEST INDIAN TOP SHELL *Cittarium pica*

KEY FEATURES To 10 cm (4 in.). Distinctively patterned with bold black-and-whitish marbling.
STATUS AND RANGE Common and widespread in the Caribbean in the rocky intertidal surf zone where it occurs on and beneath rocks. It is a popular food item throughout the Caribbean, where it is the third most economically important invertebrate after the Spiny Lobster and Queen Conch. Some species of top shells reach thirty years of age. Known in the Caribbean as *wilks* or *whelks*, they are unrelated to species of this name in the United States and Europe.

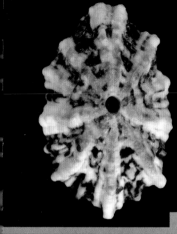
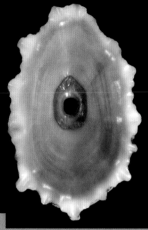

Barbados Keyhole Limpet

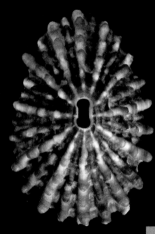

Knobby Keyhole Limpet

West Indian Top Shell

SEASHELLS (MOLLUSKS) | SINGLE-SHELLED
SNAILS (GASTROPODS)

BLEEDING TOOTH *Nerita peloronta*

KEY FEATURES To 3 cm (1.2 in.). Readily distinguished by the two to three white "teeth" surrounded by red stain. Shell coloration is highly variable.
STATUS AND RANGE Very common and widespread in the Caribbean in the rocky intertidal zone. Moving with the tides, it sometimes ranges above the high tide line. The species is most active at night, feeding by scraping algae off rocks with its very long, rasping tongue. The name derives from the appearance that it has bloody teeth, which in fact is a deposit of iron.

FOUR-TOOTHED NERITE *Nerita versicolor*

KEY FEATURES To 2.5 cm (1 in.). Note the four distinctive white "teeth."
STATUS AND RANGE Common and widespread in the Caribbean in coralline tidepools. The species frequents rocks slightly lower in the intertidal zone than does the Bleeding Tooth. It feeds by scraping algae off rocks. Unlike most snails, which release eggs and sperm into the sea, the nerite male injects sperm into the female, which lays small white eggs. There are many related species of nerites.

VIRGIN NERITE *Neritina virginea*

KEY FEATURES To 2 cm (0.8 in.). A gorgeous little shell, very variable in pattern. Note the distinctive designs. It has many small irregular "teeth" on a white or yellow inner lip.
STATUS AND RANGE Common and widespread in the Caribbean in muddy intertidal areas, including brackish waters. It feeds on filamentous seaweed. The species sometimes undertakes upstream migrations following floods. Small individuals prefer fast, turbulent flows, whereas larger individuals favor slower-velocity flows.

VARIEGATED TURRET SHELL *Turritella variegata*

KEY FEATURES To 11 cm (4.5 in.). A fairly large sea snail with a long, tightly coiled, cone-shaped shell. Very variable in color, from creamy white to a dark, blotched brown.
STATUS AND RANGE Common and widespread in the Caribbean in the shallow, calm waters of bays. Somewhat local, but where it occurs it may be found in large numbers. This snail feeds on marine plants. The first portion of the scientific name for this snail means "small turret."

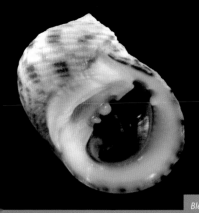
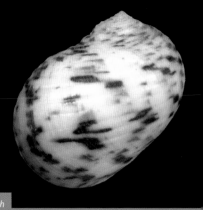

Bleeding Tooth

Four-toothed Nerite

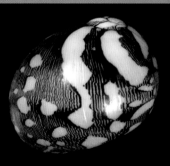

Virgin Nerite

Variegated Turret Shell

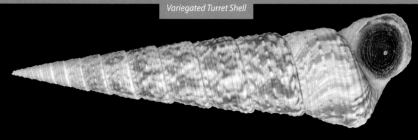

SEASHELLS (MOLLUSKS)

KNORR'S WORM SHELL *Vermicularia knorrii*

KEY FEATURES To 8 cm (3 in.). The first few connected whorls are white, while those that are detached from one another are yellowish brown.
STATUS AND RANGE The shell of this marine snail is commonly and widely found washed ashore in the Caribbean. Alive, the snail lives inside shallow water sponges. The name derives from the shell's similarity of appearance to that of a marine worm.

COMMON SUNDIAL *Architectonica nobilis*

KEY FEATURES To 5 cm (2 in.). A beautiful, distinctive, coiled, fairly flat shell. Lines of varying color trace its contours.
STATUS AND RANGE Fairly common and widespread in the Caribbean in calm, shallow waters of bays. It generally is associated with reefs, where it feeds on coral polyps. Sundials are also known as *staircase shells*.

QUEEN CONCH *Lobatus gigas*

KEY FEATURES To 30 cm (1 ft.). Among the various conch species in the Caribbean, this is best known. It is the largest snail in the region, distinguished by its distinctive shape and glossy, flared shield.
STATUS AND RANGE Formerly common and widespread in the Caribbean among sea grass beds, where it feeds on algae. A highly prized food resource as well as for souvenirs throughout the region, it is now greatly reduced in numbers due to overharvesting and is considered threatened in some areas. Females lay strands of eggs, which number up to 1.5 million eggs per season. It is also known as the Pink Conch. Vast stacks of conch shells are found where fishers congregate to extract the snails for the market.

LAMELLOSE WENTLETRAP *Epitonium lamellosum*

KEY FEATURES To 3 cm (1.2 in.). A distinctive shell with pronounced parallel ridges running down its length. Well over a dozen similar species occur in the Caribbean.
STATUS AND RANGE Generally common and widespread in the Caribbean under rocks in the low tide zone but ranging to depths of 30 m (100 ft.). A predatory snail, some species feed on sea anemones. It is primarily found washed ashore.

COFFEEBEAN TRIVIA *Pusula pediculus*

KEY FEATURES To 2.5 cm (1 in.). A dainty little shell with fine, parallel ribbing and a dorsal groove. It is pinkish, with three pairs of distinctive, brown, "coffee bean" markings.
STATUS AND RANGE This shell commonly washes up on beaches of the Caribbean. The living snail occurs in shallow offshore waters on rocks and other hard surfaces supporting sea squirts, in which the trivia deposits its eggs.

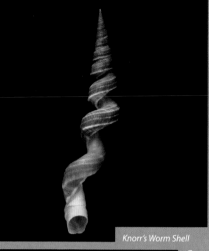
Knorr's Worm Shell

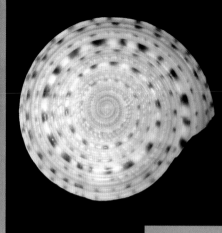
Common Sundial

Queen Conch

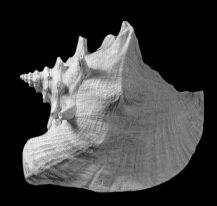

Lamellose Wentletrap

Coffeebean Trivia

SCOTCH BONNET *Semicassis granulata*

KEY FEATURES To 10 cm (4 in.). Pale tan overall, with distinctive rectangular markings that are light brown in color and arranged in an orderly pattern.
STATUS AND RANGE Common and widespread in the Caribbean on sand flats from the shallows to over 18 m (60 ft.) in depth. It is a predatory snail that feeds on sea urchins and sand dollars, the shells of which it pierces by use of sulfuric acid. The female lays a circular stack of eggs up to 13 cm (5 in.) high, reminding one of the famous Leaning Tower of Pisa. The male fertilizes the eggs, after which the hatched larvae drift in ocean currents for up to fourteen weeks before sinking to the ocean floor. This snail is primarily found washed ashore.

COMMON DOVE SHELL *Columbella mercatoria*

KEY FEATURES To 1.3 cm (0.5 in.). This shell has highly variable coloration and patterning. Note its heavy grooves.
STATUS AND RANGE Common and widespread in the Caribbean on sand flats and sea grass beds from shallow waters to about 9 m (30 ft.) in depth. The species feeds on algae and is primarily found washed ashore. It is also know as the Mottled Dove Shell.

CROWN CONE *Conus regius*

KEY FEATURES To 7.5 cm (3 in.). Usually mottled dark brown and white, but sometimes a solid pale color. It has a ring of knobs around the broadest part of the shell. There are several similar species.
STATUS AND RANGE The most common cone shell in the Caribbean. It inhabits shallow sand flats. Cones are distinctive among snails, due to their capacity to "harpoon" their prey and incapacitate it with toxic venom. Some cone snails in the Pacific Ocean have venom strong enough to kill a human being. Primarily found washed ashore.
CAUTION Live cones should be handled with care, as they produce a sting.

CARIBBEAN OLIVE *Oliva scripta*

KEY FEATURES To 4 cm (1.5 in.). A glossy shell with a purplish opening spanning nearly its full length.
STATUS AND RANGE Fairly common and widespread in the Caribbean in shallow water below the level of low tide. Generally buried beneath the sand during the day, it emerges at night to feed. Primarily found washed ashore.

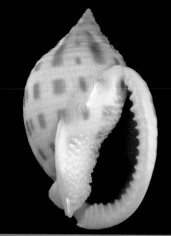

Scotch Bonnet

Common Dove Shell

Crown Cone

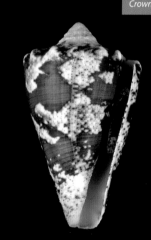

Caribbean Olive

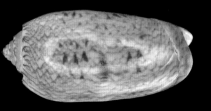
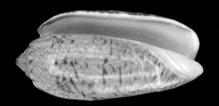

COMMON WEST INDIAN GREEN CHITON *Chiton tuberculatus*

KEY FEATURES To 8 cm (3 in.). Similar to the Squamous Chiton, but with a distinctive ridge down the center of its back and with white, greenish, and black bars on its girdle.
STATUS AND RANGE A common and widespread chiton in the Caribbean occurring in the intertidal zone, where it browses on algae attached to rocks and to which it powerfully adheres. Feeding primarily at night, chitons tend to hide under rocks during the day. Chitons are also known as Coat-of-Mail shells. Found to live up to twelve years, showing continuous growth, the average lifespan is probably less than eight years.

SQUAMOUS CHITON *Chiton squamosus*

KEY FEATURES To 8 cm (3 in.). A distinctive oval mollusk with eight overlapping plates edged with a leathery girdle barred with grayish green and white.
STATUS AND RANGE Common and widely distributed in the Caribbean. It is found tightly adhering to rocks in the intertidal zone, often remaining exposed to the air for substantial lengths of time. It feeds by scraping algae from these hard surfaces. Chitons have many rudimentary eyes, which appear to serve primarily as light detectors.

TWO-SHELLED MOLLUSKS (BIVALVES)

TURKEY WING *Arca zebra*

KEY FEATURES To 8 cm (3 in.). An asymmetrical shell covered with dark bands.
STATUS AND RANGE Generally common and widespread in the Caribbean in the shallow subtidal zone, on rocks to which it is attached firmly by hairlike filaments. Primarily found washed ashore. Fishers often use it for bait, leaving piles of shells in some locales. The species is edible. It is also referred to as Zebra Ark or Bearded Mussel.

CARIBBEAN OYSTER *Crassostrea rhizophorae*

KEY FEATURES To 15 cm (6 in.). Note the gnarly and irregular form. The smaller bottom shell fits within the larger upper shell. It has a purple muscle scar.
STATUS AND RANGE Widespread in the Caribbean, it is found attached to prop roots of Red Mangrove in channels or where water movement is calm. Occurs in clusters from the level of high tide down to where the roots contact the bottom. A popular food in the Caribbean. Born as males, members of this species change to females the following season. Thereafter, most remain female, but some revert to being males.

Common West Indian Green Chiton

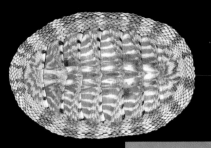

Squamous Chiton

Turkey Wing

Caribbean Oyster

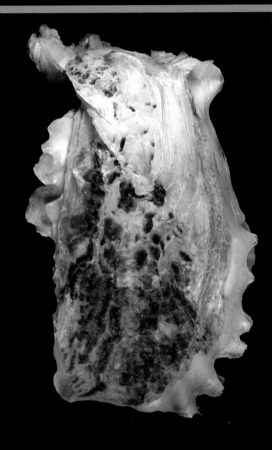

SEASHELLS (MOLLUSKS)

CALICO SCALLOP *Argopecten gibbus*

KEY FEATURES To 8 cm (3 in.). A distinctive "scalloped" shell widely known to everyone. It possesses two wings at the base. The coloration is white to pale yellow, with patches of varied colors.

STATUS AND RANGE The shell is commonly washed ashore widely in the Caribbean. The living scallop occurs on sandy bottoms offshore and among sea grass beds. Scallops are the only migratory bivalves, many, including the Calico, being active swimmers. They swim by rapidly opening and closing their shells moving as much as 0.6 m (2 ft.) per second. The Calico Scallop is a filter feeder, catching microalgae and other minute organic material in its gills. Scallops have numerous small eyes, which are better developed than most bivalves but yet are unable to see clear images. Scallops, including the Calico, are widely eaten, and this species once was the base of an important fishery.

WEST INDIAN PRICKLY COCKLE *Trachycardium isocardia*

KEY FEATURES To 8 cm (3 in.). Note the distinctive scales covering the surface. The interior is pale pink. A number of similar cockles occur in the Caribbean.

STATUS AND RANGE Common and widespread in the Caribbean on shallow sandy flats, often in colonies. The cockle is sedentary, burying itself in the sand with the exception of its siphons, which serve to draw in water from which phytoplankton is filtered. The siphons possess tentacles on which are fairly complex eyes that serve to detect predators. Primarily found washed ashore.

CARIBBEAN COQUINA *Donax denticulatus*

KEY FEATURES To 2.5 cm (1 in.). A small, glossy, elegant shell, very variable in coloration. Several similar species occur in the region.

STATUS AND RANGE Very common and widespread in the Caribbean on sandy beaches of the intertidal zone. Shallow digging in moist sand along the water's edge will reveal these mollusks, which move up and down the beach with the tides. They siphon minute algae and other detritus from the water.

COMMON SPIRULA *Spirula spirula*

KEY FEATURES To 5 cm (2 in.). A delicate, white spiral shell tapering its entire length and distinctively segmented.

STATUS AND RANGE Widespread in the Caribbean, the "shell" of the Common Spirula found along sandy beaches is only a part of the animal. In actuality, this mollusk is related to the squid, possessing eight arms and two longer tentacles containing suckers. The mouth is beaked and serves to feed on small fish and crustaceans. Live spirula, also know as the Ram's Horn Squid, occur in deep offshore waters ranging to nearly 1 km (3,300 ft.) in depth during the day to shallower depths at night, when they become more active and range closer to the surface to feed. A light-generating organ near the tail is believed to serve for communication. Unique, it is the only representative of its order.

Calico Scallop

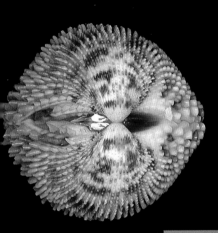

West Indian Prickly Cockle

Caribbean Coquina

Common Spirula

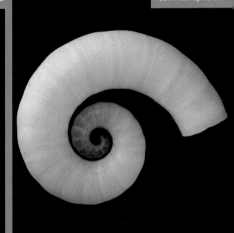

REFERENCES AND ADDITIONAL READING

GENERAL

Campbell, D. G. 1978. *The ephemeral islands. A natural history of the Bahamas.* London: Macmillan Education Limited.

Dammann, A. E., and D. W. Nellis. 1992. *A natural history atlas to the cays of the U.S. Virgin Islands.* Sarasota, FL: Pineapple Press, Inc.

DeFreitas, M. 1999. *Adventures in nature Caribbean.* Emeryville, CA: Avalon Travel Publishing.

Whittaker, R. J. 1998. *Island biogeography. Ecology, evolution, and conservation.* Oxford: Oxford University Press.

Woods, C. A., and F. E. Sergile (eds.). 2001. *Biogeography of the West Indies: Patterns and perspectives.* 2nd ed. Boca Raton, FL: CRC Press.

PLANTS

Bourne, M. J., G. W. Lennox, and S. A. Seddon. 1988. *Fruits and vegetables of the Caribbean.* London: Macmillan Caribbean Natural History.

Correll, D. S., and H. B. Correll. 1986. *Flora of the Bahama Archipelago (including the Turks and Caicos Islands).* Vaduz: A. R. G. Gantner Verlag K.-G.

Cutts, W. 2004. *Trees of the Bahamas and Florida.* London: Macmillan Caribbean Natural History.

Gloudon, A., and C. Tobish. 1995. *Orchids of Jamaica.* Kingston, Jamaica: University Press of the West Indies.

Honychurch, P. N. 1980. *Caribbean wild plants and their uses.* Barbados: Letchworth Press, Ltd.

Kepler, A. K. 1975. *Common ferns of Luquillo Forest, Puerto Rico.* San Juan, PR: Inter American University Press.

Lennox, G. W., and S. A. Seddon. 1979. *Flowers of the Caribbean.* London: Macmillan Caribbean Natural History.

Little, E. L., Jr., and F. H. Wadsworth. 1964. *Common trees of Puerto Rico and the Virgin Islands.* Agriculture Handbook No. 249. Washington, DC: US Department of Agriculture—Forest Service.

Little, E. L., Jr., R. O. Woodbury, and F. H. Wadsworth. 1974, *Trees of Puerto Rico and the Virgin Islands.* Vol. 2. Agriculture Handbook No. 449. Washington, DC: US Department of Agriculture—Forest Service.

Nellis, D. W. 1994. *Seashore plants of south Florida and the Caribbean. A guide to identification and propagation of xeriscape plants.* Sarasota, FL: Pineapple Press, Inc.

———. 1997. *Poisonous plants and animals of Florida and the Caribbean.* Sarasota, FL: Pineapple Press, Inc.

Scurlock, J. P. 1996. *Native trees and shrubs of the Florida Keys. Also South Florida, Cuba, the Bahamas, the islands of the Caribbean, parts of Mexico, South and Central America.* Rev. ed. Lower Sugarloaf Key, FL: Laurel & Herbert, Inc.

Seddon, S. A., and G. W. Lennox. 1980. *Trees of the Caribbean.* London: Macmillan Caribbean Natural History.

SEA LIFE

Alevizon, W. S. 1994. *Pisces guide to Caribbean reef ecology*. Houston, TX: Pisces Books.

Greenberg, I., and J. Greenberg. 1986. *Guide to corals and fishes of Florida, the Bahamas and the Caribbean*. Miami, FL: Seahawk Press.

Humann, P. 1996. *Reef creatures identification: Florida, Caribbean, Bahamas*. Jacksonville, FL: New World Publications.

———. 1996. *Reef coral identification: Florida, Caribbean, Bahamas*. Jacksonville, FL: New World Publications.

Humann P., and N. Deloach. 1995. *Snorkeling guide to marine life: Florida, Caribbean, Bahamas*. Jacksonville, FL: New World Publications.

Jones, A., and N. Sefton. 2002. *Marine life of the Caribbean*. London: Macmillan Caribbean Natural History.

Kaplan, E. H. 1999. *A field guide to coral reefs: Caribbean and Florida*. Peterson Field Guide. Boston: Houghton Mifflin Harcourt.

———. 1999. *Southeastern and Caribbean seashores*. 2nd ed. Peterson Field Guide. Boston: Houghton Mifflin Harcourt.

Stokes, F. J. 1994. *Divers and snorkelers guide to the fishes and sea life of the Caribbean, Florida, Bahamas, and Bermuda*. Philadelphia: Academy of Natural Sciences of Philadelphia.

SEASHELLS

Humfrey, M. 1982. *Sea shells of the West Indies: A guide to the marine molluscs of the Caribbean*. London: Viking Press.

Lipe, R. E., and R. T. Abbott. 1991. *Living shells of the Caribbean and Florida Keys*. Melbourne, FL: American Malacologists, Inc.

Magnotte, G. 1971. *Shelling & beachcombing in the Caribbean and Florida*. Hollywood, FL: Dukane Press, Inc.

Morris, P. A., and R. T. Abbott. 1995. *Shells of the Atlantic and Gulf coasts and the West Indies*. 4th ed. Boston, Massachusetts: Houghton Mifflin Harcourt.

Romashko, S. D. 1992. *The shell book: [the complete guide to collecting and identifying] Florida, Gulf, and the Caribbean*. 6th ed. Miami, FL: Windward Publication Co.

Sutty, L. 1986. *Seashell treasures of the Caribbean*. New York: E. P. Dutton.

———. 1990. *Seashells of the Caribbean*. London: Macmillan Education Ltd.

Warmke, G. L. C., and R. T. Abbott. 1975. *Caribbean seashells: A guide to the marine mollusks of Puerto Rico and other West Indian islands, Bermuda and the lower Florida Keys*. New York: Dover Publications.

INSECTS

Askew, R. R., and P. A. v. B. Stafford. 2008. *Butterflies of the Cayman Islands*. Stenstrup, Denmark: Apollo Books.

Brown, F. M., and B. Heineman. 1972. *Jamaica and its butterflies*. London: E. W. Classey Limited.

Garraway, E., and A. Bailey. 2005. *Butterflies of Jamaica*. London: Macmillan Caribbean Natural History.

Riley, N. D. 1975. *A field guide to the butterflies of the West Indies*. New York: Quadrangle Field Guide Series.

Schwartz, A. 1989. *The butterflies of Hispaniola*. Gainesville, FL: University Presses of Florida.

Smith, D. S., L. D. Miller, and J. Y. Miller. 1994. *The butterflies of the West Indies and south Florida*. Oxford: Oxford University Press.

Stiling, P. D. 1986. *Butterflies and other insects of the Caribbean*. London: Macmillan Caribbean Natural History.

———. 1999. *Butterflies of the Caribbean and Florida*. London: Macmillan Caribbean Natural History.

FISH

Bölke, J. E., and C. C. G. Chaplin. 1968. *Fishes of the Bahamas and adjacent tropical waters*. Academy of Natural Sciences of Philadelphia. Wynnewood, PA: Livingston Publishing Company.

DeLoach, N. 1999. *Reef fish behavior: Florida, Caribbean, Bahamas*. Jacksonville, FL: New World Publications.

Humann, P., and N. DeLoach. 2002. *Reef fish identification: Florida, Caribbean, Bahamas*. Jacksonville, FL: New World Publications.

Lieske, E., and R. Myers. 2002. *Coral reef fishes: Caribbean, Indian Ocean, and Pacific Ocean, including the Red Sea*. Rev. ed. Princeton, NJ: Princeton University Press.

Randall, J. E. 1996. *Caribbean reef fishes*. 3rd ed. rev. Neptune City, NJ: T. F. H. Publications, Inc.

Smith, L. 1997. *National Audubon Society Field Guide to tropical marine fishes: Caribbean, Gulf of Mexico, Florida, Bahamas, Bermuda*. New York: Alfred A. Knopf, Inc.

Took, I. 1991. *Fishes of the Caribbean reefs*. London: Macmillan Caribbean Natural History.

REPTILES AND AMPHIBIANS

Crother, B. I. 1999. *Caribbean amphibians and reptiles*. San Diego, CA: Academic Press.

Hedges, S. B. 2012. *Caribherp: West Indian amphibians and reptiles* (www.caribherp.org). Pennsylvania State University, University Park, PA.

Henderson, R. W., and R. Powell. 2009. *Natural history of West Indian reptiles and amphibians*. Gainesville, FL: University Press of Florida.

Malhotra, A., and R. S. Thorpe. 1999. *Reptiles and amphibians of the eastern Caribbean*. London: Macmillan Caribbean Natural History.

Rivero, J. A. 1978. *Los anfibios y reptiles de Puerto Rico/The amphibians and reptiles of Puerto Rico*. San Juan: Universidad de Puerto Rico, Editorial Universitaria.

Schwartz, A., and R. W. Henderson. 1985. *A guide to the identification of the amphibians and reptiles of the West Indies exclusive of Hispaniola*. Milwaukee, WI: Milwaukee Public Museum.

———. 1991. *Amphibians and reptiles of the West Indies: Descriptions, distributions, and natural history*. Gainesville, FL: University of Florida Press.

BIRDS

Benito-Espinal, E. 1990. *Oiseaux des Petites Antilles/Birds of the West Indies*. Saint-Barthelemy, French West Indies: Les Éditions du Latanier.

Bradley, P. E. 2000. *The birds of the Cayman Islands. An annotated checklist*. BOU Checklist No. 19. Tring, UK: British Ornithologists' Union.

Bradley, P. E., and Y.-J. Rey-Millet. 2013. *A photographic guide to the birds of the Cayman Islands*. London: Christopher Helm.

Evans, P. G. H. 2009. *Birds of the eastern Caribbean*. London: Macmillan Caribbean Natural History.

Flieg, M., and A. Sanders. 2000. *A photographic guide to birds of the West Indies*. London: New Holland Publishers.

Garrido, O. H., and A. Kirkconnell. 2000. *Field guide to the birds of Cuba*. Ithaca, NY: Cornell University Press.

Hallett, B. 2006. *Birds of the Bahamas and the Turks and Caicos Islands*. London: MacMillan Caribbean Natural History.

Haynes-Sutton, A., A. Downer, and R. L. Sutton. 2009. *A photographic field guide to the birds of Jamaica*. London: Christopher Helm.

James, A., S. Durand, and B. Jno. Baptiste. 2005. *Dominica's birds*. Rosseau, Dominica: Forestry, Wildlife and Parks Division.

Kavanagh, J. 2003. *Caribbean birds: An introduction to familiar species*. Phoenix, AZ: Waterford Press.

Oberle, M. W. 2010. *Puerto Rico's birds in photographs. A complete guide and CD-ROM including the Virgin Islands*. 3rd ed. San Juan, PR: Editorial Humanitas.

Raffaele, H. A. 1989. *A guide to the birds of Puerto Rico and the Virgin Islands*. Rev. ed. Princeton, NJ: Princeton University Press.

Raffaele, H., J. Wiley, O. Garrido, A. Keith, and J. Raffaele. 1998. *A guide to the birds of the West Indies*. Princeton, NJ: Princeton University Press.

———. 2003. *Birds of the West Indies*. Princeton, NJ: Princeton University Press.

Wauer, R. H. 1996. *A birder's West Indies. An island-by-island tour*. Austin, TX: University of Texas Press.

Wheatley, N., and D. Brewer. 2002. *Where to watch birds in Central America, Mexico, and the Caribbean*. Princeton, NJ: Princeton University Press.

White, A. W. 1998. *A birder's guide to the Bahama Islands (including Turks and Caicos)*. Colorado Springs, CO: American Birding Association, Inc.

MAMMALS

Hoyt, E. 1994. *Discover whale and dolphin watching in the Caribbean: A guide to meeting the whales and dolphins of the West Indies*. Plymouth, MA: Whale and Dolphin Conservation Society.

Kurta, A., A. Rodriguez-Duran, and M. R. Gannon. 2005. *Bats of Puerto Rico: An island focus and a Caribbean perspective*. Lubbock, TX: Texas Tech University Press.

Silva Taboada, G. 1979. *Los murciélagos de Cuba*. La Habana, Cuba: Editorial Academia.

Silva Taboada, G., W. Suárez Duque, and S. Díaz Franco. 2007. *Compendio de los mamíferos terrestres autóctonos de Cuba vivientes y extinguidos*. La Habana, Cuba: Museo Nacional de Historia Natural.

GLOSSARY

♂—symbol for male; ♀—symbol for female.

Buttress—An above-ground root at the base of the tree trunk that serves to support the tree.

Crustacean—A class of organisms that typically possess a hard outer shell and paired appendages. These usually live in water and have gills for breathing. Examples are crabs and lobsters.

Deciduous—Plants that lose their leaves during certain seasons.

Detritus—Deceased organisms, primarily represented by plants, which are in the process of breaking down and decomposing. This material is rich in nutrients important to the sustenance of many species.

Dorsal fin—The fin along the back of a fish.

Gorgonian—*See* Soft coral.

Initial phase—An adult phase among parrotfish and wrasses that may include sexually mature females, and males that are not sexually mature.

Intertidal zone—The area of contact between sea and land that is covered by the sea during high tides and exposed to the air when tides are low.

Muscle scar—The location on two-shelled mollusks, known as *bivalves*, such as oysters and scallops, where the large muscles that hold the shell shut are attached.

Pectoral fins—Paired fins just behind the head and gills of a fish.

Pelvic fins—Paired fins located on the undersides of fish below the pectoral fins.

Plankton—Organisms, both plant and animal, that drift in the water column and are heavily influenced by water currents for their movement. Such organisms are vast in variety and range from fish eggs and the larvae of numerous animals to minute algae and protozoans. Plankton is a basic food source for numerous marine species from sponges and corals to whales. Though most plankton is minute in size, larger organisms such as jellyfish are an element of this diverse assemblage.

Polyps—Identical individuals of these organisms grow in close association to form a coral. Each polyp is a tiny, anemone-like creature with a ring of tentacles surrounding its centralized mouth. The tentacles, some with venomous barbs, stun small fish and other organisms. The tentacles also serve to filter plankton from water currents and transport it to the mouth. Both stony and soft corals are colonies of polyps.

Primaries—The large flight feathers on the outer, rear portion of a bird's wing.

Rump—The area on the back of a bird or mammal just above the tail.

Soft Coral—Also known as *gorgonians*, these are colonial marine organisms. Each colony is made up of individual polyps, and each polyp is surrounded by an external skeleton composed of protein compounds. This soft exoskeleton allows for varying amounts of flexibility.

Terminal phase—An adult phase of parrotfish and wrasses that includes only sexually mature males.

Undertail coverts—The feathers on the underparts of a bird immediately in front of the tail.

Uppertail coverts—The feathers on the upper parts of a bird immediately in front of the tail.

Whorl—Three or more leaves, flowers, or other plant parts growing in a circle around a stem.

Zooplankton—The component of plankton that is composed of animal life such as fish eggs, copepods, jellyfish, krill, and larvae of many marine species.

PHOTOGRAPH, ILLUSTRATION, AND TEXT EDIT CREDITS

Numerous photographs were required for this project, and to that end we greatly appreciate the contributions of the individuals below:

Plants: All plant photos are by author James W. Wiley except those listed below:

Ackee, p.46: full tree; leaves—Mark W. Skinner, USDA-NRCS PLANTS Database; hanging fruit/individual fruit; fruit (open)—Pedro Acevedo-Rodríguez, courtesy of Smithsonian Institution.

African Tuliptree, p.31: full tree—Frank H. Wadsworth, International Institute of Tropical Forestry; leaves and flowers—Nils Navarro.

Avocado, p.45: full tree—Nils Navarro; hanging fruit—Álbaro J. Serrano Gutiérrez.

Beach Morning Glory, p.70: leaf (and flowers)—Richard A. Howard Image Collection, courtesy of Smithsonian Institution.

Black Mangrove, p.69: full tree; pneumatophores—Richard A. Howard Image Collection, courtesy of Smithsonian Institution; leaf—Frank H. Wadsworth, International Institute of Tropical Forestry; seed—Parker Davis, Florida Coastal Mangroves.

Breadfruit, p.47: individual fruit—Álbaro J. Serrano Gutiérrez; fruit cut open—Kevin Lock.

Bullwood, p.88: full tree; leaves—Victor Cuevas, USDA-Forest Service; trunk and roots—Peter L. Weaver, International Institute of Tropical Forestry.

Butterfly Bauhinia, p.34: full tree—Forest and Kim Starr; cluster of flowers and leaves—G. A. Cooper, courtesy of Smithsonian Institution; flower close-up, and leaf—Nils Navarro.

Calabash Tree, p.76: full tree—Forest and Kim Starr; fruit on tree—Nils Navarro.

Camasey, p.84: full plant—Carmen Galdames, Smithsonian Tropical Research Institute; leaves; flower heads—Rolando Pérez, Smithsonian Tropical Research Institute; flower head—Nils Navarro.

Caribbean Tree Fern, p.82: full plant—Peter L. Weaver, International Institute of Tropical Forestry; leaves—Frank H. Wadsworth, International Institute of Tropical Forestry.

Coffee, p.62: full tree; leaves; flower; fruit—Frank H. Wadsworth, International Institute of Tropical Forestry.

Common Guava, p.75: full bush—Robert Moreno Silva; leaves—Scott Henderson @ USDA-NRCS Plants Database; fruit on bush—Nils Navarro.

Florida Poisontree, p.90: trunk; leaves and fruit—Richard A. Howard Image Collection, courtesy of Smithsonian Institution.

Grapefruit, p.64: full tree—Robert Moreno Silva; leaves—SelecTree: a tree selection guide. http://slectree.calpoly.edu; fruit on tree—Frank H. Wadsworth, International Institute of Tropical Forestry.

Gumbo-limbo, p.74: leaves and fruit—Frank H. Wadsworth, International Institute of Tropical Forestry.

India-rubber Fig, p.36: leaves—Christian Pérez; fruit on tree—Robert Moreno Silva.

Jackfruit, p.48: fruit cut open—Richard A. Howard Image Collection, courtesy of Smithsonian Institution.

Jerusalem Thorn, p.80: full bush; flower—Frank H. Wadsworth, International Institute of Tropical Forestry; leaves—Larry Allain, courtesy of Smithsonian Institution; pod on tree—Rolando Pérez, Smithsonian Tropical Research Institute.

Leadtree, p.73: leaves—Frank H. Wadsworth, International Institute of Tropical Forestry.

Lignum Vitae, p.42: full tree—Richard A. Howard Image Collection, courtesy of Smithsonian Institution; leaves—Frank H. Wadsworth, International Institute of Tropical Forestry; flower; seedpod—Pedro Acevedo-Rodríguez, courtesy of Smithsonian Institution.

Manchineel, p.89: full tree—Richard A. Howard Image Collection, courtesy of Smithsonian Institution; fruit—Pedro Acevedo-Rodríguez, courtesy of Smithsonian Institution; leaf—Rolando Pérez, Smithsonian Tropical Research Institute.

Mango, p.43: fruit cut open—Robert Moreno Silva.

Mesquite, p.77: full tree; pods on tree—Richard A. Howard Image Collection, courtesy of Smithsonian Institution; leaves and flower—Pedro Acevedo-Rodríguez, courtesy of Smithsonian Institution.

Monkey Puzzle Euphorbia, p.71: full plant; close-up; flowers—Richard A. Howard Image Collection, courtesy of Smithsonian Institution.

Norfolk Island Pine, p.37: cones—Forest and Kim Starr.

Oyster Plant, p.59: flower—Robert Moreno Silva.

Papaya, p.44: full tree; hanging fruits—G. A. Cooper, courtesy of Smithsonian Institution; leaf—Mark W. Skinner, USDA-NRCS PLANTS Database; individual fruit—Richard A. Howard Image Collection, courtesy of Smithsonian Institution.

Periwinkle, p.54: full plant—Richard A. Howard Image Collection, courtesy of Smithsonian Institution; leaves—Pedro Acevedo-Rodríguez, courtesy of Smithsonian Institution; flower—G. A. Cooper, courtesy of Smithsonian Institution.

Pineapple, p.65: full plant; leaves—Richard A. Howard Image Collection, courtesy of Smithsonian Institution; fruit on plant—WVU Herbarium, courtesy of Smithsonian Institution; fruit cut open—Robert Moreno Silva.

Poinsettia, p.54: full bush; pale bracts—Richard A. Howard Image Collection, courtesy of Smithsonian Institution; red bracts—G. A. Cooper, courtesy of Smithsonian Institution.

Prickly Pear Cactus, p.71: close-up of pads—Richard A. Howard Image Collection, courtesy of Smithsonian Institution; flower—Pedro Acevedo-Rodríguez, courtesy of Smithsonian Institution.

Red Mangrove, p.68: full tree—Richard A. Howard Image Collection, courtesy of Smithsonian Institution; leaf; branch with leaves and fruit—Frank H. Wadsworth, International Institute of Tropical Forestry; fruit—Mark W. Skinner, USDA-NRCS PLANTS Database.

Sea Grape, p.70: fruit—Álbaro J. Serrano Gutiérrez.

Sierra Palm, p.83: full tree—Peter L. Weaver, International Institute of Tropical Forestry; fruiting body with flowers—Richard A. Howard Image Collection, courtesy of Smithsonian Institution.

Silk-cotton Tree, p.40: full tree; buttress roots—Nils Navarro; thorny bark—Jeff McMillian, courtesy of Smithsonian Institution; seedpod and kapok—Richard A. Howard Image Collection, courtesy of Smithsonian Institution.

Soursop, p.49: individual fruit, and fruit cut open—Nils Navarro.

Sugarcane, p.60: wall of cane—L. E. Bishop, courtesy of Smithsonian Institution; individual plants—R. J. Soreng, courtesy of Smithsonian Institution; stalk; flower close-up—Nils Navarro; flower spikes—G. F. Russell, courtesy of Smithsonian Institution.

Swamp Bloodwood, p.86: full tree; leaves—Roland Pérez, Smithsonian Tropical Research Institute; buttress roots—Richard A. Howard Image Collection, courtesy of Smithsonian Institution; fruit—Carmen Galdames, Smithsonian Tropical Research Institute.

Swamp Cyrilla, p.87: leaves and flowers; fruit—Richard A. Howard Image Collection, courtesy of Smithsonian Institution.

Sweet Acacia, p.78: full tree—Chris A. Martin, Arizona State University; leaves; flower—Nils Navarro; pods on tree—Richard A. Howard Image Collection, courtesy of Smithsonian Institution.

Sweet Orange, p.63: full tree—SelecTree: a tree selection guide. http://slectree.calpoly.edu; leaves—Nils Navarro.

Tabonuco, p.88: White trunks of trees—Jerry Bauer©; white trunks of trees—Noel F. R. Snyder; leaves and fruit—Richard A. Howard Image Collection, courtesy of Smithsonian Institution.

Tamarind, p.79: full tree—Richard A. Howard Image Collection, courtesy of Smithsonian Institution.

Toothed Maidenplum, p.91: full plant; leaves; leaf close-up—Nils Navarro.

Wandering Jew, p.58: full plant; leaves—Richard A. Howard Image Collection, courtesy of Smithsonian Institution; flower—Pedro Acevedo-Rodríguez, courtesy of Smithsonian Institution.

West Indian Lantana, p.81: full bush; flower; leaves—Richard A. Howard Image Collection, courtesy of Smithsonian Institution; flower—J. C. Mcmillian, courtesy of Smithsonian Institution.

West Indian Locust, p.41: full tree—Marcos Guerra; leaves—Pedro Acevedo-Rodríguez, courtesy of Smithsonian Institution; fruit—Rolando Pérez, Smithsonian Tropical Research Institute; flower—Frank H. Wadsworth, International Institute of Tropical Forestry.

Yellow Cassia, p.32: full tree—Richard A. Howard Image Collection, courtesy of Smithsonian Institution; pod—Robert Moreno Silva.

Yellow Trumpetbush, p.55: full bush—G. A. Cooper, courtesy of Smithsonian Institution; leaves—Richard A. Howard Image Collection, courtesy of Smithsonian Institution; seedpod—Pedro Acevedo-Rodríguez, courtesy of Smithsonian Institution; flowers—Frank H. Wadsworth, International Institute of Tropical Forestry.

Terrestrial Mammals: The mammal illustrations were prepared by Kristin Williams, except for the Big Brown Bat, which was provided courtesy of R. W. Kays and D. E. Wilson, *Mammals of North America* (Princeton, NJ: Princeton University Press, 2009).

Birds: All illustrations are from *A Guide to the Birds of the West Indies* (see reference list), the art produced by Tracy Pedersen and Kristin Williams.

Terrestrial Reptiles: The reptiles were illustrated by Nils Navarro, except for the Boa Constrictor, Turquoise Anole, and Jamaican Ameiva, which were illustrated by Kristin Williams.

Amphibians: All illustrations were prepared by Kristin Williams.

Freshwater Fish and Shrimp: Joe Guarisco and The Nature Conservancy provided the Mountain Mullet and River Goby illustrations. Shrimp illustration by Kristin Williams.

Terrestrial Invertebrates:
Butterflies: Gulf Fritillary and Zebra Longwing photos by James Wiley; all other butterflies photos by Rick Cech.
Crabs: Great Land Crab photo by Charlie Corbeil; Common Land Hermit Crab by Katrin Groh; all other crab photos by Robert F. Myers.
Termites: photos by James Wiley.
Snails: Live painted snail photos by Emilio Alfaro and photos of shells in shop by James Wiley.

Marine Mammals: All illustrations by Sandra Doyle.

Marine Reptiles: All illustrations were prepared by Nils Navarro.

Marine Fish: All illustrations by Ewald Lieske.

Marine Plants and Invertebrates: All photos by Robert F. Myers, except Sea Plumes, photo by Patrice Marker.

Seashells (Mollusks): Photos of Common West Indian Green Chiton, Squamous Chiton, Caribbean Coquina, West Indian Prickly Cockle, and Variegated Turret Shell were provided by José and Marcus Coltro; the Queen Conch by Naples Sea Shell Company; all other photos by Rüdiger Bieler.

For assistance in providing reference materials for artists we thank Jeremy Jacobs and James Poindexter of the Smithsonian National Museum of Natural History, Rafael Rodríguez Mojica, Alcides Morales, Padre Alejandro Sánchez, Yolanda León, Sixto Inchaustegui, Luis M. Díaz, Ernesto Reyes, Yerenia García, and Eladio Fernández. Others who helped obtain photos from collections were Dr. Ariel Ruiz Urquiola and Dra. Angela Leira Sánchez and Sonia María González Pendás of the National Botanical Gardens of Cuba.

Nick Holmes, of Island Conservation, provided data on the endangered species of the Caribbean and on the rock iguanas.

INDEX